Deep Flavors

A Celebration of Recipes for Foodies in a Kosher Style

An eclectic anthology of family recipes as well as original Jewish, regional American, and international recipes, including reminiscences and insights about food and its preparation in a Kosher style from the perspective of a southern Jew.

A BOOK FOR FOODIES, VEGETARIANS, AND JEWS WHO COOK TRADITIONAL AND NONTRADITIONAL KOSHER FOOD.

By: Kenneth M. Horwitz

Inspire On Purpose Publishing

Irving, Texas

Deep Flavors: A Celebration of Recipes for Foodies in a Kosher Style

Inspire On Purpose Publishing
Irving, Texas
(888) 403-2727
https://inspireonpurpose.com
The Platform Publisher™
"Changing Lives With Words"

Printed in the United States of America
Library of Congress Control Number: 2019940648

Hardcover ISBN-13: 978-1-941782-51-4

SPECIAL CONSIDERATIONS: 1. This book is intended to be useable in a Jewish kitchen so that each recipe can be made to comport with the user's level of adherence to Jewish dietary laws. Each user should use his or her discretion in sourcing of kosher ingredients and preparation of the recipes to the desired standard; and 2. Aside from the application of kosher rules, users should both apply needed food safety practices in the kitchen and take care to understand and observe your guests' special dietary needs including, for example, allergies such as to nuts or gluten.

For more information about the author and book, visit: https://deepflavorscookbook.com
Kenneth M. Horwitz
14801 Quorum Dr., Suite 500, Dallas, Texas 75254
(972) 419-8383
kmh@gpm-law.com

TABLE OF CONTENTS

Preface

This book was written for my son, Seth, and my daughter, Lisa, both of whom inherited my love of good food and cooking. It is intended to communicate some of what I have learned over many years of study (and practice) and to share my original recipes, family recipes, and thoughts about food in an organized fashion—from generation to generation. It gives me great pleasure that Lisa has collaborated on significant parts, both by drafting recipes and by adding editorial assistance. Also, a number of recipes are those of my wife, Bobbie—including, for example, Bobbie's Piecrust, Chopped Chicken Liver, and Apple Cake. This book is more than just a recipe compendium; it is meant to be read. I hope you read and learn from it with pleasure and use it as a resource for recipes, techniques, ideas, and other information.

I cannot count the times I have given a recipe to somebody who said, "This is too complicated" or "This has too many ingredients." Most cooking is simply not that complicated, but there are correct (read: effective to produce a delicious result) techniques, steps, and ingredients that are necessary to improve the complexity and taste of the food on the table. One of our dear friends—Ann Cole, who has tested some of the recipes—commented that she found it very useful to read the recipe through before starting the preparation process and suggested that I share that perspective with my readers.

Chapter 1: My Philosophy

I recall a radio interview of Mark Bittman, a *New York Times* food columnist; the interviewer had prepared recipes from Mr. Bittman's book with some less-than-stellar results. After the interviewer admitted to skipping some steps detailed in the book, Mark Bittman essentially (and correctly) stated that process matters. In a similar vein, my sister asked for our recipe for Mom's Chocolate Pinwheel Cake because she could not decipher Mom's recipe card. She then proceeded to bake the cake, ignoring specific instructions and changes that my wife, Bobbie, had made, including changes for updated ingredients and technology different from those popular in Mom's time. She related that the result was not fully satisfying. Cooking is worth some effort *and* attention to detail. The positive reactions from family or guests, as well as your own enjoyment, will make it worthwhile. Of course, producing delectable food is more than just process—high-quality (and this does not necessarily mean rare or expensive) and fresh ingredients are essential.

Many television shows demonstrate dumbed-down recipes, limit the number or cost of ingredients as a gimmick, or use preprocessed ingredients and the like. And then there are celebrated chefs who use so-called molecular gastronomy techniques (such as creating foams) that are totally impractical for even the advanced home cook, if only because of a lack of specialized equipment or product unavailability. I remember one *60 Minutes* segment glorifying a Michelin-starred Italian chef who, for example, deconstructed the well-known dish *tortellini en brodo* into six room-temperature tortellini on a plate with some gelatinized stock cubes; my thoughts went to the story "The Emperor's New Clothes." While it is true that enjoyment of food includes both tactual and visual components, it is my view that these situations can present incomplete, uninformed, or distorted pictures of what is included in the universe of good food.

Most cooking is not "too complicated." The steps in most recipes can be dealt with in ways that are accessible to the home cook and can be accomplished by a somewhat knowledgeable cook with normal tools to produce great food. If something is worth doing, it is worth doing right: it is important to use good ingredients and proper technique. Cooking from scratch enables control over ingredients (including, to a considerable extent, elimination of chemicals used in commercially processed foods) and control over results. Many "complicated" recipes can be broken into non-complicated steps, and the steps frequently can be done over several days or even weeks so that these "complicated" recipes become a series of reasonably simple steps that fit within your schedule. (Two examples within this book—(1) Roasted Turkey with accompaniments such as stuffing and sauce and (2) Mushroom-and-Spinach Lasagna—are multistep recipes that can be broken down into easy components susceptible of being prepared over a rational time frame and not necessarily all crammed into one day.) Many recipes can be successfully made in advance—and some can be better for the "aging," such as many stews and braises—so that one may fit the work into a busy schedule and still have great meals even on busy workdays. Multiple recipes include products that can be prepared when you have time (or when items are on sale or abundant from the garden), portion controlled, and frozen for future use (such as pesto, stocks, sautéed mushrooms, chicken parts, etc.) to reduce shopping and preparation time before service. Of course, special meals such as Thanksgiving or the seder are worth extra effort.

Not to be ignored is the difficulty of sourcing kosher ingredients, but advance planning works. With the availability of internet ordering, so much is accessible now. Information is a click away for how to create components not commercially accessible in kosher form (such as italian sausage). Of course, while making sausage sounds complicated, it is just ground beef (or lamb, chicken, turkey, or a mixture) with sufficient fat and the desired herbs and spices; there is no requirement for casing, and you can just form patties or balls.

Advance preparation of portion-controlled raw or partially processed product is an efficient use of time and effort that can also seriously reduce costs. For example, purchasing ten or twenty pounds of fresh mushrooms at a wholesaler for at least half of any price you will ever see in a grocery and then processing the mushrooms for future use allows the home chef to simply pop a plastic bag or foil packet (noting the growing concern of plastic contamination with direct food contact) out of the freezer when mushrooms are needed. Again, a significant amount of the normally last-minute work is already done. (See the discussion in Chapter 2 for acquiring and processing fresh, frozen, and dried mushrooms. Commercial frozen mushrooms "cooked in butter" are not the same.)

Similarly, when chicken is on sale, it is efficient to clean, wash, drain, dry, and freeze the pieces separately on a double layer of waxed paper; then double bag the frozen pieces for use when needed. The work has to be done anyway and might as well be on your schedule at a favorable cost. (If you do not use a double layer of waxed paper, you will have a solid mass of chicken. This double-layering technique is useful—actually, essential—when freezing many products.) Indeed, the time and cost savings possible by intelligent use of a freezer can justify the up-front capital expense if you have space.

Note: A discussion in any detail of making meat and fowl kosher is beyond the scope of this book. This book is intended to be "kosher style" and is not intended as authoritative on the application of that set of rules. The truly kosher cook will need to use his or her own sourcing to locate and acquire kosher ingredients and interpret the recipes consistent with kosher rules. Note also that I make no attempt in this book to cover the special rules for Passover.

If you want to produce an outstanding result in the kitchen, you have to (1) use the freshest and best-quality ingredients; (2) pay attention to recipe details, including reading the *entire* recipe before you start cooking (as well as understanding your ingredients—for example, you need to know to shake vanilla extract, worcestershire sauce, and liquid smoke before each use to stir up the flavor solids that settle to the bottom of the bottle); and (3) use proper procedures and techniques. There are many sources to learn procedures and techniques, including *The Joy of Cooking* and books and videos by and with Julia Child, Jacques Pépin, Martha Stewart, and *America's Test Kitchen*; the more you study and practice, the more satisfying the results. It also helps to have quality equipment. If an ingredient has degraded, it simply cannot be used to produce excellent food and is not worth your time and effort or the risk to your family's health. If an ingredient is spoiled or spoiling, use something else or make something else.

Food, population centers, and transportation have been inextricably linked at least since the Roman Army built roads that made larger towns possible. Our food supply has changed since I was growing up in Atlanta, Georgia, in the 1940s and '50s. At that time, "supermarkets" were just coming into existence. Those early stores were small by today's standards and would not be viewed today as real supermarkets. The earliest supermarkets in the 1930s era were less than 10,000 square feet, and the average size of suburban supermarkets built in the 1950s was about 15,000 square feet. A store today will frequently have 65,000 or more square feet of space and more than 60,000 different items (SKUs) on the shelves. In 2014 the median store size was 46,000 square feet, an increase of 10,000 feet in twenty years. Of course, supercenters, hypermarkets, and wholesale clubs can be much larger, and many Wegmans stores are as large as 120,000 square feet.

Stores in my childhood did not carry the variety now available in many stores around the US. The variety of ethnic markets (Mexican, Cuban, Indian, Thai, Chinese, Middle Eastern, etc.) did not exist outside of the largest cities on the coasts and even then were not available outside of ethnically concentrated parts of those cities. You could not buy many items that we now take for granted (the Roman Army rule at work: build roads, and people follow because food can be transported). While certainly food was not on President Eisenhower's mind when he pushed the interstate highway system, its broad economic effect is incontrovertible. Air transport is just another type of road that makes distant markets accessible and knowledge of distant cultures common. A few examples include availability of really fresh fish or other seafood away from the coast as well as "exotic" ingredients such as the variety of mushrooms or unusual varieties of "normal" products, including arborio, sushi, basmati, and jasmine varieties of rice. Generally, there used to only be one variety and maybe a couple sizes on the shelf. Fresh vegetables out of season simply did not exist. I remember when, as an adult, finding fresh onions for purchase was problematic at Passover or Easter. Olives came in two varieties: black, rubbery canned olives and canned (or bottled) green olives stuffed with pimentos. The now ubiquitous olive bar did not exist. The olive bar now will sometimes have a couple dozen varieties and various other marinated vegetables.

As for mushrooms, most of what was available was limited to canned mushrooms. When available, fresh mushrooms were limited to white button (Parisian) mushrooms. Now, multiple varieties of fresh mushrooms, including shiitake, cremini, hen-of-the-woods, and portobello mushrooms, are farmed and sold in regular grocery stores and ethnic groceries. Today we can also buy many varieties, fresh or dried, of truly wild mushrooms (chanterelle, trumpet, porcini, and morel are examples) as well as dried farmed mushrooms such as shiitake and even the ubiquitous white button mushrooms. At appropriate times of the year, many wild mushrooms are now available fresh and relatively widely available (albeit expensive) through such retail grocers as Whole Foods nationally and Central Market in Texas as well as specialty and ethnic grocers. Likewise, you can locate individually quick-frozen (IQF) mushrooms such as porcini.

High-quality fresh-frozen vegetables were rare in the 1950s, and items such as frozen petits pois were unavailable. Of course, the availability of out-of-season fresh fruits and vegetables flown in from South America or Asia would have been science fiction. Technology is sometimes wonderful, notwithstanding the locavore culture.

This expansion of variety is because of the shrinkage of our world by rapid transportation and communication with the parallel increase in the size of supermarkets as well as the growth of diverse ethnic populations in the US. Apples are a prime example: at some stores, twenty-five or more varieties may be available during the season as compared to maybe three varieties fifty years ago. I receive a weekly email from Central Market (an upscale grocery chain in Texas); regularly, that email shows more than forty-five varieties of citrus for sale. As a comparison demonstrating the changing times, when I lived in Washington, DC, in the early 1970s, the stores would carry Jaffa oranges, a delicious variety of navel oranges imported from Israel, with a couple other varieties. Many new foods (such as the relatively recently introduced quinoa seed from South America) and exotic tropical fruits are coming to market all the time, and we need to learn how to use and cook these foods. This variety makes for exciting eating.

Of course, it takes effort to find some of these products, as they may only be available in and around farmer's markets in large cities or at major food wholesalers. Wholesalers that normally sell to restaurants and stores will frequently sell to the individual consumer; these include Coosemans and FreshPoint. There are many others, and if you ask, you may well be surprised that local wholesalers will sell to you if you pay cash and are willing to purchase relatively large quantities. Of course, this may mean processing what is not immediately needed. Another wonderful resource that should not be overlooked is the internet. Many retailers that carry a high-quality product line have a limited number of retail stores but also sell on the internet. I buy chocolate and cocoa from King Arthur Flour, a New England company, because of the variety, quality, and value. They also sell large bottles of high-quality vanilla extract—the same brand that is locally available in small but expensive bottles (although that price has skyrocketed in the last few years). Similarly, I order tea from Ten Ren Tea, a store I found in San Francisco's Chinatown, because of the quality and variety—although if you are looking for non-Chinese teas, there are probably better sources. If you are willing to pay the cost of shipping, Harrods of London has wonderful single-source teas from India, Ceylon, and other locales, as well as wonderful blends. A great resource for high-quality spices is Penzeys, which has a number of stores nationally and a website.

Fish is now flown fresh from all of the world's oceans to all locations around the United States and is available even if you do not live near the coast; of course, be careful to purchase from retailers that have a large turnover and reliably fresh product. Good retailers will pack the fish sealed in plastic next to a separate ice bag so that it will stay fresh until you cook it, although sometimes you need to ask for proper packaging. Fish should be maintained right at thirty-two degrees Fahrenheit, the temperature of ice, until it is ready to cook. Your refrigerator is not cold enough, and the freezer is too cold—ergo, the need for ice in addition to the refrigerator. I always buy fish the day I will cook it for maximum freshness. Your market should also tell you their delivery days for fish if you ask, as you should.

High-quality and artisanal cheeses from around the world are now available from large grocery retailers and specialty stores. *Note*: Rules regarding what cheeses qualify as kosher are complex. Use your discretion in this regard, and modify the cheeses recommended in this book to kosher cheeses as needed to comply with your observance of kashruth. There are many American cheese brands that have rabbinic supervision and approval. I have even seen internet articles noting a kosher-certified parmigiano-reggiano, though it is apparently not recognized by the OU Kosher, a major US certifying body.

Even in relatively small markets such as Virginia Beach, Virginia, quality grocers such as Harris Teeter carry a respectable variety of wonderful domestic and foreign cheeses in addition to the common selection of processed and commercially prepackaged cheeses (including kosher cheeses) produced by such brands as Kraft and Tillamook. (Cheese, bread, olives, salad, and wine make a wonderful and simple meal, as does a simple sandwich of fresh bread or toast spread with mustard mayonnaise or aioli and layered with sliced ripe avocado and drizzled with lemon juice, salt and pepper, thick slices of a ripe summer tomato, basil leaves, and slices of brie. Who said great food has to be complicated?)

In speaking of positive changes, one should not overlook technological advances with the available tools. One only has to think of the changes that metal cladding and stick-free coatings have brought to stove-top pans or that electronics has brought to temperature and weight measurement to understand the revolution in our ability to minimize all sorts of difficulties that were endemic in our parents' kitchens.

On the negative side of the current food marketplace, are the limitations on some products because of the exigencies of mass production and marketing. I remember going with my mother to a chicken store a couple miles from downtown Atlanta in the late 1940s and 1950s to purchase chickens. She would select a live chicken, and then store employees would kill and clean the bird. We would leave with the whole fresh chicken, including underdeveloped eggs, the liver, the heart, the gizzard, the feet, and the whole neck (including the skin, which my grandmother would use to make stuffed *derma*—or, as it is known when made with chicken neck skin, *helzel*, to distinguish it from *kishke*, which is classically made with cow intestines. While I do not have my grandmother's recipe, there are recipes on the internet—just know that any that use a fat other than chicken schmaltz are truly inauthentic). Today, in order to get chicken feet, which are a great source of collagen for a wonderfully rich chicken stock and are not to be sneered at, you have to go to an ethnic (such as Chinese) grocery. Similarly, beef cheeks (to braise) or calves' feet (hooves) for stock are not generally available except from an ethnic (such as Mexican) market. Cabrito (goat) is generally available, at least in Dallas, only from a halal market or a Mexican market. Unfortunately, some of these products may be difficult to source in a kosher format.

Some products, such as bulk knockwurst, have fallen victim to corporate acquisition. I used to be able to obtain bulk Hebrew National knockwurst from local Jewish delis in Dallas before that company was acquired by a huge food conglomerate. The shrink-wrapped product in the grocery store now is simply not the same. A reasonable substitution for both knockwurst and knoblewurst (garlic sausage) as well as whole, uncooked, great-quality pastrami is available over the internet from Katz's Deli in New York, but you have to be determined and persistent to find such items. Flexibility and creativity are not just a part of the actual cooking process: they are also integral to the shopping process if you want a particular result.

Another negative aspect of the last thirty or so years is illustrated by the development of food risks such as salmonella, particularly in chicken and other poultry, a risk created by the production process. While this book is not a manual about food safety, cooking is, of necessity, about food safety; good safety practices should be studied and practiced—consistently. For example, notwithstanding federal regulation of our food supply, special interests were, for many years, able to block restrictions on the use of antibiotics as a matter of course in raising farm animals, a practice that increases the risk of "super" germs to all of us.

This book is intended as a practical but not encyclopedic text with many of my favorite recipes (some of which are concepts as much as "recipes") and with an emphasis on philosophy and technique; some techniques are repeated over and over, and I will try to refer the reader to the best discussion. In my cooking, I rely heavily on the many hours I have spent viewing programs put on by quality teachers such as Julia Child, Martha Stewart, and Jacques Pépin, among others, as well as reading and studying their cookbooks (and hundreds of other cookbooks and multiple hundreds of cooking magazines and websites) over the years. In this book, I will endeavor to be detailed and to avoid leaving out information essential to the production of a successful meal—a failure of many recipes. However, the reader will note that a certain basic level of knowledge is assumed.

I do remember buying a book at a famous restaurant in New Orleans on our honeymoon and being disappointed when the recipes we tried to make at home obviously left out material information; I try to avoid that type of incompleteness here. While the internet is a valuable resource, one needs to remember that anyone can put anything on the internet—a careful filter needs to be used in ascertaining the wheat from the chaff. A perfect example is the variety of nut brittle recipes available, many of which will produce a less-than-satisfactory result and none of which (at least of those I have read) are perfect—for varying reasons. Many TV food programs are, unfortunately, merely entertainment shows without adequate detail, and an insufficient amount can be learned from watching them to properly replicate the recipes, although even such programs can carry some useful information and ideas for food combinations.

Books, videos, and other informative sources go only so far; your results will improve only with experience as you hone your technical skills and determine what taste combinations work for you. For example, my daughter, Lisa, does not like cilantro, and I am sure she has figured out substitutions that work for her. In the meantime, you can enjoy the fruits of your efforts. Acquisition of skills such as the care and use of knives and other equipment is important both to production of the best-tasting food and to your efficiency of effort, safety, and enjoyment of your time in the kitchen; needless to say, this also requires practice. There is no substitute—including the myriad of special-purpose tools—to such basic skills as the proper and practiced maintenance and use of kitchen knives.

While I am not a fan of some "fusion" cuisine—with what I personally think of as weird taste combinations—my recipes are techniques and can be a base for other combinations of flavors. Are kreplach, a European-Jewish dish made with wonton wrappers, "fusion" cuisine? I do endorse experimentation with flavors, although there is a reason for the widespread acceptance of the combination of flavors in classics such as *insalata caprese*: tomato, fresh mozzarella, and fresh basil with a vinaigrette made with quality ingredients (not a store-bought dressing) and with no artificial additives. On the other hand, no one would accuse my Frijoles Refritos (Chapter 14) of being even close to authentic, although all of my additions are ingredients used in other Mexican or Tex-Mex cooking and, unlike the original, can be perfectly kosher. Unlike the ubiquitous and mostly tasteless refried beans served on every plate in Mexican and Tex-Mex restaurants, nobody would accuse these of being bland (and they not only contain no pork fat, but they are also vegan and pareve). Out of necessity, American food is made with available products, which are frequently different from the original: as an example, fresh mozzarella in the US is good but has a taste different from that available in Italy. It must be in part because of terroir—that is, what the cows eat. Thus, in a sense, all of our food is "fusion."

No matter how good your technique, and no matter how good your attention to detail, the finished product can be no better than the quality of the products you start with. By *quality*, I do not mean expensive or exotic: I mean fresh and unadulterated. As indicated above, farm produce such as tomatoes should be fully ripe and tasty. I avoid cucumbers that have been waxed, and I only wash but do not peel the unwaxed variety (but if the seeds are big or close to mature, I halve the cucumber and deseed it). I use filtered water for drinking, for inclusion in recipes, and for ice. I refrain from reliance on processed foods that may contain excessive salt and what I view as unhealthy chemical additives. I do not use salted butter and never use margarine (there are too many studies regarding its health hazards). I do use high-quality extra-virgin olive oil. I freeze butter until I am ready to use it to avoid spoilage and absorption of off-flavors. I freeze nuts in the fall (frequently after toasting them) for use later so that they remain fresh and do not turn rancid. They are then ready for use at any time. I use airtight containers to store flour, grains, sugars, etc. to maintain freshness and avoid access to weevils or other pests. As you read further, you will get some more ideas.

Cooking involves creativity, flexibility, and persistence in acquiring, storing, and using raw product. You will have occasional failures, but persevere. I remember my mom's story about the failure of the first time she made blintzes, which was corrected by her perseverance. However, there are exceptions—my failed attempt at pickling corned beef is legendary in our house, and I am forbidden to attempt another such effort.

In our house, we observe many of the Jewish dietary laws of kashruth; we do not use shellfish, fish without fins and scales, or pork, and we do not mix milk (or milk products such as butter or cheese) with meat—no cheeseburgers or cream sauces with meat. Such rules clearly impact the recipes in this book. However, we do not buy kosher beef, chicken, etc., and we do cook steaks from the loin of the beef (not traditionally made kosher outside of Israel, although it is done in the US). I intend for all of the recipes in *Deep Flavors* to be susceptible of being prepared in the observant home. For the most part, such deviances are suggestions only and should not impair your ability to cook these recipes in the most observant household. Also, as discussed later in the recipe for Charoset, we bend some of the rules, including the "Kosher for Passover" rules. While this observance, albeit modified, does place some restrictions on what we cook (for example, no chicken kiev, which is stuffed with butter, or beef stroganoff, which is finished with sour cream or crème fraîche), we nevertheless enjoy a varied diet. For example, high-quality nonkosher beef bacon is now available, as are beef sausages. These or similar products can be purchased in fully kosher packaging. They taste just as good as pork bacon or sausage (and, in my view, much better than the turkey or vegetarian simulations). Thus, a BLT—or my enhanced version, which uses beef bacon, really ripe tomato, cucumbers, salt, pepper, and my Pink Salad Dressing (Chapter 8) or mustard mayonnaise on rye, pumpernickel, or sourdough bread—is a part of our diet. A great alternative is to substitute ripe avocado for the cucumber and use a spicy, garlicky rouille as a mayonnaise variant.

As I understand the rules, for the most part, except to the extent my recipes involve cooking with wine, these recipes could also be halal, although the Muslim reader would clearly have greater knowledge of applicable rules.

Many people observe different restrictions in their diets for various reasons. Do not let such restrictions deter you from enjoying a large variety of food creatively prepared. For example, there are nondairy yogurts available that can be used in preparing meat dishes in Indian-cuisine style—perhaps not completely authentic but certainly delicious and frequently better than most Indian restaurants' food. While I am clearly not a vegetarian, one side effect of observing the rule of kashruth to keep milk and meat separate is that many of these recipes work well for vegetarians, particularly those who eat eggs and milk products. For other reasons (such as that I do not like grapefruit, blue cheese, or goat cheese, notwithstanding their current popularity), you will not read recipes in this book that include certain otherwise kosher foods. As you read this text, it will contain obvious differences from other cookbooks based on my taste and predilections—this is an invitation to you to use this as a launchpad.

Adherence to concepts discussed in this book will produce deep flavors in food you and those you cook for will enjoy. I hope you find my comments useful in your kitchen. And as Julia would say, "Bon appétit."

Garam Masala, p. 32

Chapter 2: *Ingredients*

PRELIMINARY POTPOURRI

EGGS

Selecting Eggs

When selecting eggs, you should always check the label for freshness. When you shop for eggs and other perishable foods, shop at a store with a high turnover. Examine each egg for barely visible hairline cracks. It is through these cracks that eggs become contaminated with salmonella and more. I use raw eggs for mayonnaise, for example, and Bobbie uses raw eggs for chocolate mousse (see Cold Chocolate Soufflé in Chapter 15). This is a choice you will need to make. When you get the eggs home, promptly refrigerate the eggs.

"Boiling" Eggs

People talk about hard-boiled eggs; this is a misnomer since eggs should be cooked at a bare simmer and never at a boil. What you do not want to do is put eggs in a pot with the water, turn the heat to high, and leave the eggs to boil at a hard boil for whatever period of time you choose to leave them in the water.

Before adding eggs to the water to cook, carefully pierce the shell of the large end of each egg with a thumbtack to allow any excess air to escape. This is a trick I learned from watching Jacques Pépin to (1) avoid shell breakage during cooking and (2) avoid eggs cooked with a concave area on one end.

Lower the eggs into cool, salted water in the pot. *After* you immerse the eggs, begin to heat the pot. As soon as the water reaches the bare simmer level, turn down the heat to maintain that level of temperature in the water. Then set the timer for ten minutes; certainly, do not cook the eggs any longer than twelve minutes. When the time is up, drain the eggs carefully, shake the pot to break the shells, and cover the eggs with cold water and ice.

Let the eggs sit for thirty minutes before peeling. This process avoids the green sulfurous ring that one frequently sees around hard-boiled eggs (as compared to proper hard-cooked eggs). Peel the eggs under cool, running water. Some eggs are very difficult to peel, and some eggs have the peel slip right off; I have never been able to figure out the difference in anything that I do that changes this consequence—a problem that has perplexed many commentators.

Egg Whites

Whenever you have egg whites remaining from a recipe calling for egg yolks, freeze the excess egg whites in jelly or jam (Ball) canning jars. When you are ready to use the egg whites, take them out of the freezer, and put them in the refrigerator to thaw for about one day, removing them from the refrigerator for an hour before using so that they can warm to room temperature. If you do not want to wait for the egg whites to warm, simply set the jar into a bowl of warm (not hot) water and stir or spin the jar in the water until the egg whites are liquid and warm to room temperature. Do not overheat. Egg whites whip better if they are at room temperature before whipping.

Since egg whites can accumulate, sometimes you need to look for ways to use them. Macaroons are an excellent use for egg whites, as are candied nuts. (Mix beaten egg whites with sugar and cinnamon, stir in the pecans or other nuts, spread in a half sheet pan, and roast at 350 degrees Fahrenheit, stirring occasionally until the nuts are dry and separate—*yum!*) Egg whites mixed with a sugary flavoring appropriate to the recipe makes a wonderful glaze for pies, cookies, etc. Also, some like omelets made with egg whites. Other ideas include candied "forgotten cookies" and meringue shells baked and filled.

ASPARAGUS PROCESSING

Asparagus is a wonderful vegetable, but it must be properly prepared for cooking for greatest eating enjoyment. The stems of asparagus are invariably stringy up to within an inch or so of where the tender tip of the spear begins. Therefore, asparagus should always be peeled with a vegetable peeler, a step rarely performed in restaurants and rarely demonstrated on cooking programs. Cutting off an arbitrary length of the base may save a little work and time but does not eliminate the stringiness and is wasteful.

To peel the asparagus, hold the asparagus two inches from the tip. Start peeling about two inches from the tip and peel down to about an inch from the base of the asparagus. Use a potato or vegetable peeler and take about six or eight strokes, turning the stem between each stroke to remove only the stringy surface layer of the asparagus. After the peeling process is completed, snap off the base of the asparagus at the natural breaking point about one inch from the base. This is an easy and relatively quick process. The entire asparagus spear will now be succulent, nonstringy, and a delight to eat however you cook it. After all of the asparagus being used is processed in this manner, wash the spears, and, if desired, cut the asparagus into about one-inch-long pieces or cook whole.

Note: The asparagus "waste" can be used to make Asparagus Stock (see recipe in Chapter 6). Freeze the waste until you have enough to use.

CHICKEN SCHMALTZ

There are many uses for various rendered animal fats. For many recipes in this book and for Jewish cooking, rendered chicken fat is essential. (The word *schmaltz* is German or Yiddish for "fat.") The equivalent for French cooking is goose or duck fat. Turkey schmaltz is also excellent.

To make chicken schmaltz, put chicken fat, skin, and tail into a pot with a sliced onion. When I clean a whole chicken, I save and freeze this material until I have enough to make schmaltz. Similarly, the excess skin and fat from chicken thighs should be saved for this purpose. Fat skimmed off of chicken stock is also schmaltz that should be saved for further use. Remember—waste not, want not. For those who turn up their noses at the thought of this process and product, I cite you a commentary by Jacques Pépin on his *Heart & Soul* 2015–2016 TV series, in which he extolled the flavor and health benefits of these rendered fats for use in cooking.

Add some water to the pot to start the process. Cook slowly on low heat until the fat is rendered, and the water is evaporated (about half an hour). The schmaltz will be a clear light yellow, and the chicken skin, tail, etc. will be lightly browned. The browned chicken pieces are called *gribenes* and are also a delicacy. Drain the liquid fat (schmaltz) into a jar, cool it, and refrigerate or freeze it. Sealed and frozen, the fat will store for a long time.

Schmaltz is essential to make Matzo Balls (Chapter 10), Chopped Chicken Liver (Chapter 10), Potato Kugel (Chapter 14)—I could go on. My mother used to brush schmaltz on pumpernickel bread, sprinkle it with salt, and toast it in the oven. Really good! If you are making a velouté sauce to go with chicken, schmaltz is the logical fat to use in making the roux. And these rendered fats do not make the toast or anything else more fattening than if you were to use butter or a vegetable oil—it just adds an appropriate flavor.

Note: The process for turkey fat is identical except that (1) I do not add onion, and (2) care should be taken to not cook the fat to the same doneness. I suggest stopping short of the solids browning; turkey schmaltz seems to overcook easily. Use turkey schmaltz when you want a distinctive turkey flavor; if available, it is the go-to fat for a roux used to make a turkey velouté.

If I am making chicken fried rice, I use chicken thighs—strip off the skin, and cut the meat into small pieces. Then I lay the skin in the skillet and render the fat. That rendered fat is used for cooking the fried rice. The rendered skin is crispy—a delicious garnish for the platter of fried rice. Fried rice is simply an amalgam of lightly sautéed vegetables (broccoli, cauliflower, sugar snap or snow peas, etc.), bite-sized pieces of chicken (or other meat, including beef or turkey), onion, garlic, ginger, a couple of eggs (in a simple flat omelet, just cooked and cut into pieces), and cold precooked rice—also, for a garnish, perhaps some reconstituted and sliced tree ear and/or shiitake mushrooms. Cook all separately, and then reassemble and heat, stirring with a light touch of soy sauce, hoisin sauce, fish sauce, dark sesame oil, and sriracha or garlic-chili paste, all mixed to taste. Total prep time is less than thirty minutes for a great one-pan meal.

FRESH, FROZEN, AND DRIED MUSHROOMS

There are many varieties of mushrooms, each with a different flavor. Mushrooms add great flavor to many dishes but must be properly prepared. Even though that process is easy, I like to have mushrooms ready to go and precooked to save time and make preparation of weeknight meals faster.

Preparation

By the very nature of things, raw mushrooms come with some dirt and need to be cleaned. Just brushing mushrooms simply does not do the job. Ignore myths about not washing mushrooms! Fresh mushrooms should always be washed to remove the dirt, but only immediately before use. Rinse well in a colander so that the water (together with any sand and dirt) flows through, but the mushrooms are not soaked in water. As demonstrated on the TV program *Good Eats* by Alton Brown (by weighing mushrooms before and after washing) and contrary to urban myth, using this approach does not cause the mushrooms to absorb any significant water.

Prior to sautéing, the mushrooms should be sliced or quartered or otherwise cut for the desired use. Many TV chefs eschew the use of mushroom stems. While it is true that shiitake stems will never soften or otherwise become edible in cooking and are only useful to make a shiitake stock, it is also true that most other mushroom stems are delectable and should not be discarded. Waste not, want not! Similarly, I have never found a good reason to scrape out and discard the black gills of the portobello mushroom—I am not a restaurant chef. Some TV chefs' objections to appearance do not qualify in my mind as a sufficient reason to waste good food and flavor. The gills are full of flavor, and I do not think the gills detract from the finished dish. If you are stuffing the caps and not using the stems in a recipe, the stems should be processed and used elsewhere.

Cooking

Mushrooms contain a great deal of liquid and, regardless of washing, need to be sautéed at high heat in oil or a mix of oil and butter to render and evaporate the excess water and to concentrate and intensify the mushroom flavor by caramelizing the mushrooms. If you are going to use the mushrooms with meat, omit the butter, and simply use oil. Use the minimum amount of oil needed to sauté the mushrooms without burning them. I know that some TV chefs suggest that an olive oil other than extra-virgin olive oil is acceptable since, theoretically, the flavor of the high-quality oil is altered (destroyed) by the heat. I do not subscribe to this philosophy. Salted butter never passes through the doors of my house (except for the Baklava recipe in Chapter 15). I do not use canola or other similarly flavorless vegetable oils for this purpose, although there is nothing wrong with such oils; it is a matter of flavor. I limit the use of peanut oil to primarily Asian cuisine. (Of course, some people are seriously allergic to peanuts or other nuts, so care should be taken to know your guests when you serve any peanut or other nut product.)

The mushrooms should be salted and peppered when they are placed in the hot pan. Some do not salt immediately simply because it will draw out water; however, until the excess liquid is extracted and evaporated, the process of flavor concentration cannot be completed. Unlike the process for caramelizing meat or fowl, it does not hurt to load up the pan—the browning will not start until the liquid evaporates, and then you just stir so that the process is even, and nothing is burned. The mushrooms will exude a significant amount of liquid in this cooking process. They should be cooked over very high heat until the liquid evaporates; then continue cooking at moderate heat until the mushrooms are caramelized (that is, they have browned and undergone a Maillard reaction) but not burned. It is amazing how much volume the mushrooms lose as the liquid is exuded. Before the liquid exudes, and after the liquid has evaporated, you should be at the stove, constantly stirring the mushrooms so that they do not burn. This caramelization process will cause the flavors to be enhanced and concentrated for many ingredients. Do not be tempted to add too much oil or butter to the mushrooms, because they will absorb what you give them, with the end result being overly oily mushrooms.

Preservation

Different varieties of mushrooms contain differing amounts of liquid, so you will need to pay attention to the variety that you are cooking at a particular time so as not to overcook or burn the mushrooms. Varieties should be separated for cooking and storage because they each have a unique flavor. This is particularly important for shiitake mushrooms since they have a different flavor suitable solely (at least in my view) for Asian cooking and are never appropriate for an Italian or French recipe, although many use them indiscriminately.

After the mushrooms are all cooked, they may then be cooled, refrigerated, divided into packages, and frozen for future use. Sandwich-sized baggies are excellent for this purpose, with perhaps a pre-wrap to avoid plastic contamination. The small baggies should be labeled and rewrapped in a larger bag so that the double layer of plastic will impede oxygen osmosis through the plastic, which can cause freezer burn. This is an efficient use of time and can be accomplished when you have the time to spend. It significantly reduces the prep time for a later meal. When you want to use mushrooms in a recipe, just thaw a baggie.

Acquisition

I frequently purchase a large quantity (ten to twenty pounds) of mushrooms at a wholesaler and cook all of the mushrooms. Food wholesalers exist in most large cities to supply restaurants and are not difficult to find. They will frequently sell to anyone who walks in and can pay with cash. The price is usually half of the grocery store price.

If you search diligently, you may be able to locate frozen porcini mushrooms at a food wholesaler. I have purchased them in five-pound packages from FreshPoint, a wholesale food purveyor, at less than a third of the price of fresh porcinis. They are delectable but need to be sautéed before use in a recipe in order to eliminate excess water and to caramelize them for enhanced flavor. The texture of mushrooms that were frozen before sautéing is different from that of fresh sautéed mushrooms (even after cooking), but the flavor, at least with porcinis, is worth the texture trade-off for the reduced cost and availability.

Dried mushrooms have unique, intense, and wonderful flavor. A number of dried mushroom varieties are available in one-pound packages at a rational cost. Groceries sometimes sell dried mushrooms by the ounce at an exorbitant price. I purchase dried chanterelle, trumpet, and porcini mushrooms by the pound at a local Dallas food wholesaler, and they are available over the internet—including from Amazon. I have found that fresh mushrooms are frequently sold at a different wholesaler than the dried. Dried mushrooms last essentially indefinitely until rehydrated, so storage at room temperature is easy. Also, since only an ounce or so is used per recipe, even though a pound may seem costly, the cost per recipe is reasonable. Even at thirty to fifty dollars for a pound, two ounces would only add a cost of four to eight dollars to a recipe with the payoff of an immense amount of flavor. Dried morels have an even more incredible flavor but (in 2019) cost more than two hundred dollars a pound, even when purchased from a wholesaler or over the internet. When purchased in packages of an ounce or two at a grocery store, any dried mushroom's price per pound (and particularly the non-Asian varieties) escalates enormously. Dried shiitake and tree ear mushrooms are generally available at a reasonable cost in Asian markets or over the internet. Large Asian markets sometimes carry fresh mushroom varieties not generally available in large chain groceries.

Dried mushrooms must be soaked in warm to hot water or other liquid to rehydrate and soften them. They are then drained before chopping and cooking. The soaking liquid has a wonderful flavor and should be used in the recipes or reserved for another use but never discarded. The soaking liquid should be allowed to rest for a minute and then carefully decanted to leave the sandy residue in the decanting vessel. The reserved liquid can then be used or frozen for future use if not used immediately.

TOASTING NUTS: COCONUT, PECANS, ALMONDS, PINE NUTS, AND OTHER NUTS

Nuts should always be toasted before use unless they will be subject to direct heat in the cooking of a recipe, such as for a coating in lieu of flour or bread crust for fish to be sautéed. I have seen many TV chefs who toast nuts in a skillet on the stove top. To my view, this is a surefire method to burn and unevenly toast the nuts and simply requires too much attention. Since the oils in nuts are prone to turn rancid at room temperature even if toasted, you should freeze all nuts in well-sealed containers if you do not use them immediately.

Toasting Coconut

I always toast coconut for two reasons: (1) the flavor of the coconut is enhanced, and (2) noxious chemicals put into the package of the shredded, sweetened coconut generally available in the grocery are toasted out of the coconut in the process.

With foil, line a half sheet baking pan with sides. This size pan will enable you to toast three fourteen-ounce packages of coconut at one time. Toast at 350 degrees Fahrenheit, setting your timer for eight to ten minutes, after which you should gently stir the coconut with a fork, moving the coconut from the edges to the center since the coconut at the edges cooks faster than that at the center of the pan. Be careful to not spill coconut onto the oven floor. Setting a timer is essential because you do not want to burn the coconut. Repeat for another six to eight minutes, and then repeat again for another six to eight minutes, as necessary, stirring well until the coconut is well toasted (being careful not to over-toast or burn the coconut). Cool before sealing in a storage container. The texture of the toasted coconut will be dry and flaky compared with the moist and somewhat sticky texture out of the bag.

A fourteen-ounce bag after toasting will weigh about eleven to twelve ounces. A quart Ball jar holds about nine to ten ounces of toasted coconut.

Toasting Pecans

The process for toasting pecans is basically the same as for coconut. Pecans will turn rancid, so freeze the nuts immediately after purchase and after processing. Start with the freshest pecans available. Remember that pecans are a fall crop, so if you have available freezer storage space, that is a good time to purchase a bountiful quantity for processing and storage. The half sheet pan will hold three pounds of pecan halves. I always rinse the raw pecans in a colander or sieve before roasting to remove any bitter shell dust. Let the pecans drain. Then toast, following the instructions for toasting coconut, timing and stirring several times until the nuts are toasted, and taking care not to burn them. Because the nuts start out wet, it may take longer to brown the pecans. The wet pecans may stick slightly to the foil lining the pan, so you need to take care to unstick and turn the entire bottom layer as they roast. A quart Ball jar holds about fourteen ounces of toasted pecans.

Toasting Almonds, Pine Nuts, and Other Nuts

Toast almonds, pine nuts, and other nuts as indicated for pecans, stirring occasionally until the nuts are toasted. Slivered or sliced almonds or small pine nuts can burn more easily, so set shorter times to stir and check the nuts accordingly. Almonds, hazelnuts, and pine nuts do not need to be washed. After toasting hazelnuts, lightly rub them (while warm) in a towel to remove most of the brown skin.

PRESERVED MOROCCAN LEMON

Preserved lemon is a wonderful citrusy product with a very different but delicious flavor used in Moroccan cooking. Primarily, you use only the no-longer-bitter rind (preserved) and not the flesh.

Cut the lemons into eighths. Layer the lemons in a Ball jar with generous amounts of salt. Fill the jar with lemon juice from other lemons. You may add herbs to the jar if desired to further flavor the preserving lemons. Refrigerate. Shake the jar daily for seven days. Make sure the lemons and herbs are covered with the liquid. After seven days, cover the lemons with a layer of olive oil. As long as the lemons are covered with oil, they will keep in the refrigerator for months.

SAUCES AND SPICE MIXTURES

BARBECUE SAUCE

There are probably hundreds of commercial and restaurant barbecue sauces and even more recipes for barbecue sauces online. This recipe is a Texas-style barbecue sauce, not overly sweet, and it is delicious. I got this recipe many years ago from the mother of one of the boys on my then five-year-old son's soccer team. It is reminiscent of the style of barbecue sauce from Angelo's Bar-B-Que restaurant in Fort Worth, Texas. There are as many different sauces as there are barbecue restaurants in Texas, although this style is fairly common. This sauce is very different from that found in the Carolinas or Kansas City.

Many people refer to grilling as barbecuing. Barbecue, at least in Texas, is meat cooked in a smoker at a low temperature for a number of hours, depending on the meat that is being used. Classically, in Texas, barbecue is smoked brisket, although chicken, turkey, pork ribs, and, occasionally, beef shoulder, beef short ribs, and prime rib roasts are smoked. The meat brisket is cooked at a temperature of about 250 degrees Fahrenheit for twelve to sixteen hours. Other meats that are smaller cuts, such as beef short ribs, or that do not need the time to break down collagen, such as beef prime rib or birds such as chicken and turkey, do not require this length of time to cook. The heat is an indirect, smoky wood flame, not charcoal, and the resulting cooked meat has a smoky flavor. Wood logs are used and may be oak (particularly post oak in Central Texas and the Hill Country), hickory, or pecan, but not mesquite. This recipe is for Hill Country–style smoking; in western and southern Texas, where the mesquite tree is a dominant species because trail cattle in the nineteenth century spread mesquite seeds north from Mexico, mesquite is widely used. However, I stand by my predilection. Texas is a large state with a variety in population (Mexican, American, German, Czech, etc.) and environments (the Gulf Coast, wetlands, pine forests, desert, mountain, high plains, etc.), resulting in various subcultures and food preferences.

Prior to smoking the meat, and during the cooking process, no sauce ever touches the meat. I recently viewed a televised show where the chef cooked a purported Texas-style brisket: it was not Texas style, if only because the chef coated the meat with sauce before smoking.

For brisket, a rub, depending on the end result desired, is applied to the meat for at least twelve hours prior to smoking (overnight and in the refrigerator). Some, such as Louie Mueller Barbecue in Taylor, Texas, simply use a salt-and-cracked-black-pepper rub, while others add cayenne or other spices. Similarly, for chicken, a rub is applied, and the meat is allowed to rest in the refrigerator for up to twelve hours or so prior to removing from the refrigerator for the smoking process. Angelo's spice rub is generally commercially available in grocery stores, even outside of Texas. That is what I use if I do not make my own version such as a mix of dried herbs, garlic powder, freshly ground black pepper, and salt.

Barbecue sauce is merely used as a dipping sauce on the plate or as a condiment in a sandwich; the meat is never cooked with the sauce! There is nothing prohibiting you from grilling and using sauce on the meat during the cooking process, but that is not barbecue, at least in Texas, despite the common usage of the term. When I make this sauce, I generally make up to four batches at a time and store the excess in the freezer in Ball jars, leaving a space for expansion so that the jar does not crack. Appropriately seal and label the jars and freeze. the sauce will stay fresh almost indefinitely. The work is in assembling the ingredients.

INGREDIENTS

One Batch	Ingredients	Four Batches
1½ cups	ketchup	6 cups
¾ cup	light brown sugar	3 cups
¾ cup	chili sauce (Heinz, not spicy)	3 cups
¾ cup	red wine vinegar	3 cups
¾ cup	water	3 cups
½ cup	lemon juice (fresh squeezed only)	2 cups
¼ cup	A.1. Sauce	1 cup
¼ cup	yellow prepared mustard	1 cup
2 tablespoons	worcestershire sauce	8 tablespoons
1 tablespoon	soy sauce	4 tablespoons
1 large clove	garlic (finely minced)	4 large cloves
¼ teaspoon	Tabasco	1 teaspoon
½ teaspoon	ground pepper, or to taste	1-2 teaspoons

Combine all the ingredients, and simmer for 30 minutes. Cool and store or serve.

MUSTARD-GARLIC-LIME BASTE

There are innumerable marinating mixtures for chicken and other grilled meats. This following recipe is one that I find to be delicious; it is a little bit unusual, and it is really a process with somewhat flexible ingredients.

INGREDIENTS

2-4 garlic cloves
1 teaspoon salt
1 teaspoon peppercorns
1 lime or lemon, zested and juiced
1 tablespoon dijon mustard
olive oil, sufficient to make a loose paste
optional: ¼ cup cilantro, thyme, oregano, rosemary,
or other herbs in a mixture as desired

Since it has no sugar, this baste should not create a problem of burning as you grill the chicken. I use a mortar and pestle to grind the garlic with salt, peppercorns, and lime zest (peeled off of the lime with a vegetable peeler, taking just the zest and not the white part of the pith). You can substitute lemon for the lime, particularly for use with lamb. If desired, also grind in cilantro and/or other fresh herbs: thyme, oregano, rosemary, etc. When the mixture is ground to a paste, add a liberal quantity of dijon mustard, the lime or lemon juice, and some olive oil. This finished mixture is ready to spread onto the meat. After you spread the mixture onto the chicken, coating thoroughly, let it marinate for at least half an hour before grilling (or, if you are using it on a whole chicken in an oven, before roasting the chicken). If you marinate for a longer time, add the citrus juice just before cooking so that the citrus does not precook the meat; you are not trying to make ceviche. This mixture is also excellent with lamb or beef.

CAJUN SPICE MIXTURE

This mixture is outstanding when used for various Cajun dishes, including jambalaya and gumbo. The mixture makes a bountiful amount, which should be stored in a dry, cool place, preferably the freezer.

INGREDIENTS

2½ tablespoons paprika (Spanish smoked paprika is nontraditional but is outstanding here)

2 tablespoons garlic powder

1 tablespoon black pepper (freshly ground—it loses flavor rapidly once ground)

1 tablespoon onion powder

1 tablespoon cayenne pepper

1 tablespoon dried oregano

1 tablespoon dried thyme

Combine all ingredients, and mix.

While bay leaf is a critical flavor ingredient in Cajun food, I do not grind it into the spice mixture, preferring instead to add whole fresh or dried bay leaf to the dish as it is cooking (note my preference for fresh, particularly since it is easy to grow in USDA Zone 7 and the South). Just remember to remove and discard the used bay leaf before serving. I have observed TV chefs crumble bay as they add it, which is counterintuitive since it is not eaten and must be removed.

Adding salt to a premixed spice mixture leads to the risk of oversalting, as some may want more spice flavor; if there is salt in the mixture, this limits the cook's flexibility to flavor the dish to taste.

BAHARAT

Baharat is a Middle Eastern spice mixture primarily used in Iraq and surrounding Arabic Persian Gulf countries. It is excellent in stews, providing a unique flavor addition.

INGREDIENTS

½ cup black peppercorns

½ cup coriander seed

¼ cup cassia bark or cinnamon bark (if you do not have either bark, use 2 tablespoons ground cinnamon)

¼ cup cloves (I reduce the amount of cloves to only 1 tablespoon)

⅓ cup cumin seeds

2 teaspoons cardamom seeds

½ cup ground paprika

4 whole nutmegs (approximately ¼ cup ground nutmeg)

Gently toast spices in a dry frying pan by sautéing and stirring constantly so as to not burn the spices. This releases their essential oils and enhances their flavors.

Then grind the whole spices in a spice grinder, making enough for multiple recipes and saving any not used immediately in a sealed glass jar. If you have the freezer space, the freezer is an excellent place to preserve and save ground spices.

TAGINE SPICE MIXTURE

This recipe is a version of a spice mixture used in Morocco for the broad category of foods cooked in a tagine, the pot that lends its name to the dishes.

INGREDIENTS

3 tablespoons fennel seeds

2 star anise

10 cardamom pods (or ½ teaspoon seeds)

½ teaspoon cumin seeds

½ cinnamon quill (see instructions if using ground cinnamon)

1 teaspoon black peppercorns

½ teaspoon Szechuan peppercorns

1 teaspoon turmeric

1 teaspoon smoked paprika

Toast the first seven ingredients. If you are using ground cinnamon, you can just add 1 teaspoon of that instead of the quill *after* the other spices are toasted. Cool the spices and grind them in a spice grinder or a mortar and pestle. Add the turmeric and smoked paprika.

> *Note*: I do not add saffron here; it is too expensive to tie up in a mixture like this. Add it directly to the recipe, as it is an essential ingredient for flavor. Suggestions that turmeric can fill this role because of its yellow color completely miss the point: it is about *flavor*.

PESTO ALLA GENOVESE

I add this as a special request from my daughter, who thinks my pesto is special. This recipe will be different from many recipes in that it starts in the garden. Homemade pesto is worth the effort because the commercial versions generally contain strange additions or omit critical ingredients.

Pesto is what I do with basil as a final harvest so that the basil does not go to waste. Sweet basil is used fresh in as many meals as possible during the growing season. Basil is not just a flavoring. I use it as an ingredient in salads with tomato, cucumber, fresh mozzarella, hard-cooked eggs, etc., as well as in sandwiches—essentially anywhere I think it will fit. Pesto is wonderful on pasta (including the classic combination of pasta, potatoes, and green beans with pesto) and on fresh salmon, poached or grilled. Use your imagination.

I suppose you could buy enough basil in the grocery store to make pesto, but it would be a very expensive process. I plant sweet or genovese basil because this variety is large leafed and is the type of basil traditionally used in genovese pesto—plus I like the flavor. I plant basil in my garden in Dallas in the middle of April to be used as a fresh herb and in sauces all summer until November. I generally plant at least four or five basil bushes and trim the seed heads from time to time throughout the summer so that the plant puts its effort into producing the leaves rather than seeds. We spend time during the summer at the beach in

Virginia, and we plant basil when we get to the beach. The basil at the beach does not get made into pesto unless one of the neighbors decides to cut it and make it into pesto, but it is used generously all summer. It is easy to grow and always fresh when you pick it.

The final basil harvest in Dallas is before the first frost (generally just before Thanksgiving), and the entire amount gets processed into pesto. You cannot use that amount of pesto in one or even several meals, so it gets frozen. Frozen pesto is absolutely delicious when thawed and used as a sauce for pasta, over fish, etc., and you should not hesitate to do so. During the summer and into the fall, you should clip and discard the seed heads to encourage growth—and again before final harvest of a bush so that they do not get transferred into the kitchen.

Once the bushes are harvested, the most time-consuming part of the work in making pesto is carefully removing the leaves from the stems and washing them. Discard the stems. Fill a salad spinner with water. Add the leaves to the bowl of the salad spinner so that the leaves can be thoroughly washed. The salad spinner makes it easy to lift out the leaves from the rinse water, leaving behind any dirt. Change water, and rinse as needed until the leaves are clean; do not bother spinning the leaves dry.

The next step is to place the clean leaves into boiling water for no more than five to ten seconds to blanch and just wilt them. It is quick! *Immediately* remove the blanched leaves and *immediately* shock them in a large bowl of ice water to stop the cooking process and leave them bright green. The blanching is designed to deactivate enzymes in the leaves and so to stop the pesto from browning (as it will if you use unblanched leaves).

Next, commence the process of making the pesto by grinding. Traditionally, pesto acquired its name because it was made with a mortar and pestle. Most modern cooks are not about to do this amount of work, and a food processor is ideal for the process. I have seen recipes for using a blender, but blenders are difficult to use in making a pesto because a blender will not work properly if the material to be blended is not relatively liquid (implying the need to add too much oil); this is not the case for a food processor. A traditional recipe includes the approximate proportions as listed, but basil leaves shrink enormously and lose liquid when blanched. Therefore, you must use your own judgment as to proportions—tasting as you go is an excellent idea.

INGREDIENTS

2 cloves garlic

2 cups fresh basil leaves

½ cup olive oil, split use

2 tablespoons toasted pine nuts, or more to taste (other nuts such as toasted pecans or toasted almonds are delicious, albeit nontraditional, substitutes for pine nuts)

1 teaspoon salt, or to taste

½ cup freshly grated parmigiano-reggiano cheese (except, of course, a kosher substitute as needed to comply with your observance of kashruth)

3 tablespoons unsalted butter at room temperature

Before adding any other ingredients, drop the garlic through the feed tube and into the spinning blade of the food processor so that the garlic is finely minced. You simply do not want to chomp down on a chunk of raw garlic in the pesto. Remember—pesto is an uncooked sauce when it is used, although some hot pasta water is added to thin it, and the hot pasta will "cook" the sauce slightly. (There are recipes using roasted garlic, but this changes the flavor profile.)

After the garlic is finely minced, place the blanched basil leaves into the food processor with a small amount of olive oil, close the lid, and pulse to get the desired texture, slowly adding more olive oil if needed. The pesto should be not liquidly and not completely stiff but should be relatively smooth and easily spoonable: a flowable paste. Do not add salt at this point.

At this stage, add the butter, and pulse 1 more time. Add a liberal quantity (2 to several tablespoons or so) of toasted pine nuts—or toasted pecans or almonds—as desired, and pulse lightly. Remove the pesto to a bowl. Freshly grate and stir in parmesan cheese (real parmigiano-reggiano or kosher cheese, and never the stuff in the green container. A block of parmesan will stay fresh for an extended period; this is not true for any pregrated cheese. Cheese should be properly wrapped for storage, and cheese bags made for this purpose by Formaticum really work. Add salt to taste only after you add the cheese since the cheese is inherently salty; otherwise, you can wind up with an oversalted pesto, and that cannot be fixed. Your reaction should be "Yum!"

Line ½-cup glass containers with plastic wrap, using sufficient wrap to fold over and cover the filled cups. Then fill the lined containers after tasting and adjusting the pesto. Carefully cover the filled containers with the excess plastic wrap. Put the containers in the freezer. After the pesto is frozen, decant the wrapped pesto carefully from the glass containers, and put the frozen, plastic-wrapped pesto "cubes" in a larger plastic bag. Squeeze out the air before sealing and storing in the freezer. Decanting is easier after 2 to 3 hours, when the pesto is solid but not totally frozen.

GARAM MASALA

Garam masala is one of many spice mixtures used in Indian cooking. The term *masala* means, in essence, a mixture of spices, herbs, and seasonings. One Indian vegetarian cookbook that I own has more than twenty different masala recipes; for garam masala alone, there are more than eight different recipes from different regions of India. There are a number of brands of Indian spices available in Indian food stores, just as how in American food stores, there are a number of spice brands. Three of the brands available are Bedekar, MDH, and Rajah. Many American brands, such as Spice Islands and Penzeys, have started to include spice mixtures such as garam masala in their product lines. We are all familiar with the common, very yellow curry powder (also known as "sweet" curry), which is one of a multitude of different spice mixtures. Although many Americans think of this sweet curry when they think of Indian food, this is a limited view of the complexity of Indian cooking.

Spices, when stored, should be tightly sealed in jars and labeled carefully. It is a good idea to place them in the freezer to preserve freshness, if you have space. To grind spices, many keep a coffee grinder that is labeled and used solely for grinding spices. A mortar and pestle is the classic method.

INGREDIENTS

4 dried whole chili pods, toasted and seeded before grinding (I generally use guajillo chili pods—nontraditional but delicious and not too spicy)

2 tablespoons sesame seeds, toasted

1½ tablespoons green peppercorns

1½ tablespoons white peppercorns

⅛ cup whole cloves (which I reduce by half because I am less than enamored of the intensity of the flavor of cloves)

4 3-inch cinnamon sticks (or ⅓ cup cinnamon powder)

⅛ cup cardamom seeds

⅔ cup cumin seeds

¼ cup coriander seeds

2 dried bay leaves

1 teaspoon ground ginger

2 whole nutmeg seeds

Other ingredients in other garam masala recipes include saffron (up to ½ teaspoon), fennel seeds (up to ¼ cup), ajowan seeds (up to ½ teaspoon), ground mace (up to 1½ teaspoons), black peppercorns (up to 2 tablespoons), and black mustard seeds (up to 2 tablespoons).

When you prepare any masala, toast the various components, not previously ground, in a dry pan prior to grinding, both to enhance the flavors and to enhance shelf life. Ingredients can be ground separately and then mixed, or they can be combined for grinding.

Sourdough Pancakes, p. 45

Chapter 3: *Breakfast*

DILL FRENCH TOAST

There are many recipes for french toast, including various recipes for stuffed french toast with sweet toppings and with various sweet combinations of spices and sugar, but rarely do you see a recipe for a savory french toast. This recipe is quick and easy to make using various leftover (but not stale) breads. It is a wonderful quick weeknight dinner with a salad.

Many recipes for french toast and bread puddings call for stale bread, but with the availability of freezers, why would you let bread stale? And if you did, why would you use it? If you want a dry bread to provide better liquid absorption (which is the reason for recommending stale bread), use the oven at a low heat to dry the bread.

INGREDIENTS

bread (see next page for tips)

eggs (at least 1 egg per slice of bread—extra is fine)

milk product, 2-3 tablespoons per egg (milk, heavy cream, whipping cream, or half-and-half)

salt and pepper to taste

dill weed

freshly chopped chives (optional)

unsalted butter for sautéing

For this purpose, I normally use whole milk. Dried dill weed is normally in your grocer's spice rack. This recipe is excellent and somewhat different with a liberal quantity of fresh, finely minced dill and chives.

The type of bread is an important consideration; while an ordinary good-quality bread (including challah or sourdough) can be used, this french toast is even better with a good-quality pumpernickel or Jewish rye. A sturdy bread is essential. Ordinary grocery-store white sandwich bread will disintegrate and does not fill the bill (for this purpose or much else).

The technique is simple. Add the milk product to the eggs and beat thoroughly with the salt, pepper, dill weed, and chives (optional). The dill weed sometimes is difficult to incorporate into the eggs. Use a liberal quantity of the milk product; this is more like a custard than like scrambled eggs. Soak the bread in the egg mixture. I prefer the bread to be thoroughly soaked so that the egg mixture penetrates through to the middle of the bread—*ergo*, the reason for using a sturdy bread. I generally use a generous amount of egg (more than 1 egg per slice of bread).

After the bread is soaked, heat a pan with butter. I cannot imagine for this purpose using any oil product other than unsalted butter; this is all about flavor. Sauté the bread to the desired degree of doneness. I do not like my french toast overcooked, so I cook it just to a point where the bread is still moist on the inside. My wife, on the other hand, likes her french toast cooked longer than I do. It is a matter of taste. After the bread is mostly cooked, pour the remaining egg mixture over the bread in the skillet. This is comfort food, not haute cuisine. Finish cooking the bread with the egg. Since this is a savory dish, serve as is without any syrup or other sweetener.

> *Note*: Never refrigerate bread. It stales at refrigerator temperatures.
> Either use bread right away or freeze it. Thawed bread tastes perfectly fresh.
> Thaw at room temperature; microwaving does something unpleasant
> to the bread's texture and toughens it.

> *Note*: Whipping cream has a lower fat content than heavy cream. Even heavy creams have varying fat contents depending on the brand—read labels. Purchase the one with the greatest fat content available.

SOUTHERN GRITS

Grits is a comfort food for those of us who grew up in the South. Unfortunately, all that seems to be available in most grocery stores is instant or quick grits, products that I will not buy. Quaker Old Fashioned Grits has to be cooked but takes a relatively short period of time to cook—less than ten minutes. Certainly, greater speed is not needed even for cooking breakfast on a busy morning. Having said that, it is a wonderful comfort food, and we frequently make grits and eggs for dinner.

Grits is a corn product frequently processed with lime. It is different from polenta, which is also made from cornmeal. I have come to prefer stone-ground grits. I buy it in Virginia Beach, and you might find it in specialty stores or grocers such as Central Market in Texas that cater to people who appreciate food. Given the internet and the pervasiveness of internet marketing, you easily can find stone-ground grits with a Google search. It is made using either white or yellow corn; there are subtle flavor differences between the white and yellow. I keep it in a plastic bag in the freezer to maintain freshness and flavor.

I heartily recommend stone-ground grits, even though it takes thirty minutes to an hour of cooking time. It has a more coarse texture than Quaker's ordinary, commercially available grits. Even though the stone-ground version takes longer to cook, that does not mean that you are standing at the stove, working at it the whole time.

INGREDIENTS

```
See instructions for amounts and proportions.
grits
1 teaspoon salt per cup uncooked grits
water and/or milk
butter (at least 2 tablespoons per cup of uncooked grits)
cheese (optional)

Preheat the oven to 325°F.
```

On the stove top, heat a sufficient quantity of liquid—follow the package directions. The stone-ground grits that I use calls for $4\frac{1}{2}$ cups of liquid per cup of dry grits, but other brands vary. I frequently use only water in making grits, but many people use milk or a 50/50 mixture of milk and water; the milk adds a wonderful richness. Since butter is an essential flavor, do not use chicken stock for a pareve result.

If you lightly toast the dry grits in the pan with butter, the corn flavor will be enhanced. The dry grits should be slowly added and stirred into the hot liquid to avoid lumps. Lower heat to a simmer as you stir.

When you add the grits to the liquid, you should also add 1 teaspoon (heaping if you use kosher salt) of salt for each cup of dry grits. Without this salt, the final product will be tasteless, and it is impossible to correct the failure to use the salt in the cooking process by adding salt at the table. This is why I think most restaurant-prepared grits are not worth ordering.

At this point, cover the grits, and put the pot into the oven to continue cooking. Stir every 15 to 20 minutes and add more water or other liquid as necessary. The stone-ground grits will take at least 30 minutes to properly cook, and 45 minutes to 1 hour is even better. The additional time just causes the grits to become creamier as it cooks and as you stir it. Even using the oven, it is necessary to stir occasionally to avoid sticking to the bottom of the pan but cooking in the oven avoids a necessity for constant stirring.

After cooking the grits, stir in 2 tablespoons (or to taste) of unsalted butter for each cup of dry grits that you made. At this stage, you can also stir in cheese to your taste and/or some milk if you desire.

Cheese is a delicious addition. Serve with eggs cooked as you desire. Frequently, we just make sunny-side up eggs sautéed in browned butter to serve with the grits. A cheese omelet is particularly delicious with grits. We always use butter to cook eggs if they are part of a meal that includes milk products and not meat; eggs cooked in butter just taste better, especially if you brown the butter slightly before adding the eggs.) Biscuits with honey, cornbread, toast with jam, or even bagels and cream cheese are wonderful sides.

MUSHROOM, ASPARAGUS, AND CHEESE OMELET OR FRITTATA WITH OTHER VEGETABLES AND SMOKED FISH VARIANTS

Always use butter to cook eggs unless you are going to serve the eggs with meat. I state this with the understanding as a southerner that many use bacon fat for this purpose—but never in my house. It is almost impossible to order eggs that are cooked in butter in a restaurant; most restaurants now use a flavorless oil to cook eggs, and they do not use salt and pepper, resulting in eggs that are most unappetizing. I firmly believe that butter is a superior flavor for this purpose.

Omelets or frittatas should not be overcooked. Eggs are extremely heat sensitive, and overcooking or cooking eggs at excessive heat causes the eggs' protein molecules to squeeze out the liquid in the egg, producing an egg product with an unappetizing texture and liquid runoff. I like my eggs just barely cooked—that is, cooked to the point where they are barely set and still very moist—although frittatas should be cooked until just beyond the point of runny but not beyond the point of resembling set custard. This is sufficient to render the eggs safe to eat. (Do not ignore the steps for buying eggs. This is an important safety step. See the discussion of eggs in Chapter 2.)

When cooking eggs, a nonstick skillet is preferable if you do not want the eggs to stick, although for sunny-side up eggs, a well-seasoned, flat cast-iron skillet, griddle, or comal also works well. For six to eight eggs (sufficient for two or three servings), use a ten-inch skillet; for a dozen to fifteen eggs, use a twelve-inch skillet; and for one portion (two to three eggs), use an eight-inch skillet or frying pan. It is important to use a correctly sized pan so that the eggs cook properly.

As an interesting sidenote, apparently a skillet or frying pan has flared or rounded sides, although logically it should be called a sauté pan—a pan with squared-off sides is more commonly referred to as a sauté pan. I think many people confuse the terminology, and in the 2013 season of *America's Test Kitchen*, Chris Kimball confirmed the confusion and the terminology. This is true even though you use a skillet to sauté and a sauté pan for other functions. Certainly, the kitchen equipment advertisements on the internet contribute to the definitional confusion, using the terms seemingly interchangeably. A griddle is flat with almost no sides, and a comal is the Mexican equivalent.

INGREDIENTS

This recipe can be doubled for a 12-inch pan.

<u>10-inch pan</u>

6-8 eggs

½ pound fresh mushrooms

3 shallots or ½ a medium-sized onion

2-3 cloves garlic

1-2 tablespoons butter

1 ounce dried mushrooms (porcini, black trumpet, or chanterelle)

2 cups fresh asparagus, or see recipe for alternative vegetables

fresh or dried herbs, chopped—oregano, thyme, basil, marjoram, rosemary, chives, or dill (as you desire or in combination). If using dried herbs, a mixture of ¼ teaspoon rosemary plus ½ teaspoon thyme and ½ teaspoon oregano works well. Double quantities when using fresh herbs.

salt and pepper to taste

1 teaspoon liquid per egg (water, milk, half-and-half, whipping cream, or heavy cream)

cheese as desired

Asparagus-and-Mushroom Filling

1. Omelet

An asparagus-and-mushroom omelet filling is delicious and involves a simple preparation process. To be clear, this is not the classic French omelet described by Julia Child.

See Chapter 2 for preparation of the mushrooms and asparagus. Slice and sauté fresh mushrooms until the liquid has been exuded and evaporated and the mushrooms are caramelized. Set aside.

Sauté the chopped shallots or onion in butter along with the cloves of garlic, each thinly sliced or chopped until the assembly is translucent and the aroma is intoxicating. Then combine the cooked mushrooms with the garlic and shallots or onion. Remember that a small quantity of reconstituted, dried, truly wild mushrooms makes everything better; dried porcinis, trumpets, or chanterelles that are reconstituted and chopped contribute a huge flavor burst. Reconstitute dried mushrooms with sufficient hot water to cover, with a 15-minute wait until the mushrooms are soft. Add the dried mushrooms and the reconstituting liquid (after disposing of the sandy dregs) to the cooked fresh-mushroom mixture. Cook to reduce the liquid until it is thick and syrupy before proceeding.

Add peeled asparagus stems, cut into 1-inch lengths, reserving the tender tips, and cook lightly. The asparagus should retain some crispness and green color and not be overcooked. The raw asparagus tips cook very quickly, so add them at the last minute as you add the eggs.

After you add asparagus (or other vegetable, as noted below) to the pan with the mushroom mixture, if you desire to add herbs—and you should—now would be the appropriate time. Chopped fresh oregano, thyme, basil, or marjoram (or a combination) are delicious, as would be rosemary or, for a different flavor, fresh chopped dill. Any of these herbs can be combined with chives. Be particularly careful with rosemary, both to chop it well and to not use too much, because its flavor can be overpowering. I like fresh herbs for this use, but dried work well also, except for basil, which is only to be added fresh and not dried. Herbs are very easy to grow, and if you cannot grow your own, they are now usually available fresh from a local supermarket.

At this point, the filling can be stored (refrigerated for several hours to overnight) until you are ready to cook the eggs. The eggs should be liberally beaten to break up the whites, adding salt and pepper to taste. Before cooking eggs for omelets, add 1 teaspoon of liquid per egg.

To cook on the stove top, stir the eggs to start while using a low to moderate flame or setting, and then occasionally lift the edges of the eggs as they cook, tilting the pan to allow the runny top of the eggs to flow over the edge of the cooked eggs and then under the cooked eggs so that the curds are small and the bottom does not overly brown. As the eggs approach the point where the top is barely liquid (having lifted and tilted the pan so that the liquid flows under the eggs from time to time during the cooking process), you should add grated cheese of the desired variety. For this purpose, I frequently prefer mild cheddar, although a gruyère, a young Fontina Val d'Aosta, french raclette, brie, or other similar cheese to your taste (and kosher as needed) is also delicious. To finish the cooking, place an amount of warmed vegetable filling so as to fill, but not overfill, the cooked eggs, and finish the omelet by folding the egg like a clamshell over the toppings. Slide onto a serving plate.

2. Frittata

Another easy variant for cooking a lot of eggs is a frittata. Think of it as a crustless Italian quiche. For a frittata, a somewhat larger amount of milk product added to the beaten eggs will produce a more custardy result, while cream makes the end product even richer—and better. For a 10-inch frittata with 6 to 8 eggs, ½ cup of heavy cream works well, and this can be scaled up for a 12-inch frittata. (A 12-to-15-egg frittata serves 6 generously with a salad; thus, each serving has less than 3 tablespoons of heavy cream for less than 140 calories from cream per serving.) The amount of filling for a frittata can be significantly greater than the amount that will fit as a stuffing for an omelet.

After cooking the vegetable filling as described above for an omelet, add the filling to a warm skillet, stirring so that the butter will coat the pan. Place the pan in a 350°F oven on a middle shelf. Beat the eggs and liquid as instructed above. Stir the desired shredded cheese into the egg mixture. Then add the beaten egg mixture to the pan with the vegetables. Carefully slide the pan back into the oven. Set the timer to 25 minutes, checking until the eggs are just set in the middle of the pan, puffed, and just lightly browned. (The 12-inch pan may take a few minutes longer.) Many recipes call for use of the broiler for this purpose, but I think setting the oven for baking produces a better result. The total cooking time depends on the amount of ingredients in the frittata. However, you choose to cook the eggs, the goal is that the egg not be cooked beyond a tender, moist, barely cooked stage.

Allow the frittata to cool for 10 minutes after removing from the oven. Then it should slide easily out of the pan and onto a serving plate or board. Cut into wedges to serve.

Variations

1. Spinach and Other Greens

Vegetables other than asparagus can be used in making a different-flavored omelet or frittata. Spinach is delicious. Instead of the asparagus, use ½ pound of fresh spinach or other greens such as swiss chard for a 10-inch pan or 1 pound for a 12-inch pan. The other ingredients and the process remain the same except that the lightly sautéed and drained spinach is added to the mushroom mixture at the same time as the eggs, not earlier.

The goal is that the vegetables be small enough so that each piece fits in one's forkful without cutting the vegetable on the plate. Lightly chop the spinach before cooking. Spinach should then be sautéed until it is just *barely* wilted and some of the liquid exuded; do not overcook! This liquid should then be drained off. Some of that liquid may be used in the eggs instead of water to add an additional delicious spinach flavor to the omelet or frittata. For a frittata, add the cooked spinach to the other vegetables when you add the eggs. Bake in a 350°F oven.

2. Zucchini and Other Summer Squash

Zucchini or other summer squash is best made into a frittata rather than an omelet. Use 2 small, thin zucchini for a 10-inch pan and 4 for a 12-inch pan. (Pumpkins, butternut squash, and other squash that have thick skins and hard, dense flesh are winter squash, while soft, thin-skinned squash such as zucchini, yellow squash, and crookneck squash are summer squash. Larger zucchini or other summer squash tend to have undesirably larger seeds.)

Grate the zucchini into shreds. Salt the grated zucchini lightly, letting the zucchini rest before squeezing it to eliminate much of its liquid. You will be amazed at the amount of liquid the zucchini will release when squeezed in this manner. Failing to eliminate the liquid in vegetables such as zucchini or spinach will impede the cooking of the egg and leave an undesirable and unappetizing amount of liquid on the plate and in the frittata. The texture of the end product will not be right.

Caramelize the mushrooms as described above. Lightly sweat the grated and squeezed zucchini with the garlic and onion or shallot. Add the caramelized fresh and reconstituted dried mushrooms, together with salt, pepper, and thyme or other desired herbs. Allow the sautéed mixture to slightly cool before mixing it into the eggs. Then pour the mixture back into the pan. As a safety matter, it is a good idea to add the eggs while the pan is on the oven shelf. Cook in a 350°F oven.

Frittatas are delicious hot, warm, or even cold (room temperature). Leftover frittata is delicious with sour cream and sprinkled with a little salt.

3. Smoked Fish

A final and most delicious variant addition for mixing into eggs—whether cooked in an omelet, scrambled on the stove top, or made into a frittata—is the addition of flaked or roughly diced smoked whitefish, lox, gravlax, nova, or smoked spiced sable (also known as black cod when fresh).

Simply cook the mushroom, onion, and garlic as described above. If you are using the mixture as a topping, add the flaked or diced fish to the mushroom mixture just before serving, heating only to just warm through. For a frittata, beat the eggs, add in the fish, pour the egg mixture over the vegetables, and cook. Dill is the appropriate herb for this variant. I do not add any vegetables other than onion, garlic, and mushroom. The flavor is incredible! Serve with bagels and cream cheese.

MASHED POTATO PANCAKE/FRITTATA

When I have leftover mashed potatoes, this recipe is the ultimate *easy* comfort food, yet I have never seen this described elsewhere.

INGREDIENTS

This recipe is intended for a 12-inch pan (sufficient with a salad to feed 4).

```
3 cups or so chilled mashed potatoes (remember, this is leftovers)
8 eggs (I generally use jumbo eggs)
1 cup whole milk (in addition to that already used to make the
mashed potatoes)
salt to taste (if the potatoes are well flavored, just add enough salt
to flavor the added eggs—not more than 1 teaspoon of kosher salt)
2-3 tablespoons unsalted butter
```

Proportions are approximate and not critical other than not adding too much salt, but what is important is the mashed potatoes. This recipe is easily scalable for a single serving using an 8-inch skillet or for a 10-inch skillet.

Mix the first 4 ingredients well. Lightly brown the butter in a nonstick skillet. Pour the egg mixture into the pan, filling the pan—but not so full that you cannot move it to the oven. Cook on the stove top for a couple of minutes. Then move the pan to a preheated 350°F oven to finish for about 30 minutes. (If you are using an 8-inch or 10-inch skillet, reduce the cooking time.) The pancake/frittata will be fully set in the middle and the edges lightly browned. The cooked pancake/frittata should slide right out onto a plate or cutting board. Slice and serve. Leftovers are great cold and served with some sour cream and salt.

Garlic mashed potatoes take this recipe to a special level. Boil the potatoes until just easy to pierce with a knife. If the potatoes are large, halve or quarter before cooking. For 4 pounds of Yukon Gold potatoes (which do not need to be peeled—just clean out any bad spots before cooking), melt 6 tablespoons unsalted butter in a small skillet. As the butter reaches a simmer, place 10 large, whole, peeled garlic cloves in the butter. Cook (poach) the garlic cloves in the butter at a bare simmer, stirring occasionally until very lightly tanned and just soft and mashable—do not overcook.

Add about 1 cup of whole milk to the garlic butter to heat, but do not boil. (You do not need cream, although I do recall a Julia Child recipe using heavy cream rather than butter to poach the garlic, and it makes great potatoes.)

Before adding the garlic mixture to the potatoes, drain the potatoes thoroughly. Then return them to the stove top to dry—a minute or so—shaking the pan slightly. Then turn off the heat, and add the garlic mixture to the potatoes, with salt to taste. Mash well with a potato masher by hand. A machine will ruin the texture, but a potato ricer is perfect. I know that it is a current "chefie" thing to leave the potatoes somewhat lumpy, but I do not know why anyone would want this.

SOURDOUGH PANCAKES

There is no excuse for using a premade commercial pancake mix since any pancake mixture is easy to assemble, and you will not add weird chemicals. There are many variant recipes for pancakes. However, these sourdough pancakes are the best pancakes (and maybe the easiest to prepare) you will ever eat! Of course, you do need sourdough starter. We frequently make these for dinner and serve with eggs over easy or a cheese omelet.

INGREDIENTS

This recipe makes enough for 3–4 hungry people when served with eggs. You can easily halve the recipe.

```
2 cups Sourdough Starter (see recipe in Chapter 4)
```
```
¼ cup maple syrup (the flavor and lack of added chemicals is worth
the cost of using real maple syrup)
```
```
3 tablespoons unsalted butter, melted (plus what is needed to
butter the skillet)
```
```
2 eggs (I use jumbo—use what you have)
```
```
½ teaspoon Morton's kosher salt (if using other brands or
textures, adjust appropriately because other textures of salt will
measure differently, and too much salt will ruin a recipe)
```
```
½ teaspoon baking soda
```
```
1 teaspoon baking powder
```
```
fruit, berries, or nuts (optional—see instructions for
suggestions)
```

Mix sourdough starter, maple syrup, melted butter, eggs, salt, baking soda, and baking powder, and whisk to combine. The resulting batter should be thicker than heavy cream.

At this point, if you want banana sourdough pancakes, mash up a very ripe banana, and stir it in. If you want blueberry, raspberry, or strawberry pancakes, carefully drop the fruit directly on each pancake with a sprinkling of sugar to sweeten the fruit immediately before flipping the pancake. (Strawberries need to be diced small before adding to the cooking pancakes.) These berry pancakes can be messy to cook because of the sugars that caramelize onto the pan, but they are delicious. An alternative is to cook the berries in the maple syrup, as described in the following recipe, to serve over the pancakes—easy and delicious. Another easy, delicious variant is pecan pancakes. Finely chop 1 cup of toasted pecans and stir them into the batter. Cook as normal.

Pancakes should be cooked on a buttered cast-iron skillet or griddle because once you get the pan to a proper temperature, it is relatively easy to maintain that temperature, although a nonstick pan also works. Drop ¼ cup of the pancake mix for each pancake (a 10-inch round griddle will fit 3 pancakes), or just make flapjacks that cover the pan. Pancakes are ready to turn when the top is all bubbly. After turning, they will be cooked in a few seconds.

Serve with microwave-warmed maple syrup, apple or cherry compote, or berry-flavored maple syrup.

Compotes and Flavored Syrups

These compotes and syrups are incredible spooned warm over pancakes or over ice cream—warm or cold!

1. Apple Compote

INGREDIENTS

2 large (11-to-14-ounce) apples (Granny Smith, Honeycrisp, Envy, or other variety that will retain its shape when cooked)
2 tablespoons butter
½ cup brown sugar, light or dark
1 lemon, zested
½ teaspoon cinnamon
pinch of salt

An excellent add-in to the pancake batter before cooking the pancakes is finely diced apples, sautéed beforehand in butter with brown sugar, cinnamon, and lemon zest until golden. Even better and easier is to top the cooked pancakes with this compote. You can add maple syrup as a substitute for the brown sugar. Granny Smith apples are good for this purpose. Honeycrisp or Envy apples are even better. Cool the apple compote somewhat before adding to pancake mix, or serve warm as a topping—generously, in lieu of syrup.

2. Cherry Compote

Another wonderful topping is cherry compote.

INGREDIENTS

```
24-36 ounces IQF sweet cherries (or a mixture of sweet and sour)
16-32 ounces sweet cherry juice (tart cherry juice is too sour
here)
2 cups cane sugar, or to taste
2 lemons, zested and juiced
½ teaspoon cinnamon
pinch of salt
2 vanilla pods, split to open the interior (or 1 tablespoon
vanilla extract, added after cooking if you do not have the
vanilla pods)
```

Heat all ingredients to boiling, being careful the pot does not overflow. Reduce the liquid until it is slightly syrupy, and the temperature of the compote is 218°F to 220°F.

3. Maple-Fruit Sauces

Even more simple, if possible, are maple-fruit sauces. Place 1–2 cups of washed berries (diced strawberries, blueberries, raspberries, blackberries, etc.) in a pot with some maple syrup (not enough to cover the berries, which will release their own juices), a pinch of salt, and some optional lemon or orange zest. Heat, stirring, until sauce bubbles, the berries pop or soften, and the flavors meld—it will take very few minutes.

Southern Cornbread, p. 64

Chapter 4: *Breads*

SOURDOUGH STARTER

Sourdough starter is a living organism and needs to be respected and cared for as such. The starter needs to be fed every week or two. It can be stored in the refrigerator. I do not freeze the starter, but you certainly can. I maintain the starter in a CorningWare container with a fitted glass top that is not airtight, but an airtight lid in the refrigerator is fine. The starter does not require oxygen.

There are books that describe the somewhat complicated process of creating a sourdough starter from scratch. Why would you go to that effort? A good source for a starter is from a friend who has a starter; absent that, King Arthur Flour has a reasonably priced fresh starter. King Arthur Flour's starter produces an excellent base for sourdough cooking. Just follow the easy instructions, and you will have it for years. It is truly not necessary to go through the mystical process as some writers describe of trying to grow your starter from scratch. King Arthur Flour also has a dry yeast sourdough starter, but they do not recommend that product for long-term maintenance. I have found that the persons who answer the telephone at King Arthur Flour are incredibly friendly, knowledgeable about their products, and helpful.

When the starter is at room temperature, maintain the starter in a relatively loose slurry texture—like a medium béchamel, or slightly stiffer than heavy cream. The starter will exude excess gray liquid and will be stiff when cold. To feed the starter, take it out of the refrigerator. The gray, watery liquid floating on top of the starter should be drained before feeding.

After the gray liquid is drained, add water that is filtered to remove volatile materials such as hydrocarbons, chlorine, etc. If you do not have filtered water, use distilled water and not regular bottled water. (Given the high ratio of cancer in certain US cities, one should assume that their water is particularly noxious and not fit for human consumption.) I do not consume unfiltered water, and I assume (but have no proof) that the yeast would be particularly sensitive to the chemicals in unfiltered water. Distilled water is available at any supermarket in gallon jugs.

Add enough water—approximately equal to the water that drained off plus some additional water so that after flour is added, you will have a mixture that is the texture of béchamel. Carefully stir the mixture to combine the cold starter with the added water. Since it is cold, it will be somewhat stiff. If you do not use it regularly, you may have too much starter; simply discard all but about a cup and start refreshing from that point.

There are two procedures to refresh the yeast.

(1) Stir in about ¼ cup of flour, and let the starter sit, covered with a non-airtight lid, at warm room temperature. An electric oven with only the light on or a gas oven warmed only by the pilot light are even friendlier places for the yeast. The light provides gentle warmth to activate the yeast. Over a period of several hours, repeat, adding the flour 2 to 4 times until the liquid is very bubbly and with the texture of a thin to medium béchamel. After the mixture is fully warmed, you can (but do not have to) move the container from the oven to the kitchen counter if you have a warm kitchen. Fully warmed means about 90°F as tested by your trusty Thermapen. You should not let it get much warmer than that.

(2) The second procedure is simply to add at least 1 cup of flour, and mix until very smooth. Let it rest on the counter overnight. It should be bubbly in the morning. If not, add some more flour, stir, and let rest until bubbly.

The starter is now ready for use to make bread, pancakes, etc. Immediately before putting the now vibrant starter back into the refrigerator, add and stir in slightly more flour.

SOURDOUGH BREAD (PLAIN, WHOLE WHEAT, OR RYE)

There is nothing like freshly baked bread. If you bake it on a baking stone as described in this recipe, the result is equal to the bread from any artisanal bakery. Even if you use loaf pans, the taste will be superb, although you do lose some of the wonderful crustiness. This is as much concept as recipe, and each time I bake bread, I get a somewhat different result in flavor. Unlike a restaurant or commercial bakery, I tend not to worry whether my results are replicated exactly each time I bake something.

Making the Dough

Yeast is not difficult to work with, and good bread is as much about patience as anything else. My daughter, Lisa, was recently confused because of much commentary on the internet obsessing about the critical nature of various details in producing good sourdough bread. Sourdough is very forgiving (unless you kill it with too much heat), and so—unlike baking a cake, for example—such concerns are simply not valid.

INGREDIENTS

2 cups sourdough starter

7 cups flour (I use either unbleached all-purpose flour or bread flour. I sometimes combine white flour with whole wheat. However, because of the need to ensure sufficient gluten, I do not use more than 3 cups of whole wheat or other flours in proportion to 4 cups of white flour. King Arthur Flour sells a white-whole wheat flour that can substitute for regular whole wheat flour. A cup of cornmeal as a substitute for a cup of flour adds a substantial and wonderful flavor twist. A couple cups of rye flour substituted for the whole wheat is another nice twist. Remember the cornmeal and rye flours lack gluten, so do not add too much.)

2½ cups filtered water (for flavor, you can substitute Dos Equis Amber or Modelo Negra, or use a beer that you like)

3-4 tablespoons unsalted butter, olive oil, or other oil, depending on flavor desired and pareve adherence

2 eggs (I use jumbo eggs)

1½ tablespoons Morton's kosher salt (Different salt brands have different amounts of salt per volume, so adjust amount for different textures and brands of salt. Plain table salt is more dense than any brand of kosher salt. Salt reduces the yeast activity, so defer adding it until the dough has rested for 20 minutes after the initial mixing and kneading to allow the flour to absorb the liquid and the yeast to start activating.)

Optional variations

```
¼ cup honey or molasses to add a flavor twist (the molasses works
well if you use beer)
1 onion, minced, sautéed in olive oil, and cooled before mixing
into an almost fully kneaded loaf or just before forming into
loaves
several cloves garlic, finely minced and sweated
1 cup or so minced olives
1-2 tablespoons dried herbs
2-3 tablespoons caraway seed, if you are using rye flour
```

You can start with cold, refrigerated starter. A better idea is to combine 2 cups of starter (with the gray liquid drained and fresh water added) with 1 cup bread flour, and mix, but do not knead, to make a very sticky and rough dough or leaven. Cover and let rest overnight in a non-drafty place in your kitchen. The mixture will rise and be happy when you wake up. Then continue with the recipe.

Mix and knead the staple ingredients (including the optional caraway, herbs, and honey, but not the onion, garlic, or olives), but not the salt. You have to judge how much flour to add; it is never exactly the same amount. If in doubt, add less flour at first, and then add additional after the resting and salt addition. If you heat the liquid before adding it (to no more than 105°F in the microwave), the first rise will be faster. Too much heat will kill the yeast, so use a thermometer. A Thermapen or similar instant-read digital thermometer is an essential tool in the kitchen.

After this stage, when the dough is well mixed but not yet fully kneaded, cover the dough, and let it sit for 20 minutes at room temperature, undisturbed. This allows the water to be absorbed fully into the flour. Then add the salt and knead the dough again.

If you want an onion- or garlic-flavored bread, lightly sauté (sweat, but do not brown) an onion and/or some finely chopped garlic, and then cool. Knead those flavorings in after adding the salt. Use a minimal amount of oil to sauté the onion or garlic. You can also add seeds or herbs as you desire. Add olives after kneading is basically complete to avoid crushing the chopped olives. Knead in additional flour as necessary until it is ready for the first rising.

The dough should be smooth, relatively non-sticky, and stretchy. If you are using rye flour, the dough will tend to be somewhat stickier.

Letting the Dough Rise

Take the dough out of the mixing bowl, and put it into a larger container to rise, turning it in olive oil or other oil so that it will not dry and crust over. I use a large covered pot for this purpose. Cover this container with plastic wrap or a tight-fitting lid, and place it into a warm, nondrafty place such as an electric oven with the electric light turned on but no other heat source. You are not trying to cook the dough, just keep it warm and not hot. The dough should be less than 85°F.

Contrary to every instruction I have ever seen, this rise can take 6–8 hours, particularly if your starter is directly out of the refrigerator, although I check it at about 2 hours and then from time to time as appropriate until it starts to rise. It is my experience that the first rise using only sourdough starter is much slower than if you use or add regular yeast. Sometimes, it looks like no rising is going to occur after 3–4 hours. In that case, turn the dough a little by hand to further mix up the yeast and flour. Eventually, it always rises. However, if you start with starter and flour in a bowl, rested and refreshed on the kitchen counter overnight as noted above (known as a *leaven*), the rise will be much faster.

When the dough has doubled, punch it down, and divide it into 2 or 3 loaves. This recipe makes almost 7 pounds of dough. A digital scale is very affordable. I weigh each loaf to make them the same weight, but approximation will also work. The goal is evenly sized loaves that cook evenly. Form the dough into loaves shaped in a boule or other desired shape.

After forming the dough, you can proceed directly to baking. Or, if you plan a second overnight rise in the refrigerator, place the loaves in baskets that are used solely for this purpose, with clean linen towels that are also dedicated to this purpose lining the baskets. The towels should be smooth, nontextured, and liberally rubbed with flour before placing the loaves on the towels in the baskets. Fold the towels loosely over the loaves, and place all of the baskets in a big, clean garbage bag. Puff up the bag with air, and seal by twisting the open end and tucking it under. Place the entire package on a shelf in the refrigerator overnight. This slow overnight rise adds to the bread's flavor. Magically, the next day the loaves will have risen. Gently remove the loaves from the floured towels, turning each loaf over onto a piece of unwaxed parchment paper to warm up for the next hour. Let the towels dry out. Then take the towels outside to vigorously shake them and remove the remaining flour before storing for the next use. When moving the loaves, be gentle so as not to deflate them. With a pastry brush, carefully remove excess flour. Cover the loaves during this warm-up period with a clean towel, dampened thoroughly with hot water (with excess water squeezed out).

If you want to proceed to baking the same day, just place the boules of dough on parchment paper, and cover with the warm, damp towel for a second rise, which should take about 1 hour.

Preparing the Oven

During the warming or second-rise process, prepare the oven with only 1 rack in the lowest available rack setting. Place quarry tiles (unglazed, with no lead) on the rack, close enough to each other to hold the loaves while they bake. These act like a baking stone but are much cheaper and can fill the rack. (And if a tile breaks, there is no great loss.) You may, of course, use a baking stone or steel. Heat the oven to 500°F. It takes a full hour to properly heat the quarry tiles or baking stone (and *America's Test Kitchen* ran tests to determine this time). I had a wonderful 1½ hour discussion in Mendocino many years ago with a professional baker who told me that it is the effect of heated quarry tiles or a baking stone combined with the steam process discussed below that creates a great crust.

On the floor of the oven—or, if you have an electric oven, on the first rack (noting that in this instance, you have to use 2 racks)—place a cheap aluminum pan used solely for this purpose (because it will be ruined for any other purpose) to heat during the same 1-hour period. (Other than the aluminum pan, use exactly the same procedure to prepare the oven to bake pizza.)

Baking the Bread

Near the end of the hour, bring a kettle of water to a boil. At the end of the hour, and immediately before placing the loaves into the oven, carefully score the bread with a very sharp knife or razor blade (known as a *lame*) so that the bread will expand properly. Lightly spray or sprinkle water on the loaves. Use a peel to place the bread in the oven, onto the quarry tiles or baking stone. Leave the parchment paper in place under each boule. The parchment makes the loaf slide easily off of the peel and also makes it easier to get the baked bread out of the oven. I think this method is better than the frequently suggested sprinkling of cornmeal on the peel, and it does not leave a mess. The parchment paper will become crispy but will not burn. Simultaneously, add boiling water to the pan on the shelf below the bread to create steam. Immediately close the oven. Lower the temperature to 450°F and bake for 35 to 40 minutes.

Using the peel, remove the bread, and cool for at least 1 hour on a rack before cutting, difficult as it may be to wait. The bread is not fully baked until it has cooled.

PUMPERNICKEL BREAD

Pumpernickel bread originated in Europe as a reaction to grain crop failures as early as the year 1450. The purpose was to extend available wheat flours with rye. Over time, and in America, the use of additional products such as potatoes, molasses, and cocoa occurred to achieve the dark color in the original, very different, German, mostly rye sourdough bread. I am not entirely sure where this particular recipe originated, but it contains a number of items that one would not normally associate with bread. I am sure that my European ancestors did not use chocolate. The result is a dense but incredibly flavorful loaf of bread with good texture.

Although I have used a lot of different bread recipes, in my experience, the ratios of liquid to flour in the recipes always seem to need adjustment in practice, depending on humidity and other factors. You really need to practice in your kitchen to get to a point where you understand how the dough should feel. In any event, this recipe produces dough that is dense, but it makes incredibly delicious bread.

INGREDIENTS

This recipe will make 3 boules that weigh about 2¾ pounds each after baking.

9 cups wheat flour (I split it up for added flavor: 6 cups of white bread flour—always unbleached—and 3 cups of whole wheat flour. Reserve 1 cup of the white flour to add at the end of kneading as necessary.)

3 cups rye flour

2 tablespoons salt

1 cup whole-bran cereal (I use Kellogg's whole-bran cereal)

¾ cup yellow cornmeal

2 packages active dry yeast plus 1 teaspoon sugar (or 2 cups sourdough starter)

3½ cups water, split use (2¾ cups water if you use sourdough starter. I sometimes use Dos Equis Amber or Modelo Negra as a substitute for part of the water. It is my experience that Mexican dark beers are harder to find in nonborder states, but there are many delicious beers.)

¼ cup unsulfured molasses

2 ounces unsweetened chocolate

1 tablespoon olive oil (or other unflavored vegetable oil or butter, unless you want a pareve result that can be eaten with meat)

2 cups mashed potatoes at room temperature (Sometimes I use garlic mashed potatoes, boiled simply with 2-3 pounds of potatoes, generous salt, several peeled garlic cloves, and water, draining most but not all of the water before mashing while hot. Do not add butter or milk if you want a pareve loaf.)

3 tablespoons caraway seeds

2 eggs

Combine the flours, salt, cereal, and cornmeal. Set aside.

Unless you are using sourdough starter, dissolve the active dry yeast with a teaspoon of sugar in ¾ cup room-temperature water to proof—about 10–15 minute. Set aside.

In a 1-quart (4-cup) Pyrex measuring cup, combine the remaining 2¾ cups of the water (and/or beer), molasses, chocolate, and butter, if you are using butter. (The original recipe called for margarine, which we have long since abandoned as nonhealthy.) Since this bread will frequently be used with meat, I suggest olive or canola oil instead of the butter, with the oil added after the liquid is heated. Carefully heat the chocolate mixture in a microwave until the chocolate is just melted and to no more than 105°F, stirring frequently.

> *Note*: Chop the chocolate beforehand to facilitate melting. If the chocolate mixture is heated to more than 105°F, cool to no more than 105°F before adding it to the dough mixture.

Place the melted chocolate mixture into a mixing bowl of a KitchenAid mixer. If you are using liquid oil instead of butter, add it at this time. Add the mashed potatoes and the caraway seeds to the chocolate mixture. Add the proofed yeast mixture or the sourdough starter. Use the dough hook of the mixer or stir with a plastic spatula by hand until the mixture is so thick you need to use the machine. Gradually and carefully, to avoid flouring your kitchen, add the flour mixture to the chocolate mixture. Add the eggs. Scrape the bowl frequently. Because this makes more dough than will fit in a KitchenAid bowl, split the mixture before adding the last 4 cups or so of flour. If needed, add the reserved 1 cup of white flour for use at the end of kneading, and add extra as needed. Add the flour mixture to each portion of the split dough and knead each to activate the gluten until the right texture is reached (slightly tacky but smooth and stretchy). As with most dough using rye flour, the result will be somewhat stickier than other doughs.

Knead with the dough hook until the mixture is smooth and elastic. As the bread kneads in the machine, you will probably have to use a sturdy but flexible mixing spatula to lever the dough down and keep the dough from riding up the dough hook and onto the machine. Combine and briefly knead both portions together by hand. There will be about 9 pounds of dough. Place the dough into a large covered bowl or pot so that it has room to double, oiling the bread so that a crust will not form. Place the covered bowl in a warm, draft-free place such as an electric oven with the electric light lit but no other heat source.

After the dough has doubled, punch it down, and let it rise again until it has doubled again. (Alternatively, you could divide the dough into 3 boules, and let them rise in the refrigerator overnight.) Shape the dough into boules or other desired shape and place each boule on parchment paper. Cover with a moistened (not wet) towel until the bread has doubled. If you have refrigerated the shaped breads for the final rise, you need to gently turn them out onto parchment paper and let them warm on the counter for an hour, covered with a moistened towel, before baking.

When you start to form the dough into shapes for final baking (or remove it from the refrigerator to bake), turn the oven to 500°F, using baking stones or quarry tiles as described under the recipe for Sourdough Bread (see the section on preparing the oven). It takes a full hour for quarry tiles or a baking stone to come to the correct temperature—do not shortcut the time.

When the bread is ready to put into the oven, *and* the stone is fully heated, boil a kettle of water to use with the water pan in the bottom of the oven, as described under the recipe for Sourdough Bread. Slash the tops of the bread in a design as desired to allow the bread to rise in the oven. Using a peel, put the bread—still on the parchment—into the oven. Then immediately add the water to the water pan, close the door of the oven immediately, and turn the oven temperature down to 450°F. Leave the bread on the parchment as it cooks in the oven; this makes it easier to slide in and out of the oven. Set the timer for 40 minutes, at which time the bread should be cooked. If not, continue for an additional 5 minutes.

Remove the cooked breads from the oven and let them cool on racks for at least 1 hour before slicing. As difficult as it is to wait, the bread does continue to cook and will not finish cooking properly if you do not let it cool appropriately. This is a flavorful bread that is dense and wonderful with a great crust. It is not like any other bread that you will have eaten; it is much better and more flavorful than any commercial pumpernickel. It makes wonderful sandwiches, is delicious with butter and jam or as an accompaniment with cheeses and is outstanding made into Dill French Toast (Chapter 3) or for any other use.

You can convert this bread to a sourdough pumpernickel by using a couple cups of sourdough starter rather than dry yeast. This steps up the flavor an additional notch. In such case, reduce the added liquid by about ¾ cup, and use only water, not beer.

This bread may be the easiest bread you will ever make. It is very quick from start to table. It is great for homemade pizza that is as good as or better than that from any commercial pizzeria.

INGREDIENTS

This recipe is easily doubled.

```
1 package dry yeast (I only use 1 package for 2 batches)
1 cup water, warm and not hot—less than 110°F
2½ cups unbleached all-purpose flour
½ teaspoon salt
2 teaspoons or so olive oil, with more for the rise
```

Proof the yeast in the water, and then place the proofed yeast into the mixing bowl of a KitchenAid mixer. Add the flour, salt, and olive oil. Using the dough hook attachment, knead until the dough is smooth and elastic. Place the dough into a covered bowl oiled with olive oil, turning to coat the dough. Allow the dough to rise and double in a warm, draft-free location, such as an electric oven with only the light lit. This process will take an hour or so. Deflate and turn the dough and allow it to rise a second time. This second rise can certainly be overnight in the refrigerator, a slow process that adds even more flavor and character.

Preheat the oven with baking stones to 500°F for 1 hour (see directions for using baking stones under the Sourdough Bread recipe). Roll out or stretch the dough into flat shapes. Place on parchment paper on a peel to slide into the oven. I have tried other methods of getting dough in and out of the oven, and this is by far the easiest and certainly does not make the mess that cornmeal does.

This bread, baked in this manner on blazing-hot quarry tiles or a baking stone, will cook rapidly—about 12 to 15 minutes—resulting in a flatbread with an incredible crust. Be careful not to overcook. It will be ready when it is nicely browned, and you can check simply by looking. It is most delicious and a most easy bread to make to serve at any time. Forget freezer-case pizza or delivered pizza—this dough is a base to use for the best pizza you have ever eaten, with your own selection of toppings, including dessert, for each member of your family.

Focaccia

Before baking, variations can be made. This dough is perfect for pizza or simply as a focaccia. If you are merely making focaccia, sprinkle the dough with salt, brush with olive oil (or perhaps olive oil simmered with garlic), and add herbs to taste such as dried thyme, dried oregano, or dried rosemary. Allow the dough to rise for 15 to 20 minutes, and then stipple it with your fingers before baking. Then, with the peel, place the dough into the 500°F oven. Do not reduce the oven temperature.

Pizza

If you are going to make a pizza, before baking, you can add sauce as desired, cheese, and whatever other ingredients you desire. A meat sauce or pizza with meat added is obviously not kosher if you add cheese, but there are many delectable cheese-and-vegetable combinations and unusual variants.

~ You could sauté some sliced garlic and/or shallots in olive oil with dried, chopped, reconstituted porcini mushrooms with a little bit of salt. Once this mixture is slightly cooled, spread it over the dough. Sprinkle on shredded mozzarella and freshly grated parmigiano-reggiano. Then bake this white pizza.

~ A classic pizza is the *margherita*—a simple uncooked tomato sauce with fresh mozzarella placed in slices around the pizza and liberally sprinkled with fresh basil immediately after removing from the oven.

~ Another variation is to spread some pesto over the pizza, layering on shredded mozzarella and grated parmesan before baking.

~ Instead of mozzarella and parmesan, try adding triple-cream brie over pesto. The possibilities are endless.

~ There is a wonderful sweet dessert variant not served in any pizza shop: cut seedless grapes (and/or thawed, previously frozen sweet cherries) in half, and press into the flattened dough, cut side down. Brush with melted butter, and sprinkle generously with cinnamon sugar. Bake. Serve warm. Yum!

BISCUITS

Of all the various breads, one of my favorites is biscuits made in the southern style (but with butter, not lard). This recipe produces the most light, puffy, flaky, and delicious biscuits. In one early attempt many years ago, I halved the recipe, except I failed to halve the butter. The result was not light but was incredibly rich and buttery. Although the result was luxuriously delicious despite the texture, it was an error that I have not repeated, although I have been tempted from time to time.

INGREDIENTS

2 cups unbleached all-purpose flour
4 teaspoons baking powder
½ teaspoon salt
½ teaspoon cream of tartar
2 teaspoons sugar
½ cup cold butter
⅔ cup cold whole milk

Preheat the oven to 450°F.

Whisk together the dry ingredients, and then cut in the butter using a pastry cutter or knives until the texture is soft, coarse crumbs. As with piecrust, I would not use any machines for these biscuits, notwithstanding what a TV chef might do. A pastry cutter is easy to use, and cleanup from a single bowl is easy. If the mixture is at all warm, refrigerate for ½ hour before proceeding. Pour in the milk, stirring only a sufficient amount to mix the ingredients. Do not overmix, or the texture will be impaired if the gluten in the flour is activated. Turn out the resulting dough onto a lightly floured surface and knead only as sufficient to bring the mixture together. Pat or lightly roll the dough to ½ inch thick. Cut with a biscuit cutter, or simply use a knife to cut into the desired shapes. Place on a cookie sheet lined with parchment paper.

Cook for 10 to 12 minutes until risen, golden brown, and delicious. Serve with butter and honey or jam.

I used to make corn muffins, cooking the cornbread in a muffin tin and producing separate cornbread muffins. However, I no longer do so. A much better result is obtained by placing the cornbread mixture into a cast-iron skillet preheated in the oven, which is the traditional southern method. I would not try this with any other type of skillet. Because of the heat involved, you absolutely cannot (and do not need to) use a modern nonstick skillet.

INGREDIENTS

1 cup unbleached flour
2 teaspoons white cane sugar
4 teaspoons baking powder
¾ teaspoon kosher salt
1 cup cornmeal (preferably yellow)
2 eggs
1 cup whole milk
¼ cup unsalted butter, melted, plus 2 tablespoons, split use
1-2 jalapeños (optional)
1 cup fresh corn kernels plus the "milk" from the cobs (optional)

Preheat the oven to 425°F.

First place the 10-inch cast-iron skillet into the 425°F oven while you are making the cornbread mixture. Then whisk together flour, sugar, baking powder, salt, and cornmeal. Northerners will use more sugar, but it really detracts from the taste of the cornbread.

In a separate bowl, mix together the eggs, milk, and ¼ cup of melted butter. Stir the liquid mixture into the dry ingredients. Stir until just smooth. The mixture should be a somewhat liquid batter like a thick béchamel. If desired, an addition of 1 to 2 finely diced (*brunoise*) jalapeños (with or without seeds, depending on the heat level desired) is a wonderful variant, as is a cup of corn cut from a fresh ear of summer corn, with the "milk" scraped with the back of your knife from the cob and pulsed in your blender.

Using a hot pad or insulated gloves, carefully take the heated skillet out of the oven, and place it on the stove top. Immediately add 2 tablespoons of butter, which will melt quickly. Swirl the butter around the pan, making sure to use a hot pad or heatproof glove, and then pour in the cornbread batter. Place back into the 425°F oven.

The cornbread should be cooked in 20 minutes. Cook until just brown on top. Check at 15 minutes. The cornbread should flip easily onto a cutting board. Serve hot with butter.

Seven-layer Dip, p. 74

Chapter 5: Appetizers

BABA GHANOUSH

Baba ghanoush is a simple-to-make yet complex-flavored Middle Eastern eggplant spread. It is healthy and tasty. It can be made in advance of any occasion and refrigerated, but it is better served at room temperature.

INGREDIENTS

```
1-2 firm medium purple eggplants
1 lemon, zested and juiced
1-2 large cloves garlic, mashed
¼-⅓ cup tahini
⅓ cup olive oil, or to taste
salt and pepper to taste
½ cup parsley or cilantro, chopped
```

The process is simple: Roast 1 or 2 eggplants either in the oven or on the grill. Classically, the roasting process was over a wood or charcoal fire that imparted its own flavor. Before roasting the eggplant, poke it liberally through the skin so that steam escapes; otherwise, it will explode, creating a huge mess. Roast at 350°F or 400°F, turning from time to time, until the eggplant is very soft, and the skin has turned from purple to brownish.

Cool the eggplant and cut off and discard perhaps an inch from the stem end. Slice the eggplant in half lengthwise. Scrape out the insides into a food processer. Some say that the seeds are bitter, but I do not remove the seeds, and the result is delicious. Cut the long strands of eggplant into shorter strands to assist the food processer. Alternatively, the entire mixing can be accomplished in a bowl with a potato masher. With a microplane grater, grate zest from 1 lemon into the food processer.

Before putting the lemon juice and garlic into the food processer, let the mashed garlic macerate with the lemon juice for 10 minutes to tone down the aggressive flavor of the garlic. You can achieve this goal by mashing the garlic with some salt in a mortar and pestle, or you can use a garlic press to mash the garlic and make it into a paste-like mixture. Soak the mashed garlic in the lemon juice from the lemon that you have just zested. Remove any lemon seeds. After at least 10 minutes, place the garlic-lemon mixture into the food processer. Alternatively, use the food processer to pulverize the garlic with the lemon juice, and let it sit before proceeding by adding the eggplant. For each eggplant used, add $\frac{1}{4}$ to $\frac{1}{3}$ cup or so of tahini, a Middle Eastern sesame-seed paste available in most supermarkets. Tahini separates oil from solid like natural peanut butter, so you need to stir to recombine it before measuring.

Blend the garlic, tahini, eggplant, lemon zest, and garlic mixture, adding olive oil as the processer works—at least $\frac{1}{3}$ cup or to taste for 2 eggplants. Add salt to taste, being careful if you used salt when you mashed and macerated the garlic. Add freshly ground pepper. Traditionally, chopped parsley is added to the blended baba ghanoush for serving. I like to use chopped cilantro instead of parsley. The herbs should be chopped with a sharp knife and stirred in by hand; a food processer does not serve well for this process. Serve with pita, chips, etc. I like baba ghanoush served with wonderful summer tomatoes, olives, and either cornichon pickles or Middle Eastern pickles.

HUMMUS

Hummus is now a generally available item in grocery stores. However, I still like to make my own because I am positive about what does not go into it, and I can vary the flavor as I desire. I am sure that commercial hummus does not use vegetables that add healthy flavor as I do, but that is clearly not traditional. But then I suspect that the many flavored varieties of hummus (especially chocolate) in the store are also not traditional.

INGREDIENTS

1 cup dried chickpeas (½ pound) or 2 (1-pound) cans of chickpeas
(this recipe can be made with other dried beans, although
chickpeas are the traditional ingredient)

1 onion (only if using dried chickpeas)

1 carrot (only if using dried chickpeas)

1 celery stalk (only if using dried chickpeas)

2-3 cloves garlic for cooking dry beans, plus 1-2 cloves for
making the hummus

a bouquet garni of 1 bay leaf with 2-3 sprigs each of oregano and
thyme

1 lemon, zested and juiced

salt

black pepper

extra-virgin olive oil

½ cup tahini

italian parsley or cilantro, chopped

½ teaspoon ground cumin or coriander (optional), or more to taste

dried tomato or roasted, peeled pepper (optional)

Preparing Dried Chickpeas

Pour the raw chickpeas (also known as garbanzo beans) over a large plate. Carefully examine them, looking for damaged peas, small stones, or other contaminants. Wash the chickpeas *several* times in a sieve or colander until the water is clear. Soak the chickpeas in clean water overnight in the refrigerator. The chickpeas will absorb a lot of water and will almost double their volume.

Drain the soaked chickpeas, and then put the chickpeas in a large pot. Cover with filtered water, and add the onion, carrot, celery, garlic, and bouquet garni, but *no* salt. Cook at a low simmer until the chickpeas are well cooked (very easily smashed when pressed between 2 fingers). It should take around 1 to 1½ hours to fully cook the chickpeas. Test for doneness by tasting a couple of beans. Add salt and stir, letting the chickpeas cook for another 15 minutes. When done, drain the chickpeas in a sieve, reserving the cooking water. Remove remaining vegetables, bay leaf, and any stems from the herbs. (Actually, using the vegetables, but not the bay leaf or stems, is delicious and would not hurt the hummus, but it is not traditional.)

Preparing Canned Chickpeas

If using canned chickpeas (or other beans), drain and wash before continuing with "Making the Hummus" step; note that this hummus will omit the vegetables you would use if you start with dry beans. The canning liquid is not palatable here and should not be used. Note that all canned beans are cooked and ready to use.

Making the Hummus

Puree garlic with a small amount of kosher salt, lemon zest, and black pepper in a mortar and pestle (or however you perform the task). You can grind in any other spice used, such as cumin, in this process. If you desire, you could try spices other than the cumin, such as coriander, or the cumin could be omitted. You can use commercial ground cumin or coriander, or you can toast whole seeds lightly in a sauté pan, taking them out of the pan as soon as they are toasted to avoid burning them. Then grind them for immediate use as noted.

Add lemon juice to the garlic mixture, and let it soak at least 10 minutes to take the edge off of the raw garlic flavor. This 10-minute wait is very worthwhile.

Put the chickpeas into a food processor, and process until smooth.

Add the tahini and the garlic puree (but not the cilantro) into the food processor, adding olive oil and reserved chickpea-cooking liquid until you get the desired texture. The hummus should be slightly thinner than the actual final desired texture, as it will thicken very slightly as it sits.

Blending in dried tomato or roasted, peeled peppers is a delicious variant. Add more lemon juice to taste. Add chopped italian parsley or cilantro to taste.

Season to taste.

Serve with some good olive oil drizzled on top and a garnish of chopped parsley or cilantro as well as a variety of olives, crackers, pita, and toast or croustades.

Pimento cheese is a traditional southern cheese mixture that is widely available commercially in grocery stores, at least in the South. However delicious commercial pimento cheese may be, homemade pimento cheese rises to an entirely new level. You can find numerous worthy variant recipes. This version has a more complex flavor profile than most, but it is simple to prepare. While this clearly tastes like pimento cheese, it varies from strictly traditional recipes, but the added complexity is not outside of traditional southern flavors. For example, I am positive that no one in Georgia as I was growing up ever used a jalapeño pepper (although spice heat is certainly not unfamiliar) or a smoked cheese (although smoke flavor permeates the southern cuisine).

INGREDIENTS

1 peeled garlic clove

1 small fresh jalapeño (With or without the seeds, depending on whether you want the heat. If you want even more heat, a serrano pepper can be used, but I personally do not like the serrano's flavor. I always stem and then cut the pepper, omitting the ribs or seeds. That provides an adequate amount of heat; my goal is flavor, not heat.)

¾ cup mayonnaise (not a salad spread—see Mayonnaise recipe in Chapter 8)

5 ounces smoked gouda, grated

4 ounces cheddar cheese, grated (or colby or longhorn)

4 ounces havarti cheese, grated

⅓ cup jarred pimentos, chopped (Pimentos are available in small glass jars in the grocery store. I suggest adding 1 jar—including the liquid—and tasting. If more pimento taste is desired, add a second jar.)

⅓ cup sour cream

cilantro, chopped (optional)

I generally make a double recipe, and it never lasts long. The steps are simple: First, grate the cheeses. *Note:* Freeze the cheeses for about 20 minutes before grating to make them firmer, but not solid, and easier to grate.

Put the garlic and jalapeño in a food processor as it is running so that the garlic and jalapeño are processed into miniscule pieces. Scrape the bowl, and pulse again. You really do not want to bite down on a large chunk of raw garlic or jalapeño; the jalapeño is about flavor, and most of the heat is avoided if you discard the interior ribs and seeds. Then add the mayonnaise, the grated cheeses, the pimentos, and the sour cream, and pulse just to mix. Do not overblend. Salt should not be necessary.

Pimento cheese can be eaten with various combinations of chips, Fritos, crackers, or pita that has been split open, separated by layers, brushed with a little bit of olive oil, perhaps sprinkled with dried herbs such as thyme or oregano, salted, cut into triangles, and baked in a 350°F oven until crisp (perhaps 10 minutes). It is also good as a sandwich on bread, toasted or not, or as a very easy Quesadilla (Chapter 12) filling served with Pickled Jalapeños (Chapter 7), sour cream, and Guacamole (Chapter 5).

SALMON SPREAD

This scrumptious appetizer recipe came from one of my wife's cousins in Tidewater, Virginia. We do not know the origin of this mixture, but we do know that it is easy to make and one of the most delicious and sought-after appetizers that we serve. It is also an example of how a dish can evolve over a period of time to become even better.

INGREDIENTS

1 pound (about 2 cups) of salmon (freshly poached or grilled and chilled is best, but canned also works deliciously)

1 (8-ounce) package of cream cheese (Philadelphia brand, full fat, room temperature)

1 lemon, grated and juiced (1 tablespoon of juice needed, about ½ a lemon)

⅓ medium sweet onion (Texas 1015, Vidalia, etc.)

1 teaspoon or more prepared Jewish-style (not cream) horseradish in vinegar (preferably beet colored and refrigerated, not shelf stable)

½ teaspoon liquid smoke (The smoke particles precipitate, so shake the bottle well. Add judiciously, as the flavor is intense.)

¼ teaspoon salt, or to taste

½ cup or so pecans, chopped and toasted

Originally, and still to this day, this spread used canned salmon and involved removing the bones and skin. However, lightly grilled (to medium rare) or poached fresh salmon is even better.

In a food processor, combine the salmon, cream cheese, lemon juice and zest, roughly chopped onion, horseradish, and liquid smoke. Blend thoroughly until smooth. Taste. Adjust horseradish, lemon juice and zest, liquid smoke, and onion to taste. Then add salt to taste, if needed. Stir in the chopped pecans. Chill for several hours so that the salmon spread becomes firm.

Serve with toast points, crackers, etc. An excellent base on which to serve the salmon spread is Pumpernickel Bread (Chapter 4). Alternatively, slice a french bread baguette into ½-inch-thick slices, place on a baking tin, and brush with olive oil lightly simmered with garlic (so that the garlic infuses the oil). Bake the croutons in a 350°F oven for 15 minutes until crispy. A bagel, fresh or toasted, also works.

Originally, the salmon spread was intended to be formed into a ball and coated with the pecans rather than the pecans mixed in. It is much easier to serve the spread in a bowl, and I personally like the pecans mixed in. My wife, Bobbie, does not like the pecans at all and so does not use them in the portion that she eats. It is all about your own taste preferences.

CREAM CHEESE DIPS

Anyone who entertains frequently needs simple but delicious dips for use in small or large gatherings, particularly if the gathering is to watch a sporting event. We are all familiar with the classic onion dip, but there are some other types of flavored dips that are easy to make and will receive compliments galore. These dips are so easy to make that it is almost embarrassing to put them in the form of a recipe.

INGREDIENTS

1 pound cream cheese
1 pint salsa (see recipe for variations)

Various southwestern-oriented dips can be made by taking a jar of salsa and blending with cream cheese. The proportion is 1 pound (2 packages) of room-temperature cream cheese to 1 pint of salsa. Because there are many different variations of flavors of salsa, your dips will likewise have different flavorings. If you do not want to make as much dip, you can certainly halve the recipe easily. The process could not be simpler: Blend the salsa and the cream cheese in a food processor until the mixture is totally combined. A blender will not work. Chill and serve.

If you want to get slightly more complicated, you can make your own flavor mixture instead of using a can or jar of salsa. For example, for a French Provençal twist using the classic tapenade flavors, simply blend tomatoes (preferably vine-ripe summer tomatoes), garlic, capers, olives, and chopped parsley with cream cheese in the food processor. You could also add 3 or 4 anchovy fillets to this mixture, rinsed to remove any excess salt. If fresh tomatoes of sufficient quality are not available, you can use canned whole tomatoes (packed in juice) or field-ripened tomatoes that you have frozen. The proportion of ingredients is the same as for the salsa; that is, about 1 cup of liquid ingredients to ½ a pound (1 package) of cream cheese.

Note: Lisa suggests substituting greek yogurt for the cream cheese as a healthy alternative.

SEVEN-LAYER DIP

Seven-layer dip is an easy assembly. It is a common party or game-day appetizer, at least in Texas. Unfortunately, too many times it is assembled from less-than-the-best ingredients, and the final result reflects that. Once all of the ingredients are prepared and at hand, the whole process is quick. Sometimes there are more than seven layers. The layers include the following:

1. Guacamole, the recipe for which can be found in Chapter 5—although, since Central Market in Texas makes excellent fresh guacamole every day, I frequently purchase it. However, the normal prepackaged commercial guacamole is to be avoided, and I suspect there are few sources of excellent guacamole for purchase outside of Texas.

2. Sour cream. (Daisy Brand or other quality sour cream, but not "light" sour cream.)

3. Freshly grated cheese—either a cheddar of whatever sharpness you desire, longhorn, colby, monterey jack, or, if you desire to be more adventurous, a smoked gouda. What is important is that you like the cheese. Pregrated cheese is coated with cellulose and should be avoided.

4. Refried beans. (Traditionally, most recipes call for refried beans out of a can, but I strongly prefer delicious refried beans that have real flavor; see my recipe in Chapter 14. Although the ingredients are traditional Tex-Mex or Mexican ingredients, my recipe is hardly traditional.)

5. Chopped spring onions or chives.

6. Pico de gallo (pronounced "gayo"), a fresh—not cooked, bottled, or canned—salsa made by mixing chopped tomato, finely chopped jalapeño (with or without seeds), lime juice, minced onion, and chopped cilantro. Traditional Mexican cooks use white onions, while I prefer sweet onions such as Vidalia, Texas 1015, etc.

7. Chopped, fresh, ripe tomatoes if you do not use pico de gallo. I suggest cherry tomatoes outside of summer tomato season.

8. Chopped olives. (While canned black olives of the rubbery sort are the traditional olives most recipes call for, I opt for noncanned olives whose taste I like, such as Kalamata, as well as both green and black olives of various sorts from the grocery store's olive bar that you then chop for this use, without the seeds or pits.)

9. Chopped cilantro.

Layer each of the various ingredients into a serving dish; ordering is not critical, but I usually start with the refried beans and finish by topping with the grated cheese. Serve with tortilla chips, Fritos, toasted pita chips, or other chips that are sturdy enough to scoop through the mixture and pick up some of the dip.

Of course, it is easy to make your own chips or tostadas. Brush corn tortillas with olive oil, sprinkling them lightly with salt. Some corn tortillas are thicker; these toast up tougher and should not be used for this purpose. Stack the tortillas and cut them into quarters. Place the tortilla pieces in a single layer on a baking sheet. Bake in a 350°F oven until crispy, about 10 minutes. Or cut up pita, and separate the halves, brush with olive oil, sprinkle with salt and desired herbs, and then bake in a 350°F oven for perhaps 10 minutes until crispy. The result is a very delicious chip that is better than anything you can buy in a bag.

GUACAMOLE

While I do not normally make guacamole because I can easily buy guacamole made fresh each day at Central Market in Dallas that is as good as anything that I can make, I know this is not an option to most readers. By fresh, I mean freshly made each day, not processed in a food-processing plant and sealed into a container. Such guacamole is to be avoided. *Guaca* means "avocado," and *mole* means "sauce," and that is what guacamole is—it is primarily avocado with a few flavoring items mixed in.

The recipe is most simple. Scoop out properly ripe avocado from the skin, discarding the skin and the seed. If there are brown areas in your avocado as you open it, discard those. Mash the avocado lightly with lime juice. (Lime juice is the proper citrus to use for this recipe; lemon simply does not taste right in guacamole.) The citrus is critical so that the avocado will not turn brown, and it has the fortuitous benefit of adding a delicious flavor. Mix with finely chopped (brunoise) sweet onion, finely chopped cilantro, totally minced and smashed garlic, and salt to taste. Prepare the garlic by mashing it to a paste with some salt in a mortar and pestle. Then add lime juice to soak for about 10 minutes so that the edge is taken off of the strong garlic flavor. You can add finely chopped tomato if you desire. Add, to taste, Tabasco sauce or finely minced jalapeño peppers. When I add jalapeños, because I am not looking just for heat, I remove the seeds, core, and ribs of the jalapeño and use merely the green walls of the pepper. The majority of the heat is in the seeds and core of the pepper; this is true for jalapeño and for other hot chile peppers also. Jalapeño adds a grassy flavor that you may not like for this use, and Tabasco or other Louisiana hot sauce may be more to your taste. A dash of a well-shaken worcestershire sauce adds an interesting depth of flavor but is not traditional.

Mix all of the ingredients together, salt to taste, and serve. It will be delicious.

Guacamole is delicious served by itself with corn chips such as tortilla chips (tostadas), in Seven-Layer Dip (Chapter 5), with Herb Grilled Salmon (Chapter 13), on hamburgers, with fajitas, with Quesadillas (Chapter 12), etc. Additional uses include as a garnish to soft (or hard-shell) tacos and as a dressing spread for a mozzarella, tomato, and basil sandwich— most delicious.

Mushroom Barley Soup, p. 91

Chapter 6: *Soups and Stocks*

ASPARAGUS STOCK AND SOUP WITH VARIANTS

As with many soups, a wonderful cream-of-asparagus soup starts with very cost-efficient (read: otherwise wasted) ingredients. At the price for asparagus and leeks, it seems a shame not to make use of all of what you buy. When you cook asparagus, you have the peel and cut end of the stem, which are frequently tossed in the garbage. (A delicious corn stock/soup can be made using the same techniques but substituting corn cobs freshly sheared of the corn kernels in the stead of the asparagus "waste.")

INGREDIENTS

"waste" asparagus trimmings plus peeled asparagus spears to finish
carrots
leek trimmings
celery
onion
garlic
potato, unpeeled
thyme
pepper
filtered or distilled water
dried porcini mushrooms (optional—see Chapter 2 for reconstituting instructions)
croutons for service

The "waste" portion of the asparagus (that is, the peel and cut end) can and should be made into a wonderful asparagus stock for use in an asparagus soup. Put the "waste" into a pot with carrot, celery, onion, garlic, potato, and the dark-green, tough but flavorful external leaves from the leek (which would also otherwise be waste, saved when preparing a leek for another use) with peppercorns, thyme, and filtered water. Chicken stock is not at all necessary or kosher. Simmer for 30 minutes to an hour. Cool and put through a food mill. The food mill processes out the stringy pulp; because of the potato, the result is a smooth and creamy-textured soup. The food mill is an essential tool and better here than a food processor or blender because it removes undesirable pulp and seeds, and it works better than a strainer, allowing you to add creamy texture even before you add cream. You can freeze the stock for future use or use immediately.

When ready for the final cooking, add heavy cream to enrich the stock. Add bite-sized pieces of asparagus just before serving, heating to just barely cook the tender asparagus.

An excellent variant is to add dried, reconstituted porcini mushrooms and, if desired, caramelized fresh mushrooms to the stock after the food mill process, at the same time that you add the cream. If you use dried mushrooms, carefully add the mushroom-refreshing liquid, avoiding the sandy dregs. Cook for 5 to 10 minutes before adding the asparagus pieces. Add the asparagus only at the end so as to not overcook.

Serve with freshly toasted croutons tossed in a skillet with olive oil or butter and garlic (minced or squeezed through a garlic press and then lightly sweated in the oil or butter).

CHICKEN STOCK

If there is anything more ubiquitous in the Jewish household than Jewish "penicillin," I am not aware of it. It is chicken soup that has pervaded our entire culture and has extended to non-Jewish households as well. I remember being in the ghetto in Venice on a Friday evening as the few remaining Jews residing in that area of Venice were preparing for the Sabbath; the air was redolent with the smell of chicken soup.

The base of chicken soup is merely chicken stock, but "merely" is an inadequate word if the stock is made properly to be rich and flavorful. This requires more than just the hour allocated by many recipes, although the extra time is unsupervised simmering—not a lot of work. You then add ingredients as desired to take the intensely flavored chicken base into the desired direction. For my Turkey Stock recipe, see Chapter 11 under the recipe for Roasted Turkey.

INGREDIENTS

```
chicken (see instructions—amount depends on the size of the pot)
carrot
celery
onion
leek trimmings
bay leaf
thyme
peppercorns
dill (optional)
filtered or distilled water
```

Since this stock is easily frozen, I suggest you start with a pot as large as you have. Use either chicken pieces or a whole chicken. See the discussion in Chapter 11 about processing and cleaning chicken. If you are using pieces rather than a whole chicken, I suggest that the dark meat provides much more flavor than the white meat. Bones are essential for flavor, and the giblets (other than the liver), including the heart, gizzard, tail, wing tips, and neck, are appropriate ingredients here. You can produce a much more flavorful chicken stock if you start with the carcass of a roasted chicken or parts that you roast for the purpose, along with roasted vegetables as a part of the base for the stock. Deglaze the roasting pan to use the fond in the stock to add to the richness and flavor. Deglazing is the simple process of adding liquid—in this case, water—to the roasting pan, heating the pan, and scraping up the stuck bits of flavor for use in the stock. Although many will turn up their noses in disdain, chicken feet add a wonderful gelatinous quality to the chicken stock and should be among the base components of a chicken soup. Certainly, that is what my grandmother used. Unfortunately, it is now difficult to find chicken feet, although you can do so at a Chinese grocer and perhaps other ethnic grocers (obviously not kosher sources, if that is what you need).

Along with the meat and bones of the chicken, add carrot, celery, onion, leek trimmings, bay leaf, thyme, peppercorns, and, if you desire, dill. It is better if the vegetables are also browned or roasted beforehand. Remember, browning adds flavor. Do not add salt at this stage. Fill the pot with filtered or distilled water, not tap water (at least not in Dallas) to cover the ingredients. My daughter, Lisa, once called me as she was making soup to inquire how much water to add; it seems that various websites try to specify the quantity. I told her this is not rocket science, and precision is not required here. Just cover the ingredients, and if necessary, as the stock simmers, add more water.

Bring the pot to a boil, cover, and lower to a simmer to gently cook for 1 hour. After simmering, the meat will be cooked. Remove the meat from the pot, and strip the meat from the bones, reserving the skin and the bones to go back into the pot.

The skin and bones are not yet fully cooked; additional cooking will continue to add gelatin and flavor to the stock. Cook (barely simmer) for another 2 hours. Let the pot cool and place it into a refrigerator overnight. Placing the pot in a sink filled with ice and cold water is a good way to rapidly cool the stock, as is freezing a nonglass bottle (not so full that it will burst when the freezing water expands) and swirling the frozen bottle in the hot stock. After cooking, the soup should be gelatinous when cooled. Be cognizant whenever you are cooling hot liquids of the need to rapidly cool through the temperature danger zone (below 40° F) where adverse organisms can grow.

After the stock is cold and the fat has congealed, remove any congealed fat at the top of the chicken stock. This fat is good schmaltz and should be frozen for future use. You want to avoid serving soup with a layer of fat—it is not "good eats." Bring the stock back up to a liquid stage, but well before it is really hot and ready to boil, remove the now spent bones and vegetables, draining them carefully. Strain the stock carefully through a very fine strainer, or if your strainer is not very fine, layer cheesecloth in the strainer to remove all particulates. Return the strained liquid back to the pot. Toss the spent cooking materials, but not in the garbage disposal, or you may wind up with a stopped drain.

This stock is now ready for further use or storage. If desired, you can reduce the stock further at this time to concentrate flavor and minimize storage space used. If you use the stock for sauces, do not salt it until you are ready to use in the sauce, because as you reduce the liquid, the salt will also become concentrated, and the final result will become too salty. This stock would make a wonderful consommé, and you can locate a recipe for the process to clarify stock in one of Julia Child's books or one of many other sources.

To serve as soup, add fresh vegetables, and cook until just done. If desired, add some of the reserved chicken meat, and heat. Add 1 or 2 matzo balls if desired—or add meat kreplach (traditionally served erev Yom Kippur). This is always wonderful for Friday night, a holiday dinner, or any other occasion. You can also use this stock to make a chicken, mushroom, and barley soup with carrots and shredded chicken, noting that dark meat is better for this purpose.

The reserved meat can be used for multiple purposes, including chicken salad, chicken sandwiches, chicken potpie, etc. Freeze any leftover stock for future use in an airtight container.

BEEF STOCK AND "GEDAEMPFTE" MEAT

Beef stock is a wonderful ingredient that makes a wonderful base for sauces and other soups, and it is useful when braising meats such as brisket or short ribs. A review of any French cookbook will reveal multiple possibilities for the use of beef stock; homemade beef stock is far preferable to any store-bought version.

When making stock, use the largest pot that you have. You can buy a 16-quart thin aluminum or steel pot inexpensively. This size pot filled with liquid is very heavy, about 35 pounds. A pot used for this purpose, always filled with a liquid that will not scorch, does not have to be an expensive, heavy pot. If you are making something such as chicken or beef stock, and since you can freeze the unused portion for future use, you should make as much as you can reasonably store.

INGREDIENTS

beef bones and meat
carrots
onions
celery
leek trimmings
bay leaf
thyme
peppercorns
tomato product—peels or paste
dry red wine
filtered or distilled water

To make a good beef stock, it is best to go to an ethnic market that carries cow hooves or calf hooves as well as soup bones that are meaty—obviously not a kosher source, if that is your need. You can purchase soup bones at any major grocery store, but sometimes the cost is high, and it is frequently much cheaper to buy such items at an ethnic market. USDA Prime or Choice beef is a waste here. The cow or calf hooves are needed for the gelatin that adds significant body to the stock.

Wash and dry the ingredients (hooves, bones, meat, etc.) carefully. Lightly oil and roast them at a high temperature (450°F) in a preheated oven. Turn every 15 minutes until the bones and meat are well browned—not burned. Do not overfill the roasting pan; if necessary, roast in two batches. Remove to the cooking pot. Brown the vegetables to be used (onion, celery, leek trimmings, and carrots), stirring the vegetables well into the rendered fat in the same 450°F oven, stirring every 15 minutes. It will not take more than 30 to 45 minutes to brown the vegetables. Remove the browned vegetables into the pot with the meat and bones. Add 1 cup or so of tomato skins that you have saved (frozen) for this purpose as you peeled tomatoes for other dishes or add a couple of very ripe tomatoes or 2 to 3 tablespoons of tomato paste.

Drain the rendered fat from the roasting pan into a jar for disposal. Deglaze the roasting pan with a full bottle of drinkable dry red wine, with the emphasis on *drinkable* and not expensive. Add the result into the pot with the meat and vegetables. Fill the pot with filtered water, a couple tablespoons of thyme, several bay leaves, and a tablespoon of whole peppercorns. Add several cloves of garlic, sliced but not necessarily peeled. Wait to add salt upon final use of the stock. Bring to a bare simmer and cook for up to 12 hours. Amounts of spice and herbs you add depend on pot size. Cooking time does not have to be continuous; you may cook for an hour or so, cool and refrigerate the stock, and then finish cooking on another day, although the safe cooling process can be tedious. Skim excess fat as you go or when cold and congealed.

After the stock is fully cooked, remove and drain the bones, meat, and vegetables. Strain the stock with a very fine strainer, using a cheesecloth if necessary, to remove the particulates. You can reduce further at this time to concentrate flavor and reduce storage space used. The vegetables after this period of time are not worth saving. However, the meat, while fully cooked—actually overcooked—is still delicious and can be served for wonderful eating.

My grandmother used to refer to this meat as *gedaempfte fleisch*, although I think that terminology normally refers simply to a braised meat such as brisket, shoulder, or chuck. Salt the meat to taste. My grandmother served this meat hot with horseradish, and I still find that delicious to this day. Alternatively, you could shred this meat. Season it to taste with chili powder, garlic powder, onion powder, cumin powder, chopped cilantro, salt, and pepper, mixing well. This now southwestern-and-Mexican-flavored meat is delicious served warmed in a soft taco (corn or flour) with Guacamole (Chapter 5), pico de gallo, shredded cabbage, Pickled Jalapeño (Chapter 7), and/or *Frijoles Refritos* (Chapter 14), in a style like the Mexican *ropa vieja*, which literally is Spanish for "old clothes," resembling strips of rags.

BOUILLABAISSE A LA JUIVE

Bouillabaisse is a classic French seafood soup or stew from the Provençal region in the South of France, originating in or around Marseille. Originally, it was essentially peasant food, prepared by fishermen from the leftover catch that they did not sell. The version in this book is perhaps better referred to as *Bouillabaisse a la Juive* (that is, in the Jewish style) since it does not contain any shellfish or other nonkosher fish that do not have fins, gills, and scales (noting that the fish stew prepared by those fishermen classically did not necessarily contain shellfish). Shellfish and other fish—for example, sharks—that do not have scales are not kosher and are not permitted to be eaten as set forth in the Bible. Thus, this soup has no shrimp, clams, mussels, or lobster. Since the shellfish, if used, would be added at the end of the cooking process, the preparation really does not differ much from an otherwise "authentic" version, and it is most delectable with a similar flavor profile to a traditional bouillabaisse. Since many have allergies to shellfish, this is also a recipe that can be safely enjoyed by those with such issues.

There are four major steps to the preparation of a bouillabaisse:

1. Preparation of fish stock.

2. Preparation of the rouille. The rouille is used as an ingredient in the soup as well as a condiment for the toast points.

3. Preparation of the final combined soup.

4. Preparation of toast points.

1. Preparation of Fish Stock

INGREDIENTS

bones, carcass, and heads of any white fish such as sole, flounder, snapper, halibut, grouper, etc. This does not include the gills, which are unpalatable and should be clipped out and discarded. Carefully wash the carcass, removing any blood or organs. Use at least 2 pounds of bones and trimmings for about 8–10 cups of final production of stock (2-plus quarts).

2 carrots, coarsely chopped

2 celery ribs, coarsely chopped

1 large onion, coarsely chopped

1 bunch of parsley, washed well, patted dry, and roughly chopped

2–3 cloves garlic

1 teaspoon whole black peppercorns

3–4 bay leaves

2–3 leeks (Tough green portions of the leaves, well washed. The dark green portion of the leaves are fibrous and not edible; this portion should be removed leaf by leaf for use in making stock. With a sharp paring knife, carefully make a light cut where the leaf turns dark green to break it off at that point, repeating until only white and light green remains. Reserve the edible white and light-green inner leaves for the final soup.)

2 tablespoons dried thyme

2–3 strips orange zest (optional)

10 cups water, or to cover

1–2 cups dry, not sweet, white wine (but not a chardonnay, which can be too oaky)

1–2 fennel bulb stalks, using these trimmings for the stock and reserving some of the fronds as a garnish for the finished bouillabaisse. Reserve the fennel bulbs for use in the soup for serving.

All of the ingredients for the fish stock should be combined in a large pot with water. *Note*: Julia Child called for orange zest as an additional flavoring, and that is certainly a locally used ingredient. Bring this mixture to a boil, and simmer at a very low heat, covered, for 30 to 45 minutes. Unlike beef and chicken stocks, nothing is browned, and the stock is totally cooked in a relatively short period of time. This stock, which is a variant of a regular fish stock because of the added fennel, should not be cooked for longer than 45 minutes. Once the stock is cooked, strain it through a fine sieve, discarding the solids. This stock is highly perishable but may be refrigerated for no more than 1 to 2 days, or it may be frozen for use at a later time. *Caution*: Do not run fish bones or leek leaves, cooked or uncooked, through your garbage disposal—you will not be happy when the plumbing clogs.

2. Preparation of the Rouille

INGREDIENTS

1 cup aioli (see Mayonnaise recipe in Chapter 8)
1 or more teaspoons smoked paprika per cup of aioli, or to taste
pinch of saffron

Rouille is a variant of mayonnaise—specifically, a variant of aioli or garlic mayonnaise. There are other variations for rouille, but this is the one I like. Additions that distinguish rouille from aioli include smoked paprika (although some cooks use a puree of roasted red peppers) plus a pinch of saffron. Mix the smoked paprika and saffron into the aioli, and taste, adjusting as you think necessary. This rouille is outstanding as a dressing for chilled, room-temperature grilled vegetables (carrots, zucchini, eggplant, onion, etc.) as well as a classic condiment for this fish soup.

3. Preparation of the Final Combined Soup

INGREDIENTS

3 leeks (White and pale-green reserved parts only, finely sliced, washed well, and drained. Slice the leeks from the root to the tip for cleaning. Leeks are infamous for the amount of sand that they can hide between layers and must be carefully rinsed, separating layers under flowing water, root end up and tip down so the grit washes freely away from the leek and down the drain.)

2 celery ribs, finely chopped

2 reserved fennel bulbs, thinly sliced

1 large onion, chopped finely

olive oil for sautéing

2 tablespoons tomato paste

4 cloves garlic, crushed and chopped

1 cup dry white wine, in addition to the wine used in the fish stock

2-3 quarts fish stock

1 teaspoon saffron threads, crumbled and softened in a tablespoon or so of very hot water or fish stock. Do not make the mistake of adding too much saffron; not only is it expensive, but while it is delicious and worth the cost in moderation, it is bitter in excess.

2 (28-ounce) cans whole tomatoes, drained and coarsely chopped

4 bay leaves

½ cup parsley leaves, chopped

1 teaspoon salt, or to taste

1 teaspoon freshly ground pepper

3 or so pounds fish fillets—grouper, halibut, sole, flounder, snapper, cod, or other white fishes—carefully boned and cut into large pieces. Black cod (also known as sablefish) and chilean sea bass are excellent for this use. I do not use salmon in this dish, as its flavor profile does not seem appropriate, but, of course, this is a matter of taste. Traditionally, a whole fish is cooked and served, but of course, this entails careful boning at the table, a task I do not want to undertake, and it is rendered unnecessary by the prior preparation of the stock to extract the flavor of the bones.

In a large, heavy pot, sauté the leeks, celery, fennel bulb, and onion in olive oil, sweating well but not browning. Add the tomato paste, and cook for a short time (a minute or so) to remove the raw flavor. Add garlic and cook for perhaps 30 seconds. Deglaze with the wine.

In a small bowl, combine some hot stock—perhaps ½ cup—and saffron. Then add the saffron mixture to the pot along with the prepared stock, tomatoes, bay leaves, parsley, salt, and pepper. Simmer for 30 minutes.

Discard the bay leaves. Using a very sharp knife, carefully remove any bones from your fish fillets. Add the deboned fish, and cover, cooking at a bare simmer for no more than 10 minutes, until the fish is barely cooked through. Add chilean sea bass and black cod (if you are using these wonderful species) first because they must be fully cooked to be edible, and they take an extra few minutes. Separate a portion of the rouille to a bowl and temper the rouille with some hot fish stock so that it will not curdle. Then stir the result gently into the soup.

Ladle the now finished bouillabaisse into individual bowls, carefully serving the fish so that it does not break up. Add the reserved fennel fronds, finely chopped, as a garnish. Serve with toast points and rouille for spreading on the toast points. Dunking is encouraged.

4. Preparation of Toast Points

Preparation of toast points (croustades) is simple and can be accomplished in advance as follows: Slice a french baguette into ½-inch slices. Brush the slices lightly with olive oil and toast them in the oven at 350°F until well toasted and crisp. Serve with the bouillabaisse, smearing the toasts liberally with rouille as you eat.

BROCCOLI CHEESE SOUP

This soup was a favorite of our children as they were growing up and remains so even though they are now adults. My son cooks this soup for my grandchildren. It is easy and an excellent recipe for a vegetable that children will eagerly eat.

INGREDIENTS

1 large head of broccoli, coarsely chopped

filtered water, enough just to cover (at least 1½ cups)

3 tablespoons butter

½ teaspoon salt (adjust to taste before serving)

⅓ cup flour

3 cups whole milk

12 ounces (or to taste) American or cheddar cheese (not Velveeta, which, in any event, is not kosher), diced into small chunks. Since this soup is intended for children, a mild cheese should be selected; if for adults, use cheese to your taste, such as a gruyère-and-parmesan mixture.

a pinch freshly grated nutmeg (optional)

Just cover the chopped broccoli with water in a pot. Simmer the broccoli until just softened; do not overcook. Since the broccoli is chopped, cooking time is short—a few minutes. Drain and reserve the cooking water. Set aside the broccoli.

Melt the butter in a pot. Then add the flour, and cook over medium heat, stirring constantly until the roux just begins to turn light tan but not brown—a minute or so. Slowly add 1½ cups of the reserved broccoli water to the roux, whisking to avoid lumps, until it becomes thickened. Then add the milk, stirring constantly. Heat the mixture over medium flame until thickened. As to the cheese, there are two schools of thought: you can add cheese over heat, and stir until melted, or as noted in the next paragraph, you can wait until the soup is almost ready to serve before adding the cheese.

Add more of the broccoli water or milk if the soup is too thick. Add back the cooked broccoli. Check flavor, and add salt (and pepper, if desired) as necessary. If adding nutmeg, grate it in now. If you have waited to add the cheese, now is the time with the heat off. It is Lisa's view that the melty chunks of cheese make the soup.

You can blend the soup if texture is an issue for your children; if so, add the broccoli before the cheese, blend, and then return it to the pot to add the cheese.

My mother and my grandmother made this classic soup (actually four different soups with a common theme but very different flavors). A variant can be found in Jewish delicatessens from time to time, although it's never as good as my mother's and grandmother's recipes.

INGREDIENTS

about 3 carrots, roughly chopped

1–1½ onions, chopped

2–3 celery stalks, diced

1–2 cloves garlic, diced

1 tablespoon oil

2 ounces dried porcini, trumpet, and/or chanterelle mushrooms

2–3 quarts stock: beef, chicken, turkey, or vegetable as appropriate

1 teaspoon dried thyme

2–3 bay leaves

2 cups medium pearl barley

2 teaspoons salt, plus more to taste

1 potato, diced (optional)

1 cup dried split peas (optional)

1 cup lentils (optional)

about 2 cups of the relevant meat (optional): beef, turkey, or chicken in bite-sized pieces

First, it is preferable to have a quality and appropriate stock. For turkey soup, a wonderful turkey stock is most preferable, although a homemade chicken stock can be used. Boxed turkey, beef, and vegetable broths, among others, are now available. See the recipe for Roasted Turkey in Chapter 11; turkey stock is a wonderful by-product of preparing and cooking a turkey. Similarly, for beef soup, a wonderful beef stock is best. The same applies for chicken stock or, for the vegetarian version, a rich vegetable stock. Recipes for beef stock and chicken stock can be found earlier in Chapter 6. There are many wonderful recipes for stock in multiple cookbooks. I recommend Julia Child's books as a wonderful resource in this regard.

Once you have the stock, the recipe is incredibly simple and the proportions flexible. For a 6-quart saucepan, peel and dice several carrots, 1 to 1½ onions, 2 or 3 stalks of celery, and 1 or 2 cloves of garlic, all into small pieces. Sweat but don't brown the vegetables in a tablespoon of oil.

The best mushrooms are dried porcini, trumpet, and chanterelle mushrooms, separately or mixed, and you should reconstitute them as indicated in Chapter 2, being sure to pick up and drain the mushrooms in a way that leaves the sand in the liquid to be settled and separated, allowing the dregs to be discarded. Use a couple ounces of dried mushrooms. I would never use an Asian-style mushroom such as shiitake, wood ear, etc. in this soup—the flavor is wrong.

Add stock and mushroom-reconstituting liquid to fully cover the vegetables, being careful to not overfill the pot. Remember that like rice, each cup of barley will absorb 2 to 3 cups of liquid. Add the chopped reconstituted mushrooms, thyme, and bay leaves. Sometimes I dice potato and add it to the soup. Sometimes I add dried split peas to this soup. Lentils would be good in this soup to be added late in the cooking process.

For beef soup, use beef chuck cut into 1-inch or smaller cubes. Brown the chuck before adding it to the soup and be sure to deglaze the pot in which the chuck was browned so as to not leave the fond behind. Cook the soup for at least 1 hour before adding the barley for another hour—the chuck (if you are using beef) will need this total time to allow the meat to become tender.

For the chicken or turkey barley soup, the meat cooks quickly. You can add diced-up raw chicken thighs or turkey thighs about a ½ hour before serving, so you can add the barley at the same time as the vegetables.

Obviously, the vegetarian version has no added meat.

Add 1½ to 2 cups of barley. Add a teaspoon of kosher salt for each cup of barley, plus more to taste as needed (remembering the other ingredients that need some salt). The barley takes at least 1 hour to cook. Barley adds a wonderful flavor and creaminess to the soup after it has fully cooked. *Al dente* is not the goal for the barley here; you want it fully cooked. These soups are seriously better the next day.

These soups are even better served the second day after they have rested in the refrigerator. Note that you will have to reseason the soups with salt and pepper, and you may have to adjust the salt because barley and potatoes will absorb a huge amount of salt. However, be careful not to oversalt. Add water if necessary.

I serve these soups with pumpernickel or rye bread. The bread is delicious with schmaltz brushed on lightly, sprinkled with salt, and toasted in the oven. This variation is a most delicious and ultimate form of comfort food, to say the least. There is nothing much better on a winter evening than one of these soups.

CUBAN BLACK BEAN SOUP

This hearty soup is one of my daughter's favorite dishes. As you read the recipe, it will become clear to you this is not a classic Cuban soup in an authentic sense because there is no ham or other pork product in it. Normally, Cubans would use a smoked ham as the meat product. Cuban food is not a variant of Mexican cuisine; it is more directly related to Spanish cuisine, including the regions influenced by the occupation by the Moors prior to the year 1500. Cubans love black beans, and the Cuban cuisine generally does not include extremely spicy foods. This soup is not "hot" but is, nonetheless, highly flavorful, qualifying for the category of *Deep Flavors*.

The quantity that I make is generally very large since the soup can be stored in the freezer and taken out for leftovers at future times. I use a very large pot (thirteen quarts), but of course you can scale down the recipe to fit the size of pot that you have in your kitchen, keeping in mind that proportions are only approximate and, unlike ingredients for baking a cake, are not intended as a rigid, precise formula.

INGREDIENTS

1 pound dried black (or other) beans, rinsed well and sorted to make sure there are no stones or other contaminants in the bag

5 pounds smoked beef sausage (available kosher online)

3 large bell peppers, diced and seeded

2 large yellow or sweet onions, peeled and diced

5-6 cloves garlic, peeled and roughly cut or diced

3 smoked turkey legs or comparable number of wings (What is generally available in grocery markets will be smoked but not fully cooked, but it does need to be cooked for this recipe. Available kosher online.)

turkey stock or smoked turkey stock to fill the pot (If not available, use chicken stock. See Chapter 11 under Roasted Turkey for my turkey stock recipe.)

3 tablespoons smoked paprika

1-2 tablespoons ground cumin

2-4 bay leaves

1 tablespoon chili powder (McCormick is kosher and is the right flavor profile, but if you want the soup somewhat spicier, you can use Penzeys's chili powder, which has the same flavor profile but is spicier and not kosher)

1 tablespoon ancho chile powder

1 tablespoon thyme leaves

1 tablespoon oregano leaves

1-2 tablespoons red wine vinegar or lime wedges as a garnish and to squeeze into the soup at the table

cilantro, chopped, as a garnish to stir into the bowls of soup at the table

salt and pepper

The day before you are going to make the soup, sort the beans, cover them with salted water, and soak them in the refrigerator. This step can be bypassed, but the cooking process will take longer.

On the day that you are going to cook the stock, slice the sausage into bite-sized coins, and sauté them to render their fat and caramelize the sausage. Remove the sausage from the pot and refrigerate it. Add the bell pepper, onion, and garlic to the pot, and sweat them. I suggest that you use the rendered fat from the beef sausages to sweat the vegetables because that fat contains wonderful flavor. Ultimately that fat will be removed from the soup before consuming, but in the meantime, it adds great flavor to the process.

Drain and rinse the black beans that have been soaked, and add them to the pot, together with the smoked turkey and stock to cover. Add the herbs and spices at this time, together with salt and pepper. Cover the pot, and simmer for about 2 hours, until the beans are tender, and the turkey is cooked. Remove the turkey legs from the pot and let them cool. Remove the bay leaves from the pot and discard them. Before the turkey and sausage are added back into the soup, and before the soup is blended, it is a good time to remove any fat that will rise to the surface of the soup.

Puree the soup while the meat is not in the pot. This may be done with an immersion blender, in a regular blender, in a food processor, with a potato masher, or even with a food mill (although this is intended as a rustic dish).

After the turkey has cooled, remove the meat from the bone, and discard any tough tendons. Put the turkey meat back into the now blended and defatted soup, together with the reserved sausage. At this time, you may add the vinegar, although I prefer to not use the vinegar and instead serve the soup with wedges of limes to squeeze into the soup at the table. Bring the soup back up to a simmer for 5 to 10 minutes so that the flavors are fully blended.

The soup should be served with rice, a plentiful amount of chopped cilantro, and lime wedges.

BEET BORSCHT

This recipe is my grandmother's recipe and has converted people who would never eat beets. I served it to a non-Jewish friend who was loath to try it; he devoured two bowls. It is vegetarian—but not vegan—and has just beets, sour salt, cane sugar, water, and eggs but no meat or other products. Most other recipes include meat and other vegetables. It is simple to make but does require care and judgment. Some years ago, a Jewish-Russian immigrant who owned a deli in Dallas told me that it originated from a small area of western Russia, but I do not remember the exact location. Served chilled, this is a fabulous summertime soup.

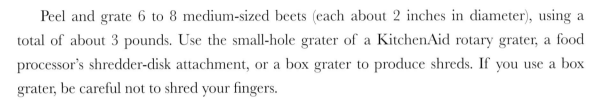

INGREDIENTS

about 3 pounds (roughly 6-8 medium-sized) red beets
filtered water to cover, about 4 quarts
3½ teaspoons sour salt
3½ cups white cane sugar
4-5 eggs (I use jumbo eggs)

For service

cucumber, diced
green onion, diced
boiled potatoes, cooled and diced
sour cream

Peel and grate 6 to 8 medium-sized beets (each about 2 inches in diameter), using a total of about 3 pounds. Use the small-hole grater of a KitchenAid rotary grater, a food processor's shredder-disk attachment, or a box grater to produce shreds. If you use a box grater, be careful not to shred your fingers.

Put the shredded beets into a 5- or 6-quart dutch oven–type of pot. Use filtered water to just cover the beets, which will total about 4 quarts. Bring to a boil, watching the pot; then *immediately* lower heat to a very low simmer. If this mixture boils over, it makes a *big* mess, so watch it, and reduce the heat immediately as it starts to come to a boil. Not covering the pot with a tight lid helps avoid an overflow, so leave the lid off or cracked open.

Do *not* add table or kosher salt (the chemical NaCl or sodium chloride) or pepper. Sour salt is a white crystalline or granular substance that rescmbles (but is not) salt (NaCl); it is dried citric acid with a seriously tart but not salty flavor.

After the beets have come to a simmer, add sour salt and sugar to taste. Start with about 2 teaspoons of sour salt and 2 cups of cane sugar, tasting as you go for a sour-sweet balance. I do not particularly like the flavor of the hot soup, and I taste only for balance of the sweet and sour with the beets. Fortunately, this taste changes dramatically and improves when the soup is cooked and cooled. Sour salt and sugar need to not only balance but also to be in sufficient quantity to add the right flavor, and you just need to add until you like the result. I estimate that I use about 1 teaspoon of sour salt per cup of sugar, with about 3 or so teaspoons of sour salt and about 3 cups of cane sugar for 3 pounds of peeled beets. You will need to taste as you add to get a result you like. Simmer for about 30 minutes until the shredded beets are very tender.

In a KitchenAid, beat 4 or 5 eggs using a paddle attachment, not a whisk. I use jumbo eggs, so adjust accordingly. Slowly drizzle in the hot beet liquid with the KitchenAid running on low to temper the eggs until sufficient beet liquid is in—double or triple the volume of the eggs. *Do not get this hot liquid on any clothes you care about—the stain is not easy to remove.* Stir the egg mixture back into the beet mixture with a spoon. The soup will be a beautiful pink color and will not look or taste like what comes in a bottle. Cool and refrigerate in a sealed glass or Pyrex container. *Note:* Even though the soup is acidic (because of the sour salt) so that botulism is probably not a concern, I do not seal the container tightly until the soup is fully cooled.

Serve cold with sour cream, diced or spoon-sized cucumbers and boiled potatoes, and chopped green onions or chives. I use cucumbers that have never been waxed, and so I do not peel the cucumber. I do remove the seeds before chopping. I suggest Yukon Gold, red new potatoes, or white boiling potatoes; since I like the peel, and it is good for you, I do not bother with that chore. Baking (Idaho) potatoes are too starchy and have the wrong texture for this purpose.

MUSHROOM SOUP

There are many recipes for mushroom soups, and the one requisite for mushroom soup, in my mind, is that it must have an adequate quantity of mushrooms. In addition, to take a mushroom soup out of the ordinary, it is absolutely necessary to use a quantity of porcini or other European forest mushrooms (such as chanterelle, trumpet, etc., but not oriental mushrooms such as shiitake, which simply have a wrong—not bad—flavor for this recipe) in addition to caramelized fresh mushrooms. There are recipes that avoid milk and cream, but I think that is a mistake. Following are two excellent iterations.

INGREDIENTS

1-2 ounces dried porcini, trumpet, and/or chanterelle mushrooms

2 pounds fresh mushrooms, diced (your choice, but not Asian mushrooms such as shiitake)

1 carrot, finely diced

½ cup shallot or sweet onion, finely diced

2 cloves garlic, finely diced

½ celery stalk, finely diced

1 teaspoon dried thyme

3 tablespoons butter, plus more as needed

unbleached all-purpose flour, as needed

salt and pepper

¼–½ cup heavy cream (optional if not using roux)

cornstarch (optional if not using roux)

Roux

2 tablespoons butter

2 tablespoons flour

1 cup dry white wine

2½–3½ cups whole milk

Reconstitute the dried mushrooms by following the steps outlined in Chapter 2. Reserve the liquid, and finely chop the rehydrated mushrooms.

Wash and slice or dice 2 pounds of fresh mushrooms (white button, cremini, portobello, etc.). Sauté the fresh mushrooms with salt and butter. Use ½ teaspoon of salt to start and use 3 tablespoons of butter. Add more if needed. Add the reconstituted and chopped wild mushrooms to the fresh sautéing mushrooms. Let the reserved hydrating liquid continue to rest. Continue to cook until the mushroom mixture is well caramelized but not burned. The fresh mushrooms will exude liquid as they start cooking that must evaporate before the mushrooms can brown and caramelize. When the liquid is gone, stir continuously, and stop the cooking before the mushrooms can burn.

Remove the caramelized mushrooms from the pan and reserve them. Add into the pan the carrot, shallot or onion, garlic, and celery. Limit the amount of celery; although the flavor is a necessary component, too much will overwhelm other flavors. Add butter as necessary. Cook until well sweated but not brown; you really want the mushroom flavor to predominate. Add the dried thyme.

For a smoother soup (except for the mushrooms), blend the vegetables before combining them with the mushrooms. If a more rustic result is what you desire, reserve the unblended vegetables to add along with the mushrooms. Alternatively, you can blend the almost final soup with all of the mushrooms and vegetables—your choice.

Once the mushrooms and vegetables are cooked, there are 2 alternatives here: you can make a soup thickened with a roux, or you can avoid the roux and instead blend all of the vegetables (and the mushrooms, if desired) to thicken and add texture to the soup, and then add some heavy cream. Both versions are good.

With Roux

For the roux/béchamel alternative, add 2 tablespoons of butter to the empty pan with 2 tablespoons of flour. Cook the flour thoroughly to a very light tan, but do not overbrown. (This is not a Cajun dish, and a brown roux is not desired.) Add 1 cup of white wine, stirring constantly to avoid lumps so that the sauce will be smooth and cooking for a couple of minutes to remove the raw wine flavor. Add the reserved mushroom-reconstituting liquid, being careful to leave any of the dregs at the bottom of the cup to discard. Continue by adding $2\frac{1}{2}$ to $3\frac{1}{2}$ cups of milk to make a thin béchamel, as desired, and more can be added after the soup is blended. The roux will not thicken the mixture until it is all hot. Remember, the blending with vegetables will further thicken the soup.

If you desire a thicker soup, you can always increase the amount of butter and flour or reduce the milk, but this is a soup and only needs a little texture. The formula for a sauce is generally 1 tablespoon of butter and 1 tablespoon of flour to 1 cup of liquid. A soup should be thinner than a sauce but still have some texture.

Without Roux

If you do not use the roux, add the wine to the vegetables first to cook out the raw wine flavor. Then add the mushroom liquid and the milk to the vegetables. You will absolutely want to blend the soup after the vegetables are cooked to thicken and add texture to the soup, which is an optional step with the roux-based process. You can also blend some or all of the mushrooms if you desire. If you do not blend the mushrooms when blending the soup with the other vegetables, add the mushrooms back later to finish the soup.

Use a blender or an immersion blender to make a smooth soup. An immersion blender will not make the soup as smooth as a blender. If you want the soup really smooth and elegant, cook the soup with the mushrooms, and then run the soup through a food mill, which does an even better job than the blender. Alternatively, you can run the soup through the food mill before adding the mushrooms. There are many choices.

Heat for a few minutes until the flavor of the mushrooms is transferred to the soup base. If you did not use the roux, add ¼ to ½ cup heavy cream. Salt and pepper to taste.

If you eschew the roux, and if, after you blend the vegetables, you want a thicker soup, you can thicken it with a bit of cornstarch slurry (water mixed with cornstarch). Add the slurry to the hot soup, whisking in the slurry slowly only until you achieve the desired thickness and texture.

Serve hot over croutons of toasted french bread. For a really delicious twist, serve with a slice of brie on the crouton. The brie and mushroom flavors are really complementary.

TOMATO SOUP

Some of the best foods are simple, and who does not like tomato soup?

INGREDIENTS

4 cups fresh field-grown summer tomatoes (or equivalent canned)
¼–½ cup of half-and-half or heavy cream
½ carrot
½ celery stalk
½ onion (preferably sweet)
chopped herbs such as fresh basil, fresh thyme, or fresh oregano, to taste
salt and pepper to taste

This soup is cooked only very briefly to preserve the fresh flavor. Freshness is critical. For this soup the strong preference is for absolutely fresh, never refrigerated tomatoes: I prefer larger, field-grown, very ripe, almost overripe tomatoes rather than roma or plum tomatoes, which have less liquid. This soup is really best using locally grown summer tomatoes. If you are outside of tomato season, use high-quality canned whole tomatoes, canned with juice, not sauce; it will still be good. All of the liquid in the soup is that in the tomatoes (other than a modicum of heavy cream or half-and-half), and this provides an intense tomato flavor.

For 4 cups of tomatoes, chop ½ a carrot, ½ an onion, and ½ a stalk of celery. Using a pan large enough to hold all of the ingredients, sweat but do not brown these vegetables in butter. Peel and core the tomatoes; that is, take out the stem end. Use all of the liquid and seeds, which not only have a lot of flavor but add the needed liquid. Peel tomatoes by blanching for about 30 seconds, shocking them in ice water, and the peel will slide off. Chop the tomatoes.

Add the tomatoes to the sweated vegetables and cook perhaps 10 minutes. After cooking, add heavy cream or half-and-half to taste (perhaps ¼ or ½ cup or so). Blend in a food processor, or even better, run the mixture through a food mill. Return to the saucepan. Heat. Add your choice of fresh thyme, oregano, and/or basil, chopped finely, and stir. Serve and enjoy. This soup is wonderful with a grilled cheese sandwich.

GREEK MEATBALL SOUP

This may be one of the most flavorful and luxurious soups you will ever eat. It is not difficult to make, although it does take time to assemble, chop, etc. It can be a complete meal, and it is very low in calories. Of course, it is far better with homemade stocks, but it can be made with commercially available stocks. It combines a mixture of rich chicken and beef stocks, meatballs wonderfully flavored with an abundance of herbs, a green leafy vegetable, and a custardy avgolemono (lemon-egg mixture) addition. As with many dishes, it can be made in parts, stored (frozen or refrigerated), and assembled on the day of service.

INGREDIENTS

Meatballs

3 pounds ground beef, 90 percent lean
1 bulb fennel, grated
½–1 cup dill, chopped
¼ cup spearmint, chopped
¼ cup parsley, chopped
1 lemon, zested
3 slices bread
4 shallots or ½ sweet onion
3 cloves garlic
olive oil
3 eggs
salt and pepper to taste

Soup

2 quarts beef stock
2 quarts chicken stock
2 bay leaves
2 lemons, zested
1 pound swiss chard or spinach leaves, not stems, chopped

Avgolemono

3 eggs
½ cup lemon juice (at least 4 lemons)

For service

2 cups rice cooked in 4 cups water
salt and pepper
chopped dill
fennel fronds

Assembling the Meatballs

For 3 pounds of ground beef in a large bowl, add a finely grated bulb of fennel (not the stalks or fronds), ½ to 1 cup of chopped fresh dill, and ¼ cup each of spearmint and parsley, chopped. Also add the grated lemon zest from 1 lemon. This mixture of herbs with a strong lemon flavor in the meatballs really makes this a unique soup.

Soak 3 slices of bread in liquid (not milk, since that would not be kosher), and mash to a pulp. Since the purpose of the bread is to lighten the texture of the meatballs, the milk is not missed. You could add almond milk, sold in many stores as a substitute, but water works fine. Squeeze out excess liquid before adding to the meatball mixture.

In olive oil, lightly sauté several shallots, chopped finely (or ½ of a finely chopped medium sweet onion), with 3 garlic cloves, finely minced. Once sautéed, add these to the meatball mixture. Add 3 eggs as a binder. Season with salt and pepper to taste. Mix well, and form into meatballs. Roast the meatballs in a 350°F oven until browned but not fully cooked, about 20–30 minutes.

Assembling the Soup

Pour 2 quarts of chicken broth and 2 quarts of beef broth into a large pot. Add 2 bay leaves and the zest from 2 lemons. Bring the stock to a simmer, and gently cook the roasted meatballs in the soup for about ½ an hour. When the soup is cooked, add 1 pound of chopped swiss chard or spinach. At this stage, the addition of a couple cups of fully cooked rice is a classic enhancement, or the rice can be added at the table. No more than 5 minutes after adding the greens, add the avgolemono mixture.

Making an Avgolemono Mixture

As the soup is cooking, make an avgolemono mixture. Separate the whites and yolks of 3 eggs, keeping both. Beat the egg whites to soft peaks. Then add ½ a cup of lemon juice, which, depending on the juiciness of the lemons, should be at least 4 lemons.

Temper the egg yolks with hot stock, and season with salt. Fold the egg whites and egg yolks together and stir them *gently* into the soup. Turn off the heat.

Place freshly chopped dill and cooked rice into soup bowls. Ladle the soup with the meatballs and greens into the bowls. Fennel fronds can be used as a garnish.

Fish chowder is a traditional New England dish, and—traditionally and indeed invariably—starts with sautéing diced bacon. That is obviously not possible in a house that does not mix milk and meat or use pork, so I have devised this substitute that produces a subtly different but incredibly delicious meal. It is, in essence, a one-pot meal because it contains vegetables, protein, and starches. It can be made on two separate days, with the first part made months in advance and frozen—that is, the fish stock that is a requisite to fish chowder. The fish for the chowder is cod, halibut, snapper, grouper, or other similar mild white-fleshed fish. Black cod (also known as sablefish) or chilean sea bass are also wonderful here. I do not think that salmon works in this recipe, but of course, that is a matter of taste. While I suppose you could use just plain water, it would not produce nearly the richness and delicacy of flavor that a wonderful homemade fish stock will produce.

INGREDIENTS

2-3 quarts fish stock (see Bouillabaisse a la Juive recipe in Chapter 6), slightly modified for this use as noted in the following instructions

1 teaspoon each dried oregano, dried thyme, and dried rosemary for preparation of the stock

butter

olive oil

2 pounds potato (preferably Yukon Gold), diced

3-4 large carrots, diced

2-3 celery stalks, diced

1 onion, chopped

3 cloves garlic, diced

1-2 cups corn, preferably fresh

1 teaspoon liquid smoke, shaken well

1 teaspoon smoked paprika (optional)

salt and pepper

1 cup heavy cream

fish (at least 6 ounces per guest)

freshly made croutons, for service

If you do not have fish stock, follow the instructions for fish stock earlier in Chapter 6, under the recipe for Bouillabaisse a la Juive. A major difference is that for any use other than bouillabaisse, you **omit** fennel as an additive in making the fish stock. The sole other difference between the fish stock for bouillabaisse and this fish stock is the added 1 teaspoon each of dried oregano, thyme, and rosemary when you add the liquid to the fish bones to cook the stock. It is not difficult to make the fish stock and the chowder in one day since, unlike beef or chicken stock, the process of making a fish stock only requires about 45 minutes of simmering the ingredients, which are then immediately fully strained, with the liquid reserved and the solids discarded.

Note: Whenever you prepare fish for cooking, including the carcass for the fish stock, you must remove the gills and any other nonbone, nonmeat parts of the carcass. For preparing a fish carcass and removing the gills, the best method is to use a very good pair of kitchen shears to clip out the gills. Gills can be somewhat difficult to remove because of the space that they are in and the fact that they are attached to the head by a bony structure. Perhaps you can get your fishmonger to remove the gills for you, which would facilitate the process. You should carefully wash the fish carcass under water, removing any red blood or other organs that may remain after the filleting of the fish.

After the fish stock is made and the liquid stock is reserved, dry the pot, and then add some butter and olive oil. Then add the vegetables for the chowder—approximately 2 pounds of diced potatoes, 3 to 4 diced carrots, 2 to 3 diced celery stalks, 1 diced onion, 3 to 4 finely minced cloves of garlic, and 1 to 2 cups of corn kernels (preferably fresh, but if fresh is not available, then frozen). Add salt and pepper. Sauté the vegetables until they are sweated but not browned. Add 1 teaspoon (and not more) of well-shaken liquid smoke. The liquid smoke flavor will be distinct at this point but will mellow as the soup simmers. An excellent spice is a teaspoon or so of smoked paprika. Ladle in fish stock to cover the vegetables, and simmer until the vegetables are just cooked. Correct the salt and pepper. Take a potato masher, and mash some of the potatoes and vegetables to thicken the broth. At this point add 1 cup of heavy cream and stir to mix.

The next step is to add the fish fillets. Add black cod or chilean sea bass first to cook an extra few minutes. Your fishmonger will probably not have removed the centerline of pin bones in the fillets. These must be removed so that you will not have fish bones in your mouth. It is an easy process to carefully trim out the centerline of pin bones with a very sharp knife, without sacrificing a significant amount of flesh, which you do not want to do since fish is expensive. Place the fully deboned fish, cut into large serving pieces, carefully into the pot so that it is covered with the soup. Depending on the thickness of the flesh, it will take no more than about 10 to 12 minutes of barely simmering—not boiling—for the fish to be fully cooked and the soup to be ready to serve. Remove the fish carefully before ladling out the soup to avoid breaking the fish too much. The soup can be served with croutons, either freshly made plain or garlic-flavored croutons, and/or with slices of fresh bread and butter. Commercial croutons are never edible and should remain in the store.

This is a most delectable and luxurious main course. One of its wonderful attributes is its ease and speed of preparation once the stock is prepared, and if you maintain a supply of fish stock in the freezer, it will always be available to you. In that case, this is a soup that can be prepared start to finish in 45 minutes. With a salad, you have a full meal.

Pickled Beets, p. 109

Chapter 7: *Pickles*

It is possible to buy pickled beets from the grocery store, and Aunt Nellie's is a brand that has a nice taste for a commercial pickled beet, but it is somewhat difficult to locate. However, there is nothing that can touch the flavor of a home-pickled beet. I use beets that I grow in my garden, but you can find excellent beets in the grocery store or at a farmer's market in middle to late summer. I generally use either wide-mouthed pint or quart jars that are intended for home canning. As with any other canning process, I do recommend that you refer to the *Ball Blue Book*, an authoritative source as to technique—available online, at some bookstores, or sometimes at hardware stores. This is critical to preserving safely; you do not want to poison your family. The process is most simple, and directions for safe canning are easy to follow, but care should be taken to produce vacuum-sealed jars that can be safely stored at room temperature.

INGREDIENTS

This recipe produces 8 pints of pickled beets.

about 3 quarts beets, cooked and peeled
2 large sweet onions
1–1½ bulbs of garlic, with cloves peeled
pickling liquid (see following recipe)

The *Ball Blue Book* recipe for pickled beets has significantly more sugar (I think too much) in the beet-preserving liquid than in this recipe. This, of course, is a matter of taste.

First, you have to have immaculately clean jars and lids. Do not reuse a lid that has previously been used (that is, the portion of the lid that has the seal on it). With respect to the screw part of the lid, you should make sure that it is clean and rust-free. You can buy lids, which are not reusable, in separate packages, as well as the screw tops, which are reusable. It is a good idea to fill jars with water and put them in a canning pot full of water so that the jars are covered by at least ½ an inch or so of water. Boil until the jars are fully sterilized. Boil the screw tops (but not the lids) at the same time. The flat portion of the lid that has the seal on it should not be boiled because the seal could be ruined, but it should be washed and rinsed carefully with soap and hot water.

Using canning tongs, lift out the jars, and let the hot water drain back into the pot. Canning tongs are very inexpensive special tongs designed to lift jars out of the boiling water. There is no reason to risk handling hot, heavy jars with a pair of tongs that are not designed for this purpose. Put the clean, boiled jars down on a clean towel on your countertop and remove the metal screw tops from the pot in which you boiled the jars. Leave the water in the canning pot to stay hot.

The beets need to be carefully washed and the leaves removed, leaving about ½ an inch of stem stubble on the leaf end of the beet. Cut off the root, leaving ½ an inch to 1 inch of root. Simmer the beets in plain, unsalted water until just barely cooked enough to slip the skins off of the beets. Depending on the size of the beet, this could take 20 to 45 minutes. You will have to test the beets with a thin skewer or knife and judge exactly when the beet is just cooked and ready to have the skins stripped off. The easiest way to remove the skin is to hold the beet under running water and to rub the skin off with your fingers. The beet itself will still be fairly hard and not fully cooked through. If you have some very small beets out of your garden, they will cook faster than larger beets and should be put into the simmering beet liquid after the larger beets have cooked for a short period of time. Dispose of the water that was used for simmering the beets.

After the skins are removed, cut the beets into desired shapes and sizes, leaving very small beets whole but cutting larger beets into slices or quarters. Put the beets directly into the jars with onion slices and garlic cloves, filling as tightly as possible. You could, of course, use whole, small, peeled onions. Finally, after the jars are filled with onions, beets, and garlic, you will need to fill the jars with a hot pickling liquid prepared in the following proportions.

PICKLING LIQUID INGREDIENTS

⅓ cup cider vinegar
⅔ cup water
1 tablespoon sugar
½ tablespoon salt

For 8 pints of beets, you can estimate that you will use at least 6 or 7 recipes of the pickling mixture. Make extra; it is cheap, and you can dispose of the excess, or you can use it for easy Refrigerator Cucumber Pickles (Chapter 7). The pickling mixture should be put in a stainless steel–lined pot and brought to a boil immediately prior to filling the jars. You should use a funnel with a very large opening at the bottom designed to fit within the pickling jars so that you do not make a mess on your counter as you are pouring the liquid into the jars. As with the canning tongs, this funnel is very cheap.

After you ladle the hot liquid over the beets, leaving at least ½ an inch headspace, jiggle the jars to remove air bubbles and to readjust the liquid level before sealing. The open space between the jar contents and the lid is critical to the creation of a vacuum for safe storage.

Wipe the edges of the jar with a clean, moistened paper towel. Screw on the jar lids, tightening only to light hand pressure. It is not necessary or desirable to overtighten, although the fit should be firm. Place the jars carefully into the same canning pot in which you sterilized the jars, using the same already hot (actively boiling) water. Using the canning tongs, place the jars in the pot so that they do not tip over. The liquid in the pot will now be at least 1–2 inches over the top of the jars. The pot should be brought to and maintained at a rolling boil and should be covered. Process for at least 15 minutes. To be ultrasafe, I process longer than the time specified in the *Ball Blue Book*.

After 15 minutes of boiling the filled and sealed jars, lift the jars out of the canning pot with the special tongs, and carefully place them on a board to cool. As the jars cool, you will hear "pops"—this is the top lid sealing to an airtight seal. If a jar does not properly seal, put it in the refrigerator, and use it first.

Because of the vinegar in the liquid, the product is acidic, and therefore there will be no opportunity for botulism to form. Botulism is a poison that can be created in an oxygen-free environment, such as a vacuum-sealed jar that has not been properly processed. Because of this I process only acidic foods such as pickles and jams and jellies with citrus or vinegar as part of the flavor. In addition to botulism, if the product is improperly processed and not sterilized, the product can spoil and become inedible. If, when you open the jar, there is obviously no vacuum, and the product appears or smells to be unsavory, or the lid is bulging, you should dispose of it; it is not safe, and do not taste or eat it.

REFRIGERATOR CUCUMBER PICKLES

If you have a garden and grow cucumbers, then you know the problem of what to do with all of the cucumbers your vines produce. I have a partial solution: make refrigerator pickles.

INGREDIENTS

cucumbers, as desired
sweet onion, as desired (Texas 1015, Vidalia, etc.)
dill, as desired
pickling liquid (see recipe for beets)

Slice cucumbers and sweet onion. I have tried this dish with sliced garlic as an addition but think the garlic (a flavor that I generally like) is too strong and detracts from the pickle flavor. If the cucumbers are mature enough to have a seed section with a significant number of seeds, cut the cucumbers in half, and remove the seeds before slicing.

Place cucumbers into a glass or Corning Pyroceram container. Sprinkle with optional dried dill weed. Add sufficient hot pickling liquid to fill about half of the container and stir. The vegetables will wilt and exude water to cover the cucumbers and onion. Cover and place in the refrigerator. Stir every day or so for 2 or 3 days, and then it is ready to eat. This continues to get better and will stay for an extended period without spoiling.

A great variant for service is to stir in some sour cream before plating. This milk version is great to serve with smoked salmon, gravlax, whitefish salad, pickled herring, or as a salad by itself.

Pickled jalapeño peppers are essential for any Mexican or Tex-Mex meal. There are a number of brands of pickled jalapeños that are sold commercially in metal cans; I would not ever purchase these products because the pickling liquid is an acid that leaches metal from the can and compromises flavor. There are also pickled jalapeños that are sold in glass jars, and some of these are actually fairly good. However, none of the commercially prepared varieties come close to matching home-canned products. This recipe is a sort of Mexican variation on an Italian spicy pickled vegetable salad or *giardiniera*, sometimes also called *sottaceti*.

See the recipe for Pickled Beets earlier in Chapter 7 and the *Ball Blue Book* for the basic process of preparing jars, filling jars, and preparing the pickling liquid. This is seriously important to both long-term preservation and avoidance of botulism, a potentially fatal poison, although probably not a risk in this recipe because the pickling solution is acidic.

I frequently grow sufficient jalapeños to make pickled jalapeños. Depending on the heat and the dryness of the soil, even jalapeños that are supposed to be relatively mild can be very spicy. Therefore, it is not always predictable as to how spicy the final product will be. Peppers grown in Texas heat are likely to be spicier than the same variety grown in, for example, New York. What makes homemade pickled jalapeños so special is that you can control the sweetness and other pickling and flavoring characteristics. The process is identical to pickling beets except that you use cross-sliced or whole jalapeños stuffed into the jars with onion and garlic. You can use either green or red jalapeños.

INGREDIENTS

3-4 jalapeños per pint, sliced into ½-inch coins
4-5 large cloves garlic, peeled
onion, as needed
carrot, as needed
pickling liquid (see recipe for Pickled Beets)

I suggest leaving the seeds and ribs for spiciness, contrary to my general practice when cooking with jalapeños. In addition, slices of peeled carrots placed into the jars with the onion, garlic, and peppers add beautiful color and wonderful flavor and texture. There is no particular formula of proportions; I simply fill the jars with vegetables until they are full, trying to have some of each vegetable in each jar. After the jars are filled with this raw product, pour the pickling liquid into the jars. Leave ½ inch to ¾ inch of headspace for the vacuum to form and seal the jar. For 11 pints of pickled jalapeños, you would need at least 10 recipes of the pickling liquid. (Remember, if you are using quart jars, 1 quart equals 2 pints.)

Jiggle the jars to remove air pockets, clean the edges of the top of each glass jar, add the lids, and seal, but do not force the lids too tight. Boil—not simmer—the jars covered by 2 inches of boiling water for at least 10 to 15 minutes. When you remove the jars to the counter, and as they cool, you will hear the lids pop as they seal airtight. Refrigerate any that fail to properly seal and use those first.

You can use other varieties of peppers, such as banana peppers, to provide color and taste variation, but I prefer jalapeños to banana peppers—and do not like the flavor of serrano peppers. It is a matter of choice and taste.

Egg Salad, p. 124

Chapter 8: *Salads and Dressings*

SALADS

CAESAR-STYLE SALAD

Various articles and books make a mystery out of Caesar salad dressing, but notwithstanding the multiple variations on its ingredients and preparation as well as the mystique of its origins, it is really nothing more than a variant of vinaigrette or, because of the egg yolk, a mayonnaise. Of course, there is the mystery of the actual ingredients in the original Caesar, a mystery I cannot solve.

INGREDIENTS

romaine lettuce
½–1 cup parmesan cheese, kosher as needed (omit for a meat meal)

Dressing (makes 2–3 servings and can easily be scaled up)
1 egg yolk
anchovy (optional—omit for a meat meal)
2 lemons, zested
½ cup acid (lemon juice or vinegar)
1-2 cloves garlic
½ tablespoon worcestershire sauce (worcestershire is a fermented sauce originally containing anchovy, but now some versions omit the fish)
1 cup extra-virgin olive oil
1 tablespoon dijon mustard
salt and pepper

Croutons

baguette
olive oil
butter and/or olive oil
2-3 cloves garlic per baguette

Dressing

If you are using anchovies, you may want to rinse the anchovies, particularly if they were packed in salt, to somewhat reduce the salt content. Remove the head and bones. You should grind the anchovies in a mortar and pestle, adding the acid, lemon zest, and garlic, previously ground. Let this mixture sit for at least 10 minutes to allow the acid to take the edge off the garlic. (I like to use a nontraditional sherry or port wine vinegar for part of the acid along with lemon juice because it tastes good.) Anchovies are highly salted, so reduce added salt to compensate. Consider whether use violates kosher rules about meat and fish.

For exactly 1 minute, place the eggs in boiling water before cracking them open to use the still liquid yolk. Separate and discard the whites. To complete the Caesar salad dressing, combine the egg yolk, worcestershire sauce (shaken well), and anchovy mixture, and drizzle in the extra-virgin olive oil, whisking vigorously. Dijon mustard is a requisite ingredient to add at this point. Add pepper to taste.

As with dressing any green salad, the Caesar salad dressing should be mixed with the greens immediately before serving. The greens for this salad consist classically of only romaine lettuce; it should not contain bacon, tomatoes, etc., added in some chef-driven restaurants or steak houses. I also know it is fashionable in some restaurants to use whole leaves, but a knife should not be a utensil required to eat a salad. The leaves should be torn into bite-sized pieces in the kitchen. Add the croutons to the lettuce with the dressing immediately before serving. Grate on cheese and toss well to coat the leaves before serving.

Croutons

The croutons should be homemade by cutting a baguette or other crusty bread into appropriately sized pieces. Drizzle lightly with olive oil, and toss. Toast the croutons in a 350°F oven until lightly browned and crispy, stirring occasionally. In a pan, lightly heat melted butter and/or olive oil, finely minced garlic, and salt to coat. Stir the toasted bread into the pan.

Classically, the salad bowl is rubbed with a cut garlic clove—I prefer adding garlic generously to the oil or butter mixed with the croutons and into the dressing. Omit the butter for a meat meal.

Add these fresh homemade croutons to the salad with a liberal quantity of parmigiano-reggiano cheese (or kosher version). If you are not inclined to make croutons, omit them; commercial croutons are not worth eating.

CHICKEN OR TURKEY SALAD

Chicken or turkey salad is delicious, but it is far from a monolithic construct; there are many variant recipes, and this is really just a compendium of ideas rather than a formulaic recipe. The chicken for the chicken salad can be either the freshly poached chicken that is produced when you make Chicken Stock (Chapter 6), or it can be chicken cooked specifically for this purpose. If you poach chicken just for this purpose, use a well-flavored chicken stock; the chicken will taste good, and the stock will become even richer and more flavorful. You can also either sauté or roast the chicken. Leftover roasted, grilled, or smoked chicken is excellent in chicken salad, and many stores now sell freshly roasted chicken—some better than others. You will need to include some time in the oven if you are cooking thighs, since they are too thick to just sauté completely through on the stove top without overbrowning the chicken. Alternatively, you can just grill thighs or breasts until they are perfectly cooked; then cool and cut up the meat for the chicken salad. Each cooking method produces a differently flavored salad. After the meat is cooked, you can shred it or cut it up in chunks as you prefer. Proportions are totally discretionary and to your taste. Turkey meat can be substituted for chicken to make a wonderful turkey salad.

American chicken salads generally have a mayonnaise-based dressing, but if you are making a Chinese or Southeast Asian chicken salad, you would use an Asian-flavored vinaigrette variant, not mayonnaise, as described at the end of this recipe. There are recipes that mix sour cream with the mayonnaise, but that is not kosher—and very unnecessary.

Chicken salads with mayonnaise are generally more about the chicken and less about the other ingredients, as the bulk of the salad is chicken—as compared to the Chinese chicken salad, which is a partnership between the chicken and the vegetable. Think of Chinese chicken salad as a salad with chicken, while many mayonnaise-based chicken salads are chicken with some additives.

A mayonnaise-based chicken salad variant that I really like includes curry powder. Another seasoning variant includes Old Bay Seasoning to taste, tasting carefully for salt before adding any salt. Liquid smoke is yet another additive to a basic mayonnaise, starting with a small amount—perhaps ½ a teaspoon for 1 pound of meat. You can always add more, but you cannot take it out.

Preparation is generally as follows: Toss the diced or shredded chicken and other desired ingredients (see below) with desired spice/flavoring, such as, for an Indian flavor, a generous amount of either curry powder (the sweet yellow curry powder that we are all familiar with) or with some other combination of Indian spice mixtures or other flavoring. This could include a garam masala, combined, perhaps, with a tandoori masala, tikka masala, or another masala spice mix. Add the spices generously to your taste. You can add more spice after you add the mayonnaise.

Various spice mixtures are available in Indian grocery stores and spice specialty stores such as Penzeys. Find and use mixtures you like for this recipe as well as for lentils and other dishes. Depending on your location, you may also find an Indian spice vendor. Many large cities now have wonderful spice shops, but these may not be kosher. There are also recipes available on the internet and in Indian cookbooks for various spice mixtures. See for example, the Garam Masala recipe in Chapter 2; it is an easy process.

Chicken salads are varied by your choice of mayonnaise, seasoning, vegetables, herbs, or nuts added to your taste. These could include carrots, diced celery, finely chopped sweet onions (Texas 1015, Vidalia, Walla Walla, etc.), green onions, or, more unusual, julienned raw (or blanched and chilled in ice water) snow or sugar snap peas, green beans (very lightly poached and chilled immediately in ice water), broccoli or cauliflower (raw or treated similarly to the green beans), cilantro, basil, etc., as you may desire to add texture and flavor. Chopped hard-cooked eggs are another common and delicious ingredient to add. Roasted nuts such as pecans or almonds are always delicious in chicken salad and add a welcome crunch. Ripe summer field-grown tomato and perfectly ripe avocado are accompaniments that seriously enhance chicken salad. I do not add fruit such as apples or raisins, although some do. You can vary the proportions of chicken to vegetables to your taste. I prefer the salad to be principally chicken.

When mixing in the mayonnaise—or, for a nice variant, use Guacamole (Chapter 5)—do so lightly because the goal is to merely lightly coat the ingredients and not to make the chicken salad gloppy. Squeeze lemon or lime juice to taste, and season with salt and pepper to taste.

A variant and more basic chicken salad replaces the curry or other Indian spice powder with dijon mustard and possibly some chopped fresh herbs. Use a very liberal quantity of dijon mustard to the amount of mayonnaise so that the dijon mustard is about a third of the dressing added. Again, lemon or lime juice squeezed into the chicken salad adds a fresh, piquant edge and reduces the amount of mayonnaise or mustard that is required in order to coat and moisten the ingredients. Add fresh, chopped herbs as desired: oregano, thyme, chives, basil, cilantro, etc. Chopped olives of your choice or cornichons change the flavor profile and add a fresh taste surprise. Chicken salad does not have to be boring!

For Chinese or Asian chicken salad, mix the chicken with various raw vegetables that have been cut up, diced, or julienned neatly. Good ingredient options include carrots, snow peas, shredded Chinese cabbage, green onions, cucumbers, radishes, cilantro, diced celery, and roasted nuts such as peanuts, almonds, or pecans—all tossed with an Asian-flavored vinaigrette just before serving. If you do not like cilantro—and some people, including my daughter, experience cilantro as soapy tasting—then use another herb such as spearmint or basil. The vinaigrette should consist of ¼ cup of either rice wine vinegar or Chinese black vinegar as the acid and an equal amount of soy sauce, a teaspoon or less of a dark Chinese sesame oil, a teaspoon of sugar, a garlic paste mashed with ginger (1 tablespoon each), and a neutral-flavored oil such as peanut oil. Although the goal is an Asian-flavored dressing, the formula of 1 part acid to 2 or 3 parts oil for the vinaigrette still holds (see Vinaigrette recipe later in Chapter 8). Whisk to combine and toss the vinaigrette with the salad. Depending upon the amount or the saltiness of soy sauce used, you may not need to add salt, so you should taste the vinaigrette before tossing with the chicken salad to test the saltiness as well as the acid-oil balance of your vinaigrette. Tasting as you cook is always critical to achieving the desired delicious result. Grind black pepper to taste.

I find many commercial types of coleslaw too sweet, but this slaw is not too sweet and is always delicious. It does not contain sour cream and can be served with a meat meal.

INGREDIENTS

Slaw

```
3 cups red or green cabbage, finely shredded
1 medium-sized sweet onion, grated
2-3 carrots, peeled
2 celery stalks
```

Dressing

```
⅔ cup mayonnaise (not Miracle Whip or other commercial salad
dressing—see my Mayonnaise recipe later in Chapter 8)
2 or more tablespoons red (or sherry or port) wine vinegar to
taste (I like a tart mixture, so we add more vinegar after
carefully tasting)
2 teaspoons white cane sugar (The slaw is also good without any
added sugar. It is a matter of taste. This amount smooths the
vinegar flavor but, to our taste, does not make the salad sweet.)
1 teaspoon salt
½ teaspoon celery seed
freshly ground pepper
```

To shred the cabbage, you may use a knife, but the KitchenAid vegetable-grater attachment makes the process much easier. A similar blade is available with the Cuisinart mixer. Finely grate the onion and celery, and peel and grate the carrots. Unlike for most purposes, grating (particularly the onion), not chopping with a knife, is best because of the released onion juices.

Mix all of the grated ingredients.

Mix all of the dressing ingredients until the dressing is well combined and the salt and sugar are dissolved. Mix the dressing into the cabbage mixture and refrigerate until use. Mix occasionally until the dressing has caused the cabbage mixture to wilt slightly.

Many people will add other vegetables to coleslaw such as green peppers or even apples or raisins. I do not like these as ingredients in coleslaw, although many do.

This slaw is excellent to accompany smoked meats such as brisket or chicken, hamburgers, grilled hotdogs, or knockwurst, as well as on pastrami or corned beef sandwiches.

PENNSYLVANIA DUTCH COLESLAW

This coleslaw is perfect for those who eschew the use of mayonnaise or want a change of pace. It is tart but with offsetting sweetness—vinegary and delicious.

It is almost a pickled coleslaw, and if you use artificial sweetener instead of sugar, it is incredibly low in calories. This recipe is for about three pounds of coleslaw. As the slaw ages, the cabbage will exude moisture and will wilt, which is fine. This slaw can last for weeks in a refrigerator without fear of spoilage. However, if you make the coleslaw with artificial sweetener rather than sugar, it will not store as well as if you use sugar since sugar is a natural inhibitor of pathogens that cause spoilage.

INGREDIENTS

Slaw

1 head of cabbage, shredded (use your choice of savoy cabbage, regular green cabbage, red cabbage, etc.—all taste great)

3 medium carrots

3 green onions

1 celery stalk

½ medium-sized sweet onion

Dressing

2 large cloves garlic

1 cup white or cider vinegar

½ cup sugar (if you are using sugar and not artificial sweetener)

¾ cup vegetable oil or olive oil

1 teaspoon salt

½ teaspoon pepper

1 teaspoon celery seed

Shred 1 head of cabbage (a knife works quite well, or you can use the food processor or KitchenAid mixer with a shredder blade). Peel and shred the carrots, dice the green onions, shred the celery, and grate the onion.

In the manner that you choose (in a mortar and pestle, with a knife edge, or a garlic press), mash 2 large, peeled cloves of garlic. If you want a very garlicky slaw, use more garlic. Macerate the minced or mashed garlic in a little bit of vinegar for at least 10 minutes to take the edge off of the garlic flavor before adding to the salad dressing.

The salad dressing is most simple: Add all dressing ingredients, including garlic mash, to a pot. *Note:* If you are using artificial sweetener, do not add the sweetener until after the mixture is boiled. Different artificial sweeteners vary in their sweetness compared to sugar; for example, I think that 1 package of Equal (aspartame in the blue package) has approximately the same sweetening as 1 teaspoon of sugar, while saccharin (Sweet'N Low) is significantly sweeter. You need to adjust the amount to your taste and which of these products is acceptably kosher.

Heat the marinade to a boil. If using artificial sweetener, add it after turning off the heat. Pour the marinade over the shredded vegetables. Toss well. Store in a glass or Pyroceram container and refrigerate. Use plastic wrap to seal the flavors from everything else in the refrigerator unless your container has an airtight seal. Stir occasionally to redistribute the marinade as it macerates.

EGG SALAD

One might wonder why anyone needs a recipe for egg salad because everyone knows how to make it, but I happen to think that egg salads are among those special constructs that are supremely enjoyable—and the variety of the possible constructs deserves exploration. As a general rule, for me, egg salad frequently requires the availability of delicious tomatoes—if not as an ingredient, then to be served with the egg salad. Fortunately, since the tomatoes in egg salad are generally in relatively small pieces, you can use cherry or other small tomatoes that are grown frequently in hothouses, are available year round, and have an intense sweet flavor—although nothing can replace field-grown and sun-ripened summer tomatoes.

Ingredients always include hard-cooked—not hard-boiled—eggs, and I assume 4 eggs per person as the base for a generous main course serving. There is a right way and a wrong way to make hard-cooked eggs. Please see the discussion on eggs in Chapter 2.

Proportions in making egg salad are not intended to be set forth precisely, because in such a construct, everything depends on your taste.

Mayonnaise is a significant flavor component in most egg salads. Different brands of mayonnaise have different flavors, and none of the commercial brands can come close to the flavor of homemade mayonnaise—particularly, homemade mayonnaise made with a significant percentage of the oil being a quality extra-virgin cold-pressed olive oil, with dijon or another tasty mustard and a quality vinegar and/or citrus as an acid (see Mayonnaise recipe later in Chapter 8). In addition, it should be clear that when mayonnaise is referenced, it is not a call for a commercial salad dressing such as Miracle Whip, which is entirely too sweet, and a product never used by me for any purpose whatsoever.

It is widely recognized that mayonnaise is a southern tradition, and everyone has a favorite brand. I favor Kraft, while my wife insists that, for egg salad especially, Hellmann's is the brand to use. There are other brands that are favorites in the South such as Blue Plate and Duke's, while there are many other brands such as Best Foods that are favorites in other regions. Some manufacturers now produce mayonnaise with different additive flavoring variations, but my practice is to purchase plain mayonnaise; you can add your own flavor variation if you want.

One of my favorite egg salads is simply 4 hard-cooked eggs, diced and mixed with (1) 1 or 2 strips of beef bacon, diced and cooked until crispy and carefully drained; (2) ½ a celery stalk, diced finely; (3) ¼ to ½ cup of the ripest and most delicious tomato, chopped; and (4) just sufficient mayonnaise and dijon mustard in a 3:1 proportion to bind the egg salad, with salt and pepper to taste. One optional delicious addition is finely diced sweet onion, a couple tablespoons per 4 eggs. Other wonderful options can include a couple tablespoons of capers, 1 or more varieties of olives, finely diced cornichon, or even finely diced dill pickles. You should mix all of the ingredients together and taste before adding salt because some additions carry their own salt. The same rule applies before adding the dressing of mustard and mayonnaise because some ingredients add liquid, and you may not need much dressing to cause the egg salad to bind together sufficiently.

Another variant is 4 hard-cooked eggs mixed with tomato, celery, onion, and 1 or 2 tablespoons of sweet curry powder with just sufficient mayonnaise to bind, with salt and pepper to taste. If you are going in the direction of Indian flavorings, instead of using sweet curry powder, you could insert a combination of garam masala and some other masala of either mild or very spicy flavor, such as tikka or tandoori masala, to your egg salad. Remember that while some brands may be kosher, many spice blends are not certified kosher—the solution is to find a kosher brand or find a recipe and make your own blend. Yet another variant is to use smoked paprika in lieu of the curry powder. Smoked paprika has a wonderful smoky flavor, adding piquancy. Yet another variant is to use Old Bay Seasoning as a variant for the curry powder or smoked paprika. If you are using Old Bay Seasoning or any other prepared spice mixture, be careful before adding salt because a mixture such as Old Bay Seasoning frequently has quite a salty component.

And finally, a variant that is an Eastern European Jewish tradition: eggs and onions. The preparation is simply chopped hard-cooked eggs with finely minced (preferably sweet) onions or shallots mixed in, in the proportions desired. The binder, however, rather than mayonnaise, is a couple tablespoons of chicken schmaltz, melted or very loose at room temperature. Add salt and pepper to taste.

A variant with a classic Eastern European twist is to add reconstituted, diced, sautéed porcini mushrooms (reserving the reconstituting liquid for future use) or some chopped, well-caramelized, domestic mushrooms. Chill before serving. My mother made this dish using yellow onions, but I assure you it is much better with a sweet onion variety. Serve this delicacy on toasted pumpernickel or rye bread—even better with a light spread of schmaltz lightly salted on the bread before toasting in the oven.

POTATO SALADS

There are multiple varieties of delicious potato salad.

First, use only Yukon Gold or white or red boiling potatoes. Baking or Idaho potatoes are too starchy and mealy for this use. I personally do not ever peel potatoes for potato salad; it is simply too much trouble, plus I like the flavor of the peel, and it is good for you. The potatoes should be simmered, starting with cold water until just cooked. Add salt liberally to the cold water used to boil the potatoes. This is your one chance to completely flavor the potatoes, and the salt in the water that does not flavor the potato is discarded. If you do not start with cold water, then by the time the center is cooked, the outside will be overcooked.

Do not cook potatoes until they fall apart; it is sufficient that a knife just pierces and slides out easily. Add several cloves of peeled garlic and salt to the water to boil with the potatoes.

The garlic infuses and flavors the potato, as does the salt. The cooked, now very mild garlic is then mashed and added into the salad to add a wonderful flavor. I also frequently cook eggs to the hard-cooked stage with the potato for inclusion in the potato salad. Eggs cooked with the potatoes should be removed once they are hard-cooked, about 10–12 minutes after the water starts to simmer. See the discussion in Chapter 2 for achieving hard-cooked eggs.

After the potatoes are perfectly done, they should be taken out and sliced or cut as desired. They should immediately be doused while hot with vinegar or lemon juice because they are in a perfect state for the flavor of the acid to be absorbed into the potato. A red wine, port, or sherry vinegar is delicious, but balsamic vinegar has too strong and sweet of a flavor for this purpose. At the time the potatoes are sliced, the eggs are also sliced or cut into the potato salad. Adjust the salt to taste at this stage, along with the vinegar or lemon juice. As I watch chefs prepare potato salad on TV, they seem to wind up with beautiful pieces of potato in the salad ready for service. I do not seem to be able to achieve this result unless the potato is undercooked, but the salad is nonetheless delicious.

Set forth below are a couple of very different recipes for potato salad.

1. "Normal" American Potato Salad

INGREDIENTS

2 pounds cooked potatoes (see Potato Salad introduction for cooking steps)

4 hard-cooked eggs (see Chapter 2 for cooking steps)

¼ cup vinegar, or to taste

1 celery stalk, minced

½ cup sweet onion, diced (Texas 1015, Vidalia, Walla Walla, etc.)

mustard powder or yellow mustard (not necessarily dijon or other "gourmet" mustard)

celery seed to taste

black pepper to taste

dill pickles (optional)

cornichon (optional)

smoked or garlic beef sausage (optional)

mayonnaise to taste (not ever a sweet salad dressing like Miracle Whip—see Mayonnaise recipe later in Chapter 8)

Combine the ingredients. For this salad, diced kosher dill pickles or cornichon make a delightful addition, and you can add some of the pickle liquid to the hot potatoes along with the vinegar. Actually, the mustard and dill pickle addition makes this sort of a German-style salad.

Claussen pickles are crisp and fresh tasting. They are sort of similar to what are referred to as "half-dones" in a Jewish delicatessen but with a slight twist that you need to taste to understand because they do not taste barrel-cured. Claussen pickles can be found in the refrigerator case in the grocery. Regular barrel-cured dill pickles (or "hamburger dills," which are really sour and not the same), while good in their own way, do not work (at least for me) in potato salad. Thus, Claussen is my favorite brand for use here, but your cooking is always a matter of your taste.

Many people use sweet pickles or relish in their potato salads, but those are not products I like or would ever use—certainly not in a potato salad. I also never use bell peppers in a potato salad, although many do.

A delicious additive is to cut smoked or garlic beef sausages into coins that you then cook until rendered and caramelized before draining and adding to the potato salad. The salad then becomes a main course.

Add mayonnaise to taste. I use just enough to make the assembly moist. If you add mustard, use less mayonnaise. I do not use sour cream in potato salad, although many do. The reason for this is because my mother did not use it. Of course, my mother did use sweet pickles in her potato salad, and I do not follow her lead there simply because I do not like sweet pickles. It all boils down to taste. In any event, because potato salad is normally eaten with meat, the use of sour cream or another milk product would not be kosher; thus, sour cream is not appropriate for this salad in our house.

2. "Italian" Potato Salad

INGREDIENTS

2 pounds cooked potatoes (see Potato Salad introduction for cooking steps)

½–1 cup (or more to taste) mix of freshly picked thyme, marjoram, oregano, and basil

several green onions or ½ cup chives

¼–½ cup Vinaigrette (see recipe later in Chapter 8)

4 hard-cooked eggs (optional)

salt and pepper to taste

This potato salad is very different from what I refer to as an American-style potato salad and really has no relation to Italy. It has no mayonnaise or sour cream. It uses an oil-and-vinegar dressing or vinaigrette variant. Chopped fresh herbs are not just a flavoring; they are also an ingredient.

Strip the leaves from the stems of thyme, marjoram, oregano, and basil, freshly picked. Mince the herbs finely. Dice several green onions, using both the white and green parts, or finely chop about ½ cup of chives. Add vinaigrette to the hot potatoes first. Then add the optional 4 hard-cooked eggs, chopped or sliced. Add salt and pepper to taste. Stir in the herbs and green onion just before service. This is best served warm. If you have leftover salad, refrigerate it, and then nuke it lightly to bring to room temperature before serving.

CAPRESE SALAD

There are few ingredients in *insalata caprese*, and this salad emphasizes a standard theme in this book: use the ripest, preferably field-grown and field-ripened, best-quality tomatoes or other ingredients, the best and freshest mozzarella, and a liberal quantity of fresh basil leaves, drizzled with a homemade vinagrette. Otherwise, the result will inevitably be disappointing rather than the ethereal combination it can be. Even here, variations can be successful: fresh oregano and/or marjoram and/or thyme (all of which can be picked fresh year round, at least through USDA Zone 7) as a substitute or addition to fresh basil (a summer-only product, unless your grocery store imports a supply in the winter, as many now do) and cucumber and/or avocado (or even roasted garlic, room-temperature grilled vegetables such as carrots, eggplant, zucchini, and a variety of olives) as additions to the tomato also result in delectable food. While dried thyme and oregano have a place in the kitchen—but not in this salad—I find that both dried basil and parsley are flavorless and not ever to be used. The bottom line is that you should cook what tastes good to you—and a kitchen garden, at least for herbs, is a great way to go. I always look forward to summer, when I can get field-grown and field-ripened tomatoes, cucumbers without wax, etc., and I can gladly make a meal of variants of this salad with some freshly baked bread and butter.

It is difficult to buy unrefrigerated, ripe, field-grown tomatoes from most supermarkets even in the summer and is more difficult in the winter. Tomatoes should *never* be refrigerated; I was recently disappointed to see a TV cook take a basket of tomatoes from the fridge. If you can, buy ripe (not "ethylened") tomatoes. Even though they may appear unripe with stripes of green, once tomatoes have at least a pink blush, they will normally fully ripen to bright red on the counter and acquire a reasonably good flavor. If you have tomatoes in your garden, just before the first freeze, pick all of the tomatoes, even green tomatoes. Many will magically ripen on your counter—not summer tomatoes, but still good. Greenhouse tomatoes are frequently available, and although they may be ripe and adequate if the "real" thing is not available, they simply do not have the flavor of field-ripened fruit. Cherry tomatoes with good flavor are frequently available. If possible, shop at farmer's markets from stalls manned by local farmers selling their own product—not commercial vendors—during season.

DRESSINGS

MAYONNAISE (AND VARIANTS)

Mayonnaise is really simple to make. Homemade mayonnaise tastes so much better than store-bought mayonnaise that it can hardly be compared as the same product—and you control the ingredients, which certainly do not include weirdly named chemicals. Of course, it has a limited shelf life, but that is a trade I will make every day. Mayonnaise is one of the classic "mother" sauces in French cuisine. It has multiple variations, many with their own names such as aioli, a garlic-flavored variant.

BASIC FORMULA

This recipe can easily be scaled up.

```
1 cup oil (mixed: ½ cup olive and ½ cup flavorless vegetable)
1 raw egg yolk (see the discussion regarding the purchase of eggs
in Chapter 2)
at least 1 teaspoon dijon mustard or other mustard (including
mustard powder), depending on flavor desired
acid (such as lemon or vinegar) to flavor
salt and pepper to taste
```

For Aioli Variant (Optional)

```
1-2 cloves garlic per cup of oil
1 tablespoon lemon juice or other acid
salt
lemon zest (optional)
```

Crack the egg, and separate the egg yolk from the egg white. Place the egg yolk into a mixing bowl. Either hand whisk or use the whisk attachment in an electric mixer such as a KitchenAid; the latter is by far easier. Egg whites can be stored in a glass jar and frozen for later use, such as for Coconut Macaroons (see recipe in Chapter 15).

The mustard acts as an emulsifier for the oil and egg and is important for this reason as well as for taste. Add mustard right before you add oil to the egg yolk, and whisk.

Contrary to popular uninformed belief, this emulsification is not at all difficult. I have never had a failure of emulsification with this process using the KitchenAid mixer. Some people try to make a mystery out of some cooking processes and imply that things are more difficult than they really are. Be adventuresome; you will be rewarded.

Use 1 cup of oil per egg yolk. To my taste, using olive oil exclusively provides too intense an olive oil flavor to the mayonnaise. Drizzle the oil slowly into the mixture as you start to whisk the egg yolks and mustard by machine or otherwise. Add about a teaspoon per yolk of liquid such as lemon juice or vinegar (or water, although I vote in favor of flavor) as needed for taste at this stage and as the mayonnaise is close to completion. Certainly, some finely grated lemon zest as emulsification proceeds also adds great flavor. Taste as needed.

After emulsification is in progress, you can speed up the addition of oil (but not too fast). As the process proceeds, you can observe that the oil and egg are absorbed together (emulsified), and then you can add more oil. Then mix in more of the desired acid (lemon juice, white or red wine vinegar, port wine vinegar, or some combination) to taste. I add more mustard and more lemon juice and/or vinegar and salt as needed, tasting frequently, because I like the flavor and tang, but if I am making aioli, I hold off on adding salt and extra acid until the mashed garlic mixture is added. I frequently use a mixture of acids: lemon juice and red, port, or sherry wine vinegar.

If you are making an aioli, now is the time to add the garlic paste, discussed below.

Add water as necessary to reach the thickness you desire. You may add minced herbs such as dill, basil, thyme, etc., depending on desired flavor. If you start with a commercial mayonnaise, do not let this deter you from modifying it to taste with additional acid (using lemon or vinegar), various kinds of mustard, herbs, etc. However, the commercially available variants never taste right to me.

Aioli

If you are making an aioli, a garlic paste (1 or 2 cloves of garlic per cup of oil in the mayonnaise) is an essential component. Using a mortar and pestle, pound the garlic with kosher salt, or use a garlic press, or mash the garlic and salt with the side of your knife blade. Squeeze some lemon juice or other acid into the paste and let the lemon or other acid macerate with the garlic paste for 10 minutes or so to soften the edge on the garlic flavor prior to using in the recipe. I personally like lemon, so I usually also add lemon zest, which is where the lemon oil and flavor is, even more so than in the juice.

Remember, the process of making a garlic paste inherently uses salt, so defer adding salt to the mayonnaise until you add the garlic mixture. Also remember that the acid used in the garlic paste is part of the acid used in the mayonnaise.

PINK (OR RUSSIAN) SALAD DRESSING

I own several editions of *The Joy of Cooking*, and the original base for this recipe (which is significantly modified here) is in each edition. This is a sauce that has enjoyed great acceptance in our family. It is very easy to make—maybe five minutes, including chopping or grating the onion. Measurements are to taste and not precise. My use of brand names is simply because those are what I like; however, it is simply a matter of personal taste. It is slightly different each time I make it. As noted below, this dressing has many uses as a sauce (and, I suppose, could be regarded as a mayonnaise variant), in addition to its use as a salad dressing.

INGREDIENTS

```
2 cups Kraft mayonnaise (not low fat, not flavored)
1 cup Heinz ketchup
½ large sweet onion, finely chopped brunoise or grated
1-2 tablespoons worcestershire sauce to taste
½ teaspoon (or to taste) Tabasco sauce or other hot sauce
2 tablespoons (or to taste) horseradish in vinegar (preferably
red)
```

Start with mayonnaise. I use regular, full-fat, unadulterated, and unmodified Kraft mayonnaise, and not some variant that they now make with different tastes. I have used other brands that also produce a good result. However, do not use Miracle Whip; it is too sweet. I do not use homemade mayonnaise for this purpose, although I am sure homemade mayonnaise would taste good. If you use homemade mayonnaise, as in all mayonnaise products, it has to be refrigerated, but it has a very limited shelf life because of the raw egg yolk, plus it lacks the chemical stabilizers in commercial mayonnaise.

Grate or very finely chop (brunoise) ½ a large onion. I now use sweet onions year round since they are now always available. There are many varieties of sweet onions available at varying seasons, such as Texas 1015, Vidalia, Walla Walla, and more. While I no longer use a regular, spicy, yellow, red, Spanish, or white onion here, you should absolutely use a nonsweet variety if you want a stronger onion flavor.

Add about 1 tablespoon of worcestershire sauce (shaken well because it settles as it sits) or adjust to taste. Stir in Tabasco or other hot sauce, including, for example, sriracha to your taste (½ teaspoon or more). Sriracha adds a sweet flavor you may not want. I like the dressing spicy but use the hot sauce to your taste. It adds taste as well as spice, and you might like a different brand.

Add horseradish (preferably beet-flavored for color). Use up to several tablespoons of horseradish, adjusting to your taste, in a total quantity of dressing equal to about ¾ of a quart. Do not use a cream-style horseradish sauce. While the Kraft brand contains no milk product—despite the "creamy" descriptor—the horseradish should be nonsweet horseradish in vinegar because of flavor, not any dietary law. The original recipe called for a relatively small amount. I use a much larger amount of 2 or more tablespoons, adjusting to taste depending on the freshness, which affects its spiciness. Freshly purchased horseradish tends to be spicier. Horseradish that is purchased for Passover and is so labeled tends to be the spiciest commercially available. I currently use Silver Spring's horseradish because that is what is available in Dallas. Ba-Tampte is another brand with the right flavor. Freshly grated horseradish is much spicier than commercial varieties. It can be a challenge to grate because of the fumes—like cutting onions on steroids.

Mix thoroughly, and taste. Add ingredients as needed to produce the desired flavor. I do not use salt or pepper in this recipe. Refrigerate the dressing in a jar that has a good seal, such as a Ball jar.

This dressing is good on salads, in BLT sandwiches (using beef bacon), on cold poached salmon, with hamburgers, on pastrami or corned beef sandwiches with coleslaw, on room-temperature grilled vegetables, and for other uses as a dressing. Be creative.

VINAIGRETTE

A vinaigrette is a salad dressing that can also be used as a marinade. This is more a very simple formula than a recipe. Basically, a vinaigrette is a mixture of oil, acid, and flavorings. The trick is to use quality ingredients you like in a flavor combination you like. If you do not like the vinegar (or other acid) or the oil, you will not like the finished vinaigrette—taste and adjust to your preference. If you use too much or too little oil, the flavor will not be balanced. Remember that balance is to your taste, and the 3-to-1 oil-to-acid standard is merely a starting guide.

I generally like a more tart result and use about 2 parts of oil—or less—to 1 part of acid. This is a matter of taste, but reducing oil has the additional benefit of a reducing calories. Taste the mixture and reseason with salt as needed. The completed vinaigrette can be stored in the refrigerator in cruet bottles or other sealed containers almost indefinitely. Because of the acid, do not use leaded glass or crystal storage bottles. The lead, a poison, can leach out of the glass, and as Alton Brown would say, "That is not good eats." Take the vinaigrette out of the refrigerator a few minutes before using it to allow the oil to re-liquify before shaking vigorously to re-emulsify the mixture for use.

This is so easy to make and so much better, and without the chemical additives, that I cannot imagine buying a bottled salad dressing.

The vinaigrette that I generally prefer is made with quality cold-pressed extra-virgin olive oil, vinegar (which may be a port wine, sherry, red wine, or balsamic vinegar, or a vinegar flavored with, for example, herbs or raspberry, depending on the ultimate flavor desired), salt, pepper, and other flavorings. In addition to or as a substitute for vinegar, I frequently use lemon flavoring, consisting of lemon zest and freshly squeezed lemon juice. The juice is a flavored acid. The zest is flavoring that is derived from citrus oils in that part of the lemon. I never use the bottled lemon stuff because it has a vile flavor. Orange is also an appropriate flavoring, although you may find it too sweet for your purposes. Garlic crushed into a paste and macerated for 10 minutes in some of the acid for the dressing is frequently a desirable additive. Dijon mustard adds flavor and enhances emulsification. Dried or fresh herbs can be a useful variant or enhancement to the flavor profile. If you add fresh herbs, it will not store well, and you will need to use the vinaigrette relatively quickly. Fresh herbs (oregano, thyme, chives, basil, etc.) are better added directly to the salad.

The process is as follows: First mash garlic, if you are using it, into a paste with kosher salt. The salt crystals are sharp and facilitate the grinding process. There are a number of methods of achieving this result, but I like a mortar and pestle. As long as you are using a mortar and pestle, you can also grind in black pepper and citrus zest and/or any herb that you may be using. There is also a process for smashing the garlic clove on a cutting board with a knife and mashing and chopping the garlic and salt with the back and side of the knife to achieve a paste, which I have done, but it is not my preferred method. I am amazed whenever I see the skill Jacques Pépin brings to this process. You can achieve a similar but not quite as satisfactory result with a garlic press.

The final result is materially enhanced if you then let the garlic paste macerate in lemon juice or vinegar for about 10 minutes to tone down the raw garlic edge. I suggest the following procedure: (1) grind lemon zest into the garlic paste, or use a fine microplane grater to grate zest into the mixture; (2) squeeze the lemon juice or other acid into the garlic paste; and (3) let the garlic sit in the acid for 10 to 15 minutes before processing further. This maceration process softens the edge on the raw garlic flavor, making it much more palatable in the finished recipe.

Dijon or other mustard, including mustard powder, in the mixture for the vinaigrette adds not only flavor but also assists the vinegar and oil in emulsifying with each other. This is a matter of taste.

Mushroom Risotto, p. 144

Chapter 9: *Grains*

KASHA AND KASHA VARNISHKES

Kasha is a grain (buckwheat groats) and is cooked, as are most grains, with salt and a liquid. However, the process for making kasha is different from making rice or other grains. It is highly desirable for the cooked kasha to be fluffy and for the grains to be separate. Kasha is not bland and has a wonderful nutty flavor, very different from other grains.

Beat 1 egg for each cup of kasha and mix the egg and the kasha so that each granule of kasha is coated with egg—I use a whisk.

Place the raw kasha in a cold skillet. Use a heavy cast-iron skillet or a heavy aluminum or steel pan clad with aluminum. The pan needs to heat evenly so as not to burn the raw-egg-and-kasha mixture before you add the liquid. You will need a cover that fits tightly on the skillet.

The liquid should be premeasured and by the stove, ready to add. You can use chicken stock or beef stock, but I think the kasha flavor is wonderful with just water as the liquid. Use the ratio of liquid to grain as set forth on the box. The brand we use is Wolff's Kasha, in a coarse granulation. The proportion of kasha to liquid is 1 cup of kasha to 2 cups of liquid. The recipe on the box provides for addition of a fat product, such as butter, but I have never used a fat product in cooking kasha and would not use butter because kasha is usually a side dish for meat.

Place the skillet with the egg-coated kasha on a burner. Cook and stir constantly until the grains are all separated and dry. The kasha will become slightly toasted in this process, so be careful to (1) not overcook and to (2) continuously stir. Then add the suggested amount of salt (1 teaspoon of kosher salt per cup of raw kasha) and the liquid. Since the pan will be intensely hot at this stage, it will boil immediately. Lower the flame to a very low simmer and cover tightly. The kasha will cook in 5 or so minutes.

Mix with cooked bow tie pasta and caramelized chopped onion to make *kasha varnishkes*. I do not use pepper for this dish, but that is a matter of taste. Kasha is frequently served with roasted or braised meat such as pot roast, brisket, or chicken. Ladle the meat's sauces generously over the kasha. Another wonderful use is as a filling for knishes instead of the more frequent potato-onion mixture.

LEMON COCONUT RICE

Rice is a natural base for adding flavorings, and Indians are masters of this art. Basmati or other naturally flavored varieties of rice, such as jasmine or Texmati, are better for this dish—or, actually, many rice preparations—but plain long-grain American rice will also work. Short-grain rice—such as the Italian arborio or carnaroli varieties used for risotto or the Spanish rices used for paella, such as valencia—are too starchy and do not work here.

INGREDIENTS

This recipe can easily be scaled up.

1 cup rice
½ onion, finely diced
2 large cloves garlic, minced
1 tablespoon fresh ginger, minced
1 teaspoon olive oil
2 cups filtered water
1 teaspoon kosher salt
1 teaspoon turmeric
1 lemon, zested and juiced
2-3 tablespoons whole black mustard seed
½ cup coconut, toasted
½ cup almonds, toasted and roughly chopped or slivered
½ cup cilantro, chopped
1 cup raisins (optional)

Wash the rice carefully to remove surface starches. Soaking the rice for 15 to 30 minutes before cooking will enhance its cooked texture, but this step is not essential.

Dice the onion and garlic cloves. Lightly sauté the onion, garlic, and ginger in a teaspoon or so of olive oil until the onion is translucent and the aroma is wonderful—a couple of minutes. Add the rice into the sautéed onion and garlic. Cook the rice lightly to coat it. Then add 2 cups of filtered water for each cup of rice. For each cup of rice, add 1 teaspoon of kosher salt. If you use other salt, such as plain table salt, you will need to adjust the measurement to avoid over-salting. Add a teaspoon of turmeric. It is desirable to zest a lemon and add the zest during the cooking process. Stir only to combine. Cover and simmer lightly until the rice is cooked and the liquid absorbed, about 15 minutes. If using raisins, stir them in after the rice is cooked.

Toast 2 or 3 tablespoons of whole black mustard seed in a dry skillet, stirring constantly by swirling the pan, a 30-second-to-1-minute process. The mustard seed will "pop" as it toasts, and you may wish to use a cover as you swirl the pan. Do not burn the mustard seed. Immediately remove to a cool plate. Toss into the cooked rice.

Toss ½ cup each of toasted almonds—slivered or chopped—and toasted coconut into the cooked rice. After the rice is cooked, squeeze in juice of 1 lemon for each cup of raw rice used. Toss with ½ cup (or to taste) of chopped cilantro leaves. Fluff lightly with a fork to mix all of the ingredients.

MUSHROOM-BARLEY CASSEROLE

Barley is a totally underused starch that has a mild delicious flavor and melds well with other flavors, particularly with mushrooms.

INGREDIENTS

This recipe yields 3–4 servings as a side dish.

½ ounce dried wild European mushrooms (chanterelles or porcini, but not shiitake)

¾ cup hot filtered water to reconstitute mushrooms

1 cup medium pearled barley

2 cups liquid (unsalted beef, chicken, or turkey stock, or water for a vegetarian option)

1 teaspoon kosher salt

bay leaf (for vegetarian option)

dried thyme (optional)

dried oregano (optional)

onion, chopped and sautéed (optional)

garlic, chopped and sautéed (optional)

Mirepoix (optional vegetarian variation)

1 carrot, finely chopped

1 celery stalk, finely chopped

Soak mushrooms in the hot filtered water. The barley should be washed in a strainer before assembly. In a large bowl, combine the barley and 2 cups liquid. If you want a vegetarian dish that you can serve with a meal containing milk, you could certainly use a vegetable stock, or you can add a mirepoix (carrot, onion, and celery, finely chopped) with water, perhaps a bay leaf, and some dried thyme. Flavor will vary depending on what stock you use.

Drain the mushrooms, preserving the soaking liquid. Chop the rehydrated mushrooms and add them to the barley and stock. Add 1 teaspoon of kosher salt. Let the mushroom-soaking liquid settle before adding the clear liquid to the barley, being careful to stop pouring before you reach the dregs in the bottom, which include sand and dirt. At this stage you can add dried herbs (thyme or oregano or such other herbs as you desire), some chopped, sautéed onion, and garlic, if using. Mix carefully and pour the barley mixture into a 9-inch square casserole dish.

Cover with foil and cook in a 350°F oven until the liquid is absorbed and the barley is tender and done (about 45 minutes to 1 hour).

Since we do not use cheese or milk products with meat, this risotto is somewhat different from anything that you will have in an Italian restaurant. It is, nonetheless, quite delicious and stands on its own. With a vegetable and salad, it makes a wonderful meal. (Or you can maintain the Italian ambiance and merely serve a platter of room-temperature grilled vegetables with recommended dressings.) As with other risottos, you should use an arborio, carnaroli, or other similar short-grain Italian rice intended for use in risottos. More and more of these rice varieties are becoming available, at least in specialty stores, and arborio is generally available even in normal grocery stores.

INGREDIENTS

2 pounds fresh beef italian sausage without casing, either sweet or spicy or mixed

olive oil, as needed

2 cups short-grain rice (arborio or carnaroli)

1 onion, diced, or 3 shallots

2-3 cloves garlic, thinly sliced

1-2 tablespoons tomato paste

1-2 cups red wine

1 teaspoon thyme

2 teaspoons oregano

1 bay leaf

1 teaspoon salt

pepper to taste

4-5 cups stock, preheated (vegetable, chicken, or beef)

While beef italian sausage is difficult to find, if your butcher makes other sausages, he or she may be willing to make beef italian sausage for you. Ask not, and ye shall not receive. If your butcher is not kosher and uses pork casings, simply buy the meat without casings, and cook it as balls or patties.

The process is simple. Poke the sausages so that they do not burst in the sautéing process, or you can just roll bulk sausage into bite-sized balls. With olive oil, lightly coat a heavy pot in which you will be cooking the risotto. Heat the pan so that the oil is clearly hot and shimmering. Then put in the sausages. Brown the sausages or sausage balls on all sides, but do not complete the cooking. Remove the sausages from the pan and set them aside while you cook the risotto.

Put rice in the pan, together with the onion (or shallot), and lightly toast the rice at medium heat. Add a little olive oil if needed, although there may already be sufficient, very flavorful oil when you remove the sausage. As the risotto becomes toasted and translucent, stir in the garlic and the tomato paste. When aroma of the garlic becomes apparent (less than 30 seconds), add 1 or 2 cups of the red wine. Stir. The red wine will be absorbed very quickly. After you add the red wine, add the dried thyme, dried oregano, bay leaf, and 1 teaspoon of kosher salt. Grind in fresh pepper.

Start adding preheated liquid (water, vegetable stock, chicken stock, or beef stock) until the risotto is almost cooked. Add the liquid 1 cup or so at a time, stirring frequently. Cook at low heat. The liquid you use will certainly impact the flavor of the finished risotto. This risotto made with a wonderfully rich homemade beef or chicken stock is incredibly flavorful. Slice the partially cooked sausages into coins and place them or the sausage balls into the almost-cooked risotto to finish cooking. The sausages need to cook at least 5 minutes. Serve hot, and drizzle with olive oil.

MUSHROOM RISOTTO

Mushroom risotto is a wonderful and sumptuous dish that can be made in less than an hour, provided that you already have the mushrooms prepped. The taste of the risotto is seriously enhanced by porcini or other European wild mushrooms such as trumpets or chanterelles. These can be purchased at a rational price wholesale in one-pound portions. Fresh wild mushrooms sautéed in butter are wonderful but probably too costly for most and seriously limited seasonally. Truly wild mushrooms add incredible flavor. Portobello, cremini, shiitake, or other cultivated mushrooms (Oriental or European), however exotic, are not "wild," even though they may be so described on many menus. Cooking any risotto does require careful attention at the stove for about twenty to twenty-five minutes until the risotto is cooked.

INGREDIENTS

This recipe is flexible—while it calls for 2 cups of rice, you can use 1 cup of rice and scale the other ingredients proportionally. The full recipe will make 8 generous appetizer servings.

1-2 ounces dried porcini (also known as cèpes) or other dried wild European mushrooms

unsalted butter and olive oil for sautéing, plus a couple tablespoons for service

1 cup water, heated to reconstitute the dried mushrooms, then reserved

2 large shallots or ½ large sweet onion, finely chopped

3 cloves garlic, finely chopped

2 cups short-grain rice (arborio or carnaroli)

1 cup drinkable dry white wine (such as sauvignon blanc, but not chardonnay)

2 teaspoons kosher salt

pepper

2 teaspoons dried thyme

5-7 cups or so of hot water or low-sodium vegetable stock (*not chicken*)

1-2 cups fresh mushrooms, sautéed until the liquid is evaporated and the mushrooms browned (these would include, for example, cremini, portobello, or white button mushrooms, but not any Asian variety such as shiitake)

1 cup or more parmigiano-reggiano cheese, generously and freshly grated

Prepare all of the ingredients, including the hot stock and the sautéed mushrooms. Do not use a domestic or other nontraditional cheese unless needed for kosher compliance. Soak the dried European wild mushroom (porcini, trumpets, and/or chanterelles) in the hot water until they are softened. Lift them out of the liquid carefully, leaving any sand and reserving the liquid. Let the reserved soaking liquid rest so that the dirt can settle to the bottom. Chop the reconstituted mushrooms roughly and reserve.

In about 2 tablespoons total of butter and olive oil, sauté the onion and garlic lightly with the rice. Sauté the rice until it is sort of translucent and is fully coated with the oil and butter. Then deglaze with the cup of white wine before adding any other liquid, letting the wine evaporate and absorb. Add 1 teaspoon of salt for each cup of rice. Add the thyme. Add pepper to taste.

Stir the rice frequently, simmering slowly, and do not abandon it at the stove. As the wine in the pot is absorbed, add another cup or so of liquid, starting with the mushroom-reconstituting liquid—but toss the dregs from the reconstituting liquid. Add the chopped, reconstituted mushrooms. Continue stirring and adding vegetable stock until the rice is fully cooked. You can tell when the rice is fully cooked by tasting it; it should be creamy and not crunchy. As you near the completion of the cooking process, add the previously sautéed fresh mushrooms. When the rice is cooked, turn off the heat, and add grated parmesan cheese to taste (at least 1 cup or more) and a couple tablespoons of butter. The rice mixture should not be completely stiff before you finish cooking but should be slightly soupy.

An additional idea, perhaps less traditional but nonetheless delicious, is to mix in snow peas, sugar snap peas, or asparagus (peeled and cut into 1-inch pieces) a few minutes before turning off the heat. These vegetables should be served bright green and somewhat crisp. None should be cooked long.

Serve promptly and hot with a salad.

Jewish-style Stuffed Cabbage
(a.k.a.. Prakas or Holishkes), p. 166

Chapter 10: *Jewish Food—Traditional*

CHAROSET

Charoset is a wonderful concoction of fruits, nuts, spices, and wine, traditionally served at the Passover seder. Even though it is a delicious dish, it is usually not made at any other time of the year. Two recipes are set forth: first, my mother's recipe, which is an Ashkenazic version, and second, a variant of a Sephardic version. Ashkenazi Jews descend from the Jewish population of western and central Europe—the Holy Roman Empire, generally understood to also include Jews living in and from Eastern Europe who migrated east to Russia, Ukraine, etc. Sephardic Jews are descended from Jews previously living in Spain and Portugal prior to expulsion during the Inquisition and include Jews of North Africa and Asia Minor.

My mother's version can be easily made kosher for Passover, which requires all foods for the Passover to be prepared after the house is cleaned of chametz. Chametz is leavened foods that are not just forbidden to be used during Passover but are forbidden to be owned or to have unsealed in the house during Passover; thus, all breads and other leavened products, including flour, are disposed of before the Passover commences in a prescribed ceremony. Because of this tradition—in order to use flour before the holiday of Passover—baked goods for Purim are prominently featured, including the well-known and delectable Hamantaschen (see recipe in Chapter 10).

My version is sort of Sephardic and can be made kosher for Passover by limiting the period for soaking the dried fruits and nuts in wine (such as by heating the wine in the microwave before pouring over the dried fruits to accelerate absorption), is much better with a two- or three-day maceration—obviously not kosher for Passover unless you kosher your kitchen early.

When I was a child, my mother would clean the house, and we had the ceremony of disposing of the chametz the day before Passover began, and the cooking occurred thereafter. My mother changed the dishes, the silver, and the pots in the house so that everything was fresh and kosher for Passover, even though we did not keep kosher during the rest of the year. Although my wife and I are unabashedly Jewish and observant of many, though not all, of the traditions, our observance does not rise to that level of detail in that particular matter. Moreover, as my wife and I have gotten older, we have concluded that it is impractical and difficult to put on a large meal without significant advance preparation.

We do subscribe to the view that Judaism is a community- and family-centered religion, and much of family life is centered around the table. The Passover seder and meal is—for us, as with many Jews—one of our favorite traditions. For example, we prepare brisket or beef short ribs and Potato Kugel (Chapter 14) weeks in advance without contact with flour or other chametz, and we freeze those mostly cooked foods in a container ready for reheating, final cooking, and service at the seder. Many foods do have to be made at the last minute. For example, Egg Salad (Chapter 8) and Chopped Chicken Liver (Chapter 10) simply cannot be made ahead because they would spoil, even with refrigeration. Of course, food safety is paramount.

First, Mom's recipe:

Peel, core, and chop apples (preferably Red Delicious) into $\frac{1}{4}$-inch or $\frac{1}{2}$-inch squares or other convenient shape. Add raisins and chopped pecans to taste. Add cinnamon to taste. Stir in Manischewitz Concord grape wine (kosher for Passover). Adjust the amount of raisins and nuts to the amount of apples so that it looks right, and no ingredient dominates. Stir and let sit in the refrigerator until the seder.

Now for my version:

I have found myself incapable of making an amount of charoset that is less than 3 or 4 quarts by the time I add in all of the ingredients. However, charoset keeps well, and any leftovers can be slightly reengineered after Passover for an incredible dessert use.

INGREDIENTS

Amounts are approximate.

1 cup each of dried stone fruits of various sorts: apricots, sour cherries, and dates, plus raisins (dark or light or both) and/or dried cranberries. I do not use prunes here because of my personal taste preference, but if you like, go for it. Use whole dried dates when selecting dates. Do not use dates that have been precut; they are dusted with a flour mixture that makes the texture of the charoset wrong and not kosher for Passover.

1-2 apples, preferably crispy with tart flavor such as Honeycrisp or Granny Smith

1 pear (optional—the pear should be ripe but not overripe and a firm, crunchy variety such as Bosc or Anjou, but not Bartlett, which is delicious but tends to be soft)

1-2 cups each of a variety of unsalted nuts, all toasted and roughly chopped (including pecans, almonds, hazelnuts, pistachios, etc. but not peanuts, which are legumes and therefore not kosher for Passover)

1 teaspoon cinnamon

½ teaspoon ginger

¼-½ teaspoon nutmeg, or to taste, freshly grated (nutmeg loses its flavor rapidly once it is grated, so always buy whole nutmegs and use freshly grated)

½ teaspoon kosher salt

¼-½ teaspoon allspice (optional)

¼-½ teaspoon mace (optional)

a very small amount of clove (optional—clove, in particular, can be an overpowering flavor)

about 1 bottle of sweet, kosher-for-Passover wine such as Concord grape

This is assembly more than cooking, and amounts are approximate. If you are missing one of the types of dried fruit or one of the nuts, do not let that deter you. Remove the pits from the dates; then quarter the dates. Apricots also should be quartered. I personally love apricots and usually add extra. The cherries, raisins, and cranberries are left whole. The apples and pear should be peeled, cored, and diced into ¼-inch pieces. Add toasted, chopped nuts as desired. A mixture adds texture and complexity. Add spices as desired. Test using a small quantity of spices at first, stir, and add to balance to your taste as the mixture macerates.

As with all sweet dishes, add a pinch of salt. Add wine, stir well, cover, and refrigerate. It takes several days for the tastes to meld and for the wine to be absorbed. I use the same sweet wine as for my mother's version. I have tried sweet kosher blackberry and cherry wines, and they are okay but not as good as the Concord grape, to my taste. For my taste, Carmel edges Manischewitz for flavor, but it is a matter of taste. If this is done erev Passover in accord with the rules, heat the wine before adding to accelerate absorption for use that evening. For 4 quarts or so of charoset, I start with at least ½ bottle of wine, and over the next couple of days before the seder, I add more as necessary, stirring well every day, since the wine will be absorbed by the fruit. You may use a whole bottle of wine before you are done. Wine adds sweetness, and as you add wine and let it sit, the charoset sauce will become syrupy, and the dried fruits will hydrate and soften. Taste to adjust the seasonings. Stir several times over this period.

This recipe is a variant from a Sephardic version of charoset, which is commonly served finely chopped or ground and thus could be made and served the same day, since the ground fruit would absorb the wine rapidly. The fruit is ground to be reminiscent of the mortar it is supposed to emulate. However, I like to leave the fruit and nuts in visible chunks.

Unless you have 30 or 40 guests at the seder, you will have leftovers. Despair not; charoset is excellent served over ice cream. Add even more wine before microwaving. This modified charoset will be somewhat saucy in texture. Cool (or not) and serve over ice cream.

CHEESE NOODLE KUGEL

This kugel (or pudding) is truly comfort food and incredibly easy and quick to make.

INGREDIENTS

1 pound pasta (traditionally egg noodles; although nontraditional, I like shaped macaroni pasta that has holes or spaces that the cheese filling will fill, such as tubular penne)

Cheese blintze filling

1-2 pounds farmer's cheese (not cream cheese or cottage cheese; the cheese should be Friendship or Breakstone brand farmer's cheese)

1-2 cups sour cream (At least 8 ounces. Do not use a low-fat version. The amount depends on the moisture in the cheese and the texture needed, and the eggs will loosen the texture of the uncooked filling.)

salt to taste (1-3 teaspoons kosher salt, mixing and tasting as you add before adding eggs)

4 eggs (I use jumbo eggs)

Boil pasta to al dente; that is, slightly undercook the noodles. Follow the filling instructions under the recipe for Cheese Blintzes (Chapter 10).

Lightly butter a baking dish appropriately sized for the amount of kugel being cooked. Cook the noodles to al dente. Mix the hot noodles well with the cheese mixture. Bake at 325°F for 20 to 30 minutes or until the noodle kugel is hot and bubbly and the top is lightly brown.

Some people (including my daughter, Lisa) add cinnamon and sugar to the cheese filling. I do not. Obviously that addition changes the profile from savory to sweet.

Fresh pasta does not work here if you are baking the kugel. However, if you omit the eggs in the cheese mixture—and do not bake the cheese mixture with the pasta—then fresh pasta or dried, shaped pasta cooked and *then* mixed with the cheese, sour cream, and salt is even easier and most unctuous. The flavor profile is similar, but the texture is somewhat different. Since you omit the eggs for this unbaked version, 1 pound of cheese to about 8 ounces or so of sour cream and 1 teaspoon or less of kosher salt to taste is a good proportion. Mix the cheese, sour cream, and salt, starting with less salt. Then taste for the salt, and then mix in the pasta. This eggless cheese mixture literally takes no more time to assemble than the pasta cooking time. Cold leftovers are also yummy, particularly served with some more sour cream and salt.

This is wonderful hot. It is a delicious side dish to serve with fish—either grilled or dusted with flour, lightly seasoned with salt and pepper, and sautéed in butter. It is also great served cold with sour cream and salt. It makes an excellent quick and easy meal with a salad.

BREAD AND FARMER'S CHEESE

Another delicious use for the cheese, sour cream, and salt mixture (without the raw egg) used in the previous recipe for Cheese Noodle Kugel is as a generous topping for toasted rye or pumpernickel bread. Bread well toasted takes on a wonderful character very different from its untoasted version.

You can also top the cheese with either a flat omelet (egg whipped with a touch of milk, salt, and pepper and cooked in a nonstick skillet with lightly browned butter without stirring, flipped once when mostly set). Or you can add smoked fish (smoked salmon or gravlax, sablefish, flaked whitefish, or whitefish salad). Slices of onion and muenster or American cheese work well with the fish.

Of course, bagels are more than acceptable here. While in New York, wonderful, dense, flavorful, chewy bagels are the rule, in Dallas we have to search for a source for acceptable bagels that are not just round, fluffy bread with a hole in the middle. Many prefer their bagels toasted, but if the bagel is really fresh, it shines on its own without toasting.

MATZO BALLS/KNAIDEL

I do not personally make matzo balls, which I sometimes refer to by the Yiddish word *knaidel*. Since I regard them as an essential food and recipe for this book—and certainly a family tradition—I turned to an expert: my daughter, Lisa. Lisa learned to make great matzo balls the traditional way—from her mother and grandmother. Following in Lisa's voice is her rendition of what she has learned and, as I can attest, learned well.

Matzo balls were traditionally made by Grandma—my mom's mom—with me taking the occasional turn on her hand-cranked eggbeater and snatching small tastes of the raw dough. While I have followed her recipe of using one egg to one tablespoon of schmaltz, then adding matzo meal until it feels right and salt until it tastes good, I also understand most people did not learn to make matzo balls by feel, and a recipe helps. After experimenting with recipes, I have found the following ratios produce matzo ball dough that "feels right."

INGREDIENTS

For variations, see the recipe below.

1 egg
½ teaspoon salt, or to taste
1 heaping teaspoon Chicken Schmaltz (Chapter 2)
¼ cup matzo meal
3-4 quarts cooking liquid (water or broth)

Lightly whisk the egg, salt, and schmaltz together. Then slowly incorporate the matzo meal. You can start this step with the whisk, but as it thickens, you will likely need to switch to a fork or other sturdy utensil. Combine everything thoroughly. Rest the mixture in the fridge for at least ½ hour. This resting time is critical for the matzo meal to soak up the liquids and to let everything come together. Or you can cook your dough immediately at your own peril.

This is your basic kosher-for-Passover version, and it will produce tasty, fairly dense matzo balls. From here, we have options on leavens, seasoning, and cooking method. While it is possible to use other fats besides schmaltz (and here comes your Jewish guilt), it just will not be the same. If you do not feel like making schmaltz or using the fat layer produced when you make chicken soup, a number of supermarkets (particularly in neighborhoods with a significant Jewish population), Jewish delicatessens, or butchers carry schmaltz in most American cities. So, while my father might grumble about it not being homemade, you will get the flavor at least.

Variations

For an airier matzo ball (a.k.a. floaters), there are a few different options: baking powder, seltzer, and egg whites. Contrary to popular belief, all of these leavens are still kosher for Passover, except for maybe a few more orthodox Jews. As authority for this view, see the *New York Times*'s article "It's Passover, Lighten Up."[1] Since I usually have it around the house, I am a fan of baking powder. Depending on how fluffy a matzo ball you want, your baking powder addition can range from $\frac{1}{8}$ teaspoon to $\frac{1}{4}$ teaspoon (or more) per $\frac{1}{4}$ cup matzo meal. I like my matzo balls on the substantial side, so I keep the baking powder to $\frac{1}{8}$ teaspoon or even slightly less.

Seltzer is another good, simple option, with an easy-to-remember ratio of 1 tablespoon of liquid per $\frac{1}{4}$ cup matzo ball batter.

Lastly, you can separate half your eggs and whip up the whites, folding them into your batter. Personally, I think this is a little too much effort, but it is a solid method if your cupboard is lacking in baking powder and seltzer.

For seasoning, I have done versions with no added seasonings and some with garlic powder. Both have been delicious, and the conclusion I have come to is your soup is likely to be a bigger contributor to flavor. Speaking of which, we come to cooking method.

---

1   Joan Nathan, "It's Passover, Lighten Up," New York Times, April 5, 2006,
        https://www.nytimes.com/2006/04/05/dining/05leav.html.

Cooking

Cooking matzo balls has 2 distinct aspects: cooking liquid and technique. My parents have always cooked their matzo balls in a large pot of salted water, which worked well and produced no complaints. My theory is that Dad's homemade broth, in which the matzo balls were served, contributed to the overall flavor. However, not everyone has the foresight or freezer space for homemade broth, which is where my alternate method comes in: cooking in a quality commercial stock. The matzo balls get more flavor as they soak up the stock, which gives just a bit more oomph to your final product. Necessary? No. A nice option? Definitely. (A father's note: Bobbie tried Lisa's suggestion to cook the matzo balls in commercial broth, and it seriously enhances the flavor of already good matzo balls.) A couple things to remember here: cooking in the stock will (a) use up a bunch of that liquid, so make sure you buy extra for the final soup, and (b) make the stock cloudy, so if you care about have a clear stock for serving, buy even more extra, or use your homemade broth for the soup.

Now we have come to the actual cooking. After resting the matzo ball dough in the refrigerator, take it out just as you are ready to form the matzo balls and put them in the pot. With the liquid at a rolling boil, form your balls quickly, and drop them in. Some people like perfectly spherical balls, which you can do by rolling them into 1-to-1½-inch balls in your hands, wetting your hands as necessary to keep the dough from sticking. However, this method will take longer and result in a bit more uneven cooking than simply using 2 teaspoons to scoop, roughly shape, and drop the balls in the cooking liquid. While ours are not the most symmetrical, in our house looks do not matter so much as taste.

Cover the pot, lower the heat to higher than a gentle simmer but not so high as to boil over, and cook for 30 to 40 minutes. While it is fine to open the lid and check on them every now and again, it is important to keep the matzo balls covered during cooking, since otherwise they'll dry up and will not expand fully (and then all of your efforts at making floaters would be wasted!). Test for doneness by cutting a matzo ball: the center should look done and not be a doughy color or texture.

Serving

Lastly is the issue of how to serve your matzo balls. As I was growing up, we ate matzo ball soup primarily at Passover, so the matzo balls were served simply in Dad's homemade broth.

Nowadays, I like to make matzo balls occasionally as part of a main course, in which case, I give it the full chicken-soup treatment—i.e., chicken and vegetables poached in the stock, with the matzo balls replacing noodles or rice. Either way, they are a wonderful comfort food.

As a significant variant, my dad's family also serves matzo balls separate from soup, garnished with a liberal serving of horseradish (made with vinegar, not the creamy variety), a custom the rest of us regard as somewhat peculiar.

MATZO BRIE (FRIED MATZO)

Fried matzo is a dish prepared primarily during Passover (an eight-day holiday), when leavened bread is not only not permitted to be eaten but is not even permitted to be present in the house. There are a number of variations for preparation of fried matzo; this is not a dish with precise proportions. The variations can primarily be separated into (1) fried matzo that *does* contain milk or milk product and is cooked with butter and (2) fried matzo that does *not* contain milk or milk products and can be cooked with Chicken Schmaltz (Chapter 2), as my mother did. While it is a dish designed to be eaten during Passover, we make it for dinner from time to time because it is simple, easy, and delicious comfort food. Traditionally, in America it is a breakfast food, or at least that was the case in our family.

The process is simple, and the ingredients are few. I know some people who sauté onions and add them to the mixture also, but that is not our family tradition.

INGREDIENTS

This is a proportional "formula" and can be scaled up as needed.

2 pieces matzo
½–1 cup milk
3–4 eggs
½ teaspoon salt, or to taste
pepper to taste

Break the matzo into pieces and soak it, usually in hot water, until it is soft. Then squeeze out and discard the liquid. Occasionally I will soak the matzo in milk, which, if it is not hot, makes the soaking process somewhat longer—maybe ½ an hour. The excess milk is combined with the eggs.

Beat the eggs with milk, adding milk until it looks like a custard. (I like my matzo soft and moist, which is very different from the way my wife, Bobbie, likes her fried matzo.)

Add the salt and pepper to the egg mixture at this time. The amount of salt that needs to be used will seem inordinately large, because for 2 pieces of matzo you will need about ½ a teaspoon of kosher salt. If you do not use a sufficient amount of salt, the fried matzo will be very bland. It is difficult to add sufficient salt at the table. You will have to adjust the salt to your taste as you proceed. Cook a small amount, and taste before cooking the bulk of your recipe.

The egg mixture and matzo are stirred together and then poured into and cooked in a nonstick pan with butter (more is better). When frying the matzo, turn it after the matzo is cooked on the bottom—that is, non-liquid. If you are using a large amount for the pan, it will be somewhat thick and will need to be turned and perhaps broken up during the frying process, although I personally like the matzo to be in large chunks or in a "cake," almost like a frittata, and not chopped up when it finishes cooking. As with an omelet, you should lift the edges and let the uncooked liquid on top flow over the edge of the cooked matzo, then underneath it. You can cook it to whatever degree of doneness you prefer. For me, I prefer that eggs be just set and not runny. Bobbie prefers that her eggs reach a drier stage.

After it is partially cooked, it is an easy process to pop it into a 350°F oven for about 5 minutes. To that extent my wife's recipe and my recipe are similar, except that she adds very little milk and cooks hers to a much drier state than I cook my matzo. It is a matter of your taste.

Variations

Some of my friends use much less egg to the amount of matzo (2 eggs for every 3 or 4 pieces of matzo, with some adding onions). Some also make a sweet version with cinnamon and sugar or with applesauce or jam as a garnish. I have never made it with either onions or as a sweet version, but I am sure that either would be tasty.

These recipes are milk based and are the way our family makes fried matzo today. This is very different from the way Mom made fried matzo with schmaltz and no milk. I suspect that some of the differences in the oil used may have originated in what part of Europe or Russia our families came from. Originally, schmaltz was cheaper and more available. I have seen suggestions that matzo brie was invented after Ashkenazi Jews came here, and it was unknown in Europe.

Mom started, of course, with the same hot-water-soaking process described. After discarding the extra liquid, she added eggs, salt, and pepper, but no milk. She fried the matzo in a pan with chicken schmaltz, not butter. (We do not mix milk and meat, and chicken schmaltz is, of course, a meat product.) I remember that I liked it at the time, but I have not made it this way in probably 40 years, in part because, I suppose, our tastes have changed—but also, in part, because chicken schmaltz was demonized due to perceived cholesterol and other health issues. Indeed, for some time we used margarine and avoided butter for the same reason until we came to understand the health risks of margarine and other artificial products. My brother still likes the version with schmaltz, so at least some carry on that tradition.

SALAMI AND EGGS

An easy, quick (about 15 minutes), and unbelievably flavorful breakfast or dinner is salami and eggs. I learned this recipe at my grandmother's knee; it was a favorite in my house as I was growing up. This seems to be a cross-cultural concept, because I recently saw an online recipe using an italian salami rather than kosher beef salami. My preference is Hebrew National salami. There are many other beef salami brands, each with a different flavor profile, that work in this situation. The salami and eggs can be made into a sandwich between layers of rye bread and deli mustard (not yellow ballpark mustard and certainly not dijon or another gourmet mustard). Or you can serve it just as it is, with a dollop of deli mustard on the side. It is excellent served with American Potato Salad (Chapter 8) and dill pickles, in which case it is delicious to dice the dill pickle into the Potato Salad.

I buy whole salami and do not have the store thinly slice the salami. Once the salami is opened, the plastic must be completely removed to store any unused salami, or the meat will quickly mold and be inedible. Leave the papery wrapping and put it in the refrigerator uncovered. The salami will dry, its texture will harden, and its flavor will change slightly, but the meat will still be wonderful to eat. Go into a proper Jewish deli, and you will see salamis hanging in various stages of drying.

Slice beef salami into pieces about ⅛ inch thick and cut into bite-sized pieces. For 6 to 8 eggs, use about ½ a pound or so of salami. Sauté the salami until it has rendered some of its fat. If you desire, before you add the egg to the salami, you may wish to add ¼ to ½ a cup of finely diced onion, although that is certainly not required. Cook the onion until it is well sweated but not browned.

In a separate bowl, beat the eggs vigorously with 1 teaspoon of water per egg. Salt and pepper to taste. A very nice addition, though unusual, is 1 or 2 teaspoons of dried or chopped fresh dill. Pour the eggs into the hot pan with the salami (and the onion, if using). Stir the salami and eggs until the eggs are cooked. I prefer the eggs very soft but cook to your desired degree of doneness. Serve as indicated.

As an additional variation, many people like corned beef or pastrami made with eggs in much the same manner. One difference in cooking is that the meat should be chopped and then barely warmed prior to adding the eggs. Since the meat will not render fat like the salami, you may have to add a trace of oil to coat the pan.

CHOPPED CHICKEN LIVER

At our house, Bobbie makes chopped liver only with fresh chicken liver and never with the liver from any other animal. This is a matter of flavor, except of course that pork is forbidden. Clean the chicken liver of all parts that you would not want to eat, including the yellow fat, connective tissue, any bloody portion, etc. If you buy the liver more than a day before cooking, the liver should be cleaned and washed immediately, drained carefully, and then frozen . Even more than with most meats, you should buy the freshest liver. Look carefully at the sell-by date. Liver must be koshered, and because liver has a high concentration of blood, that process includes broiling the liver. To make chopped liver kosher, the cooking process described here would need to be modified from sautéing the meat to broiling first.

INGREDIENTS

This is proportional and can be scaled up easily.

```
9 eggs, hard-cooked and cooled, plus extra for garnish (We use
jumbo eggs. See Chapter 2 for instructions for hard-cooked eggs.)
1 pound liver, uncooked
2 large sweet onions, split use (Vidalia, Texas 1015s, Walla
Walla, etc.)
extra-virgin olive oil
salt to taste
2 tablespoons Chicken Schmaltz (Chapter 2), room temperature
```

Slice up 1 whole onion and cook that in a couple tablespoons of olive oil until well caramelized. Remove the onion, and then use the same pan to cook the chicken liver, adding olive oil as necessary. Wait to add salt until after the ground liver is cooked and assembled.

The chicken liver is cooked traditionally with schmaltz, but Bobbie, until recently, had used a neutral-flavored liquid vegetable oil that is kosher for Passover (not corn oil or peanut oil unless, of course, it is not Passover). However, Bobbie serendipitously recently used olive oil, which is our general default oil, and the result was superb.

The chicken liver must be sautéed until it is done; that is, the pink is completely eliminated, the livers are firm, and there is no blood coming from the liver, but the liver is still moist. If the chicken liver is cooked until it is completely well done and dry throughout, it becomes tough, with an off-taste. There should be no liquid that may have been exuded from the liver in the pan used to cook the liver, or the texture of the chopped liver will not be right.

Add the cooked liver to the cooked onion, cool, and refrigerate covered with plastic wrap until well chilled (at least an hour or so) before grinding. After the cooked liver and cooked onion are cold, the order for grinding is as follows: (1) the chicken liver intermixed with the cooked onion, (2) followed by the raw onion, and (3) followed by the hard-cooked eggs. A mixer such as a KitchenAid with meat-grinder attachment is best for this purpose. The meat-grinder attachment for the mixer is preferable to using a processor such as a Cuisinart because it results in the proper finished texture. Use the small-hole grinding plate part of the attachment and not the large-hole plate of the attachment (that is, the piece that fits on to the grinder after the blade is inserted to determine the grind of the meat as fine or less fine).

After the liver mixture is ground, mix thoroughly with 2 tablespoons of room-temperature chicken schmaltz, and salt to taste. Cover tightly, and chill well before serving. This product is very perishable and should not be left at room temperature except to serve. Grate some hard-cooked egg yolk over the top for garnish. It should be consumed within 2 to 3 days.

For this recipe, chicken schmaltz is an essential ingredient for texture and flavor. There are recipes for chopped liver that include, for example, mayonnaise, which is a concept that I cannot grasp. Any milk product (such as cream, butter, or sour cream) would never be appropriate here because it is not kosher to mix milk and meat, even though that would be the norm for a French-style chicken liver pâté. This is very different from pâté.

For Passover, serve with matzo or celery stalks. In a non-Passover setting, I prefer to eat the chicken liver with Hi Ho, Ritz, or other crackers, although many people eat it with rye or pumpernickel bread. As the saying goes, "Whatever floats your boat."

MEAT KREPLACH (AND A WONTON OR POT STICKER VARIANT)

Meat kreplach are traditionally served at the High Holidays in chicken soup (the Jewish version of *tortellini en brodo* but with no cheese). Many cultures have their own filled pasta (such as the Italian ravioli or Chinese pot stickers) and variants. Kreplach are a Jewish (Russian) version. The technique is the same—to change the name and culture, use appropriate fillings and flavorings.

INGREDIENTS

Filling

1 pound ground beef (chuck or shoulder has the best percentage of fat and good beef flavor; the beef should have a finer grind such as for hamburgers and not chili, which uses a courser grind)

vegetable oil, as needed (canola, corn, or other vegetable oil, but not olive oil because olive oil has a wrong taste for this dish)

½ onion, very finely chopped (small brunoise cut)

1 carrot, finely shredded (or small brunoise cut) using a box grater or the fine shredding blade of the KitchenAid mixer or a very sharp knife

celery, no more than ½ stalk, shredded or small brunoise cut

2 cloves garlic, very finely minced, then ground to a paste in a mortar and pestle or put through a garlic press

½–1 cup water or beef stock

bay leaf

salt

pepper

1–2 eggs

Dough (For instructions, see the Cheese Kreplach recipe later in Chapter 10)

1 egg

2 cups flour

½ teaspoon salt

water or flavorless vegetable oil, if necessary

A clear time saver is to purchase kosher wonton wrappers, which are now generally available, or fresh sheet pasta, available from an Italian market in many cities. It takes about 100 wonton wrappers for a recipe using 1 pound of beef since each wrapper will contain only 1 to 1½ teaspoons of filling.

For the filling, sauté 1 pound of ground beef in a light amount of vegetable oil to coat the pan until the meat is fully browned. Use a heavy pan such as a pan that is aluminum-clad with steel inside lining or a cast-iron pan, but preferably not a nonstick pan. My grandmother would use leftover pot roast or brisket and grind that for the filling.

Remove the meat from the pan, draining excess rendered fat and oil but leaving a small amount to cook the vegetables. Add to the pan the onion, carrot, and celery, with only so much oil as needed to cook the vegetables. Sweat the vegetables until translucent. Add the garlic at the end of this process so that it does not burn.

Add the browned ground beef back into the pan with ½ to 1 cup of water—or, even better, beef stock—and a bay leaf, salt, and pepper. Cover the pan, and simmer on low heat until the beef-vegetable mixture is cooked, and the meat is tender (30 to 40 minutes). Uncover, and cook until the liquid has evaporated but the filling is still moist. Taste for seasoning (salt and pepper). Remove the bay leaf. Cool and refrigerate the mixture. When cold and ready to use, add 1 or 2 eggs per pound of meat to bind.

Following the instructions detailed in the Cheese Kreplach recipe (Chapter 10), prepare the dough. Fill small squares of dough and seal the beef mixture in the kreplach dough by folding it over and making triangles, then sealing the edges. Kreplach are traditionally triangular, at least in my family.

For a wonton wrapper variation, use around 1 teaspoon of filling. With a finger dipped in water, moisten 2 adjacent sides of the wrapper and opposing corners followed by gently but firmly pressing the sides to seal. After sealing one edge, carefully pick up the kreplach, and push in the filling to clear and seal the other edge. (If you have seen a Chinese chef make dim sum and aspire to that expertise and speed, then I wish you good luck. It takes me about 2 hours to fill the kreplach to use up the pound of beef, but there are a lot of kreplach.)

If you are not cooking the kreplach immediately, freeze on a half sheet pan with double layers of waxed paper between the kreplach layers. Because these are somewhat fragile when frozen, transfer to an airtight sealable plastic or Pyroceram freezer container for storage.

The kreplach can be cooked in salted, simmering water and served in chicken soup as is traditional for the High Holidays, or they can be fried like pot stickers (see below) or baked in the oven. Since the dough or pasta is fresh and the filling cooked, the cooking process, particularly in water, does not take but a very few minutes—just enough to heat the filling and cook the egg.

To bake the kreplach in the oven, brush them lightly with oil or schmaltz, and put them on a greased or parchment-covered baking sheet. Silpat is also a good nonstick surface to bake on. My mom would roll out the dough, add the filling, roll it into a log, and brush it lightly with schmaltz before baking—certainly less work than forming a lot of little kreplach. Bake at 350°F until the dough is cooked (lightly browned) and the filling is hot, about 15 to 25 minutes.

Alternatively, the kreplach could be sautéed (as are Chinese pot stickers) in a lightly oiled sauté pan. After the bottoms are browned, add a small amount of water, and close the top of the sauté pan quickly, lowering the flame to low. Cook for perhaps 5 to 10 minutes; then remove the lid, raising the flame until the water has evaporated and the kreplach are cooked through. These can also be served in chicken soup.

Wonton or Pot Sticker Variant

To convert kreplach to an Asian pasta (wontons or pot stickers), include Asian flavoring listed below.

Filling

```
1-2 tablespoons ginger, finely chopped
up to 6 green onions, finely sliced
bok choy, finely chopped
2 teaspoons dark sesame oil
2 tablespoons of either soy sauce, hoisin sauce, and/or vegetarian
oyster sauce
¼ cup cilantro, finely chopped
```

Dipping sauce (combine all ingredients)

```
¼ cup soy sauce
¼ cup rice vinegar (clear or black)
1 tablespoon sesame oil
1 tablespoon ginger, chopped or grated
1 tablespoon fresh garlic paste
1 tablespoon green onion, chopped
```

In addition to the vegetables used for kreplach (or as a substitute), add finely chopped bok choy. The bok choy cooks quickly and merely needs to be completely wilted. For flavoring, add finely chopped ginger to the garlic. At the time you add the stock to the browned beef, add 2 teaspoons of dark sesame oil and 2 tablespoons sauce as noted above. Because the soy or hoisin sauce contains a lot of salt, you will need to reduce or eliminate any added salt. When the meat and/or vegetables are finished cooking, take them off the heat, and stir in the finely chopped cilantro and very finely chopped green onion. Chill completely before adding the eggs as a binder.

To cook as wontons, you may steam or boil in salted water and serve in chicken soup or serve as dim sum with a dipping sauce as included in this recipe.

To cook as pot stickers, lightly coat a nonstick sauté pan with a flavorless vegetable oil and lay the pot stickers into the hot pan. Cook for 1 to 2 minutes; then add $\frac{1}{2}$ cup of water, clamp on a lid, lower the heat, and cook for 5 to 10 minutes. Then remove the lid and let remaining liquid evaporate. A handful of chopped cilantro added after the heat is off is a great finish.

1. Asian

For the Asian variant, omit the bay leaf, but add a couple star anise and 1 teaspoon of five-spice powder. A $\frac{1}{4}$ cup of Shaoxing wine or dry sherry is also a desirable addition.

2. Vegetarian

The filling can be made completely vegetarian (a delicious variant) by adding a finely chopped bulky vegetable such as bok choy to the filling (which wilts just prior to completing the filling) as a substitute for the meat. For the vegetarian version, 2 or 3 ounces of sautéed, chopped, fresh or reconstituted shiitake mushrooms adds great texture and umami flavor in lieu of the beef. Add the mushroom-reconstituting liquid or vegetable stock, noting the vegetarian filling cooks very quickly (just to wilt the vegetables) and needs little added liquid to facilitate the process.

All ingredients must be very finely chopped to fit into the wrapper. As with kreplach, cool the filling, and then mix in 1 or 2 whisked eggs to act as a binder immediately before assembling the wonton or pot stickers.

3. Chicken

Ground chicken thigh meat can be substituted for the beef. In this case, use chicken stock and not beef stock, noting that chicken is more tender than beef, so the cooking time for the filling would be only 10–15 minutes. As with kreplach, cool the filling; then mix in 1 or 2 whisked eggs to act as a binder immediately before assembling the wonton pot stickers.

JEWISH-STYLE STUFFED CABBAGE (A.K.A. PRAKAS OR HOLISHKES)

Jewish-style stuffed cabbages are in the multicultural tradition of vegetables stuffed with meat and other fillings. The Italians stuff zucchini flowers, zucchini, eggplant, and other vegetables. The French and Eastern Europeans stuff cabbage (primarily with pork, which is obviously not what we do). Mexicans have *chile rellenos* or stuffed poblano peppers, filled with either a meat or various sorts of cheese. Stuffed cabbage in the Jewish style generally has a sweet-and-sour flavoring. In my family, the sour comes from sour salt—essentially citric acid—and sugar, but in my wife's family, the sour comes from lemon, also sweetened with sugar. Some recipes also call for the sour to be derived from addition of vinegar, also offset with sugar.

Prakas (or holishkes) are served at the Jewish holidays of Sukkoth (the harvest festival) and Simhath Torah, the celebration of the Torah and the completion of the cycle of reading through the entire Torah at services and the start of the recitation and reading of the Torah for the following year. The custom of serving stuffed cabbage at Sukkot implies richness or plenty, while at Simchat Torah, it is the symbolism of two pillows of cabbage placed side by side that is evocative of the Torah scroll.

Apparently, the term *prakas* is a name given to holishkes or stuffed cabbage leaves by American Yiddish-speaking Jews in Philadelphia and Baltimore. My mother's family used the term *prakas*, but as far as I am aware, we had no connection on that side of the family with either Philadelphia or Baltimore.

Whatever the dish is called, it is comfort food that is most delicious.

INGREDIENTS

1-2 large heads green cabbage (about 2 pounds each—you should find the largest head of cabbage that you can because the larger leaves make the nicest pillows of filled cabbage)

2 cups yellow onion, finely chopped, split use (I use sweet onion)

3-4 large cloves of garlic, finely minced

2½ pounds finely ground chuck

3 large eggs

1 teaspoon salt

½ teaspoon freshly ground black pepper

3 (28-ounce) cans whole tomatoes, packed in juice, not sauce

1 lemon, juiced, with the pits removed and the rind added to the baking dish

1 cup white cane sugar, or to taste

salt to taste (probably 1-2 teaspoons)

1½ teaspoon sour salt, or to taste

2 bay leaves

Prior to removing the leaves of the cabbage, you will need to cut around the core (the stem end) carefully and remove the core from the cabbage. This will facilitate the removal of the outer leaves from the cabbage, exposing inner leaves.

The cabbage leaves need to be separated from the cabbage without tearing since they need to be whole in order to be stuffed. The leaves need to be softened prior to their removal from the head. This can be achieved in 1 of 2 ways: (1) you can freeze the cabbage, and then let it thaw (an idea from Julia Child); or (2) you can boil a large pot of water, and place the cabbage (with the core removed) into the pot of water until the outer leaves are softened, repeating as necessary as the outmost leaves are removed, exposing the uncooked, unsoftened inner leaves that also need to be removed. If you freeze the cabbage, remove it from the freezer, and allow it to thaw so that the leaves are all softened.

Once the usable leaves are removed, coarsely chop the remaining cabbage to add to the baking dish. (The core of the cabbages should be given to your dog as a special and healthy treat.)

You also need to make the filling for the prakas. Mix about ½ cup or so of the finely minced onion and garlic into the finely ground beef. Add the salt, pepper, and eggs, and mix thoroughly. Many recipes call for adding ½ to ¾ cup of uncooked white rice to the ground beef mixture. My mom did not do this, but my wife and I tried this one time many years ago. We simply did not like the texture of the final product. However, it is your choice, and if you like that addition, you can certainly feel free to add the rice (uncooked) to the ground beef. Alternatively, you could soak 2 or 3 slices of bread (but not the crusts) in water to make a panada to mix with the meat to lighten the filling and help it stay moist, if you desire.

Once the leaves are fully separated from the cabbage and the filling is mixed, place a cabbage leaf on a flat surface, and measure about ⅓ to ½ cup (or less for smaller leaves) of the ground beef mixture. Place this filling into the cabbage leaf.

Fold up the bottom of the leaf, pushing the beef mixture down and making a packet. Next, fold each side across the folded-over base of the cabbage, and roll the cabbage until the packet becomes a nice pillow.

Add some of the chopped tomatoes and liquid to a roasting pan so that the prakas do not stick. Then place the folded packets seam side down in the pan. Continue folding until all of the meat is used. If you run out of cabbage before you run out of meat, simply roll any excess into meatballs, and place them into the roasting pan. If you have excess cabbage, chop up any remaining cabbage, and place it on top of the packets in the roasting pan. Sprinkle the remaining 1½ cups of finely chopped onion over and around the packets of stuffed cabbage. Pour the lemon juice over the packets and place the rind into the roasting pan.

Cut the remaining tomatoes into smaller pieces, or crush the tomatoes with your hand. Stir the sour salt and the sugar into a can of hand-crushed tomatoes, and then pour the mixture over the filled roasting pan. Pour the other cans of hand-crushed tomatoes over the packets of stuffed cabbage. Add the bay leaves into the sauce in the pan. Grind pepper and add salt as necessary. You should taste after the cabbage has cooked for a period of time, and you may wish to adjust the seasoning.

Preheat the oven to 350°F. Cover the roasting pan tightly with aluminum foil. Cook for 90 minutes. Adjust the sour salt–sugar balance as needed to taste. Adjust salt and pepper if necessary. Serve with white rice.

> *Note:* Sour salt is pure, granulated citric acid. It is available in spice racks (and certainly from Penzeys) in a white crystalline form that looks like, but has no taste relationship to, regular salt (sodium chloride) crystals. It has a neutral flavor but very sour impact on your taste buds that is really indispensable in this dish.

CHEESE KREPLACH (A.K.A. VARENIKI)

Cheese kreplach are different from cheese blintzes in that they are traditionally cooked in boiling water and can be viewed as the Jewish (or Russian) variant of ravioli. These cheese kreplach are traditionally served at Shavuot or Purim but are good at any time of the year. Shavuot is the holiday in the spring that celebrates God giving us the Torah (that is, the first five books of the Bible) at Mount Sinai. My daughter-in-law, who grew up in eastern Ukraine, refers to this delicacy not as *kreplach* but as *vareniki*. Stuffed dumplings have many names in many cultures.

INGREDIENTS

This recipe is proportional and can be scaled up easily. You will need 3–4 batches of dough for the amount of filling.

Dough

```
1 egg
2 cups flour
½ teaspoon salt
water or flavorless vegetable oil, if necessary
```

Filling

```
1 loaf of farmer's cheese (Slightly less than 3 pounds. Not cream
cheese or cottage cheese. The cheese should be Friendship or
Breakstone brand farmer's cheese . I like the cheese that has salt
in it as opposed to unsalted; as with butter, the taste is just
different. If you cannot locate the full loaf of cheese, sometimes
1-pound or 7½-ounce blocks are available. The cheese must be fresh
because it will quickly mold and will be unusable after a very few
days once the sealed plastic wrapping is opened. For that reason,
I buy only unopened packages.)
1-2 cups sour cream (not a low-fat version)
1-3 teaspoons kosher salt
4 eggs (I use jumbo eggs)
```

The dough my mother made is essentially pasta dough rolled into a sheet. Mix flour, salt, and egg. Knead the mixture, and if necessary, add a very slight amount of water to make the dough come together to be kneaded. If you use oil, use a tablespoon or so of a flavorless vegetable oil and not olive oil. A mixer with a dough hook makes mixing and kneading easy. The dough should be smooth, elastic, and rollable after it is kneaded. Refrigerate the dough for at least ½ an hour or overnight to relax the gluten and let the flour absorb the liquid. This resting is standard for any pasta dough and produces a better product.

My mother rolled the kreplach dough by hand, although that task is made much easier with a pasta roller. Pasta rollers are available with hand or machine cranks. A version for use with a KitchenAid mixer is available and relatively user friendly. Roll the dough as thinly as possible but not so thin that it falls apart. My mother's dough was not as thin as a pasta sheet, but her kreplach were, nevertheless, unctuous.

Make the cheese filling when you roll out the dough and are ready to fill. For instructions, see the recipe for Cheese Blintzes later in Chapter 10. The filling is the same in both recipes.

Cut the dough into squares or other desired shape, and fill with the cheese filling. I use squares because it makes efficient use of the dough easier and is easy to fill and seal. Do not use too much filling—use about 1 to 1½ teaspoons. Paint the edges with water or egg wash as a sealer. Fold the dough over to make triangles, crimping the edges carefully so that they do not fall apart when cooked.

The filled dough is then cooked in water in the same fashion as ravioli, or it can be frozen before cooking. (To freeze, place on a half sheet pan covered with a *double* layer of waxed paper and use another double layer of waxed paper to separate layers of kreplach to be frozen. Store the frozen kreplach in a rigid airtight freezer container.)

When cooking, keep the water at a simmer rather than a rolling boil to avoid having the kreplach come apart. The cooking process is relatively short (no more than 3 to 5 minutes). It will only take so long as needed to cook the fresh pasta dough and the filling so that the egg acts as a binder and is not raw.

Serve with sour cream and salt. I prefer kosher salt here because it is easier to control.

Variation

An alternative and easy cooking method, albeit nontraditional, is in the style of the Chinese pot sticker or Polish pierogi. Melt a little butter in a Teflon sauté pan and add a single layer of uncooked or even frozen kreplach. Cook, shaking the pan lightly to loosen the kreplach, for a couple of minutes. Unlike with pot stickers, you are not looking for the pasta to stick or for a strongly caramelized bottom. Add ½ cup of water or so, clamp on a lid, and cook for 3 more minutes, approximately. Remove the lid and evaporate any remaining water. This method also has the advantage that the filling always stays in the kreplach.

Substitutes such as commercially available wonton wrappers are used by many as a labor-saving product. Fresh pasta sheets are another time-saving and certainly acceptable substitute. Wonton wrappers are really easy to use and are available—at least in Dallas—in regular grocery stores, frequently in or near the fresh vegetable area, as well as in Chinese or Asian markets in refrigerated cases. The amount of filling will make 100 to 125 kreplach using square 4-inch wonton wrappers.

CHEESE (AND OTHER) BLINTZES

When my son was in AZA (a Jewish youth group for teenage boys), his chapter had a gathering at our house with a BBG Chapter (a parallel group for girls). My wife and I were making blintzes, and a couple of the girls, about thirteen years old, asked what we were doing. When we told them, one said, "I have never seen anyone actually making blintzes." Hopefully this recipe will inspire some to remedy that loss of our culture. Blintzes are true soul food.

Crepe Batter

INGREDIENTS

This amount of ingredients should be doubled to produce enough batter to make crepes for the amount of filling made with 1 full loaf of farmer's cheese (about 3 pounds).

4 eggs
1 cup flour
enough milk to make a very loose slurry—about 1½–2½ cups (whole milk and not a low-fat milk)
½ teaspoon salt

Combine the ingredients above, but do not add all of the milk at once. The mixture will thicken as it sits and may need to be thinned with more milk. The consistency of the batter is the same as that for french crepes. We frequently make 3 or 4 loaves of farmer's cheese at a time and freeze the blintzes for future use. One loaf weighs slightly less than 3 pounds and will make about 25–28 blintzes.

The filling for blintzes included here is also used for Cheese Kreplach (Chapter 10) or Cheese Noodle Kugel (Chapter 10).

Blintze Filling

INGREDIENTS

1 loaf farmer's cheese (slightly less than 3 pounds), not cream cheese or cottage cheese. (The cheese should be Friendship or Breakstone brand farmer's cheese. I like the cheese that has salt in it as opposed to unsalted; as with butter, the taste is just different. If you cannot locate the full loaf of cheese, sometimes 8-ounce blocks are available. The cheese must be fresh because it will quickly mold and will be unusable after a very few days once the sealed plastic wrapping is opened. For that reason, I buy only unopened packages.)

1–2 cups sour cream (At least 8 ounces. Do not use a low-fat version. The amount depends on the moisture in the cheese and the texture needed, and the eggs will loosen the texture of the uncooked filling.)

1–3 teaspoons kosher salt, mixing and tasting as you add

4 eggs (I use jumbo eggs)

If you do not want to taste the filling with raw eggs with it, combine the ingredients before adding eggs, or cook a little in unsalted butter. Add salt as necessary to taste. Mix well. The flavor should be fresh, mild, and delicious, but without the tang that many cheeses have. I do not add pepper, sugar, cinnamon, or any other flavoring, although many do. Then add the eggs. Mix thoroughly again. The filling should be somewhat solid, not overly stiff, but not saucy or flowable like a batter. If it is too stiff, add more sour cream. Remember that the eggs will loosen the mixture and that it must hold its shape somewhat inside the blintze.

As I first wrote this recipe, I looked at the original recipe card from my mom. She apparently did not use eggs but did use butter. Early on when Bobbie (my wife) and I made blintzes, I added about 2 tablespoons of melted butter, but I have ceased to do this on the theory that the cooked blintzes have plenty of butter, richness, and taste—butter is used to cook the crepes and to cook the filled blintzes. Readers of this book who know me will find that elimination of butter an incredible choice since I subscribe to the Julia Child philosophy in respect to butter: "Everything in moderation . . . including moderation."

Jewish farmer's cheese becomes difficult to find outside the eastern part of the US. I suppose that if you cannot find Jewish farmer's cheese (Breakstone's or Friendship's), this recipe could be made with a fresh, dry ricotta as a substitute, although the flavor would be somewhat different. Many cities have Jewish or Russian delis, and they will frequently source farmer's cheese for you. Potted cottage cheese is too liquidly and is unsatisfactory for this use. I remember my grandmother making the cheese in our house, so I know it is possible; there is a recipe on www.allrecipes.com for farmer's cheese that I suspect comes close to what she did.

If you have no source for farmer's cheese, you could drain a high-quality small-curd cottage cheese in a strainer lined with cheesecloth. I personally like Daisy Brand cottage cheese, and it is kosher, so that might be a good source to start. I know that some people use cream cheese and other products as a substitute for farmer's cheese. I have yet to taste such a blintze where I want to repeat the experience. Actually, unlike many dishes, the only blintzes I will eat are the ones I make: the difference is that great—and most cooks use sugar and cinnamon, which I do not like in blintzes and therefore eschew.

Assembly

The batter mixture for the crepes should be made first and should sit for a few minutes to allow the flour to absorb the liquid. It should then be re-stirred. If it is too thick, thin it with additional milk. If you are familiar with french crepe batter, that is the desired consistency: like thin pancake batter.

In our house, we make the blintzes as an assembly line. I stand at the stove and cook the crepes in an 8-inch, lightly buttered nonstick skillet (a pan with sloped sides), using 2 pans at a time. The pans should be hot, but the butter should not be browned. You will need to experiment to get the right heat in the pan.

Heat a small amount of butter in the pan. Then put a small amount of batter into the pan, swirling the pan until the bottom is *lightly* covered with batter. Dump the excess liquid batter back into the batter container. Cook the crepe until it is done. This happens when the top is just barely dry. It must be carefully watched because the correct interval is a matter of seconds. Unlike with a french crepe, do not flip the crepe. Instead, gently bang the crepe out of the pan and onto a wooden or plastic cutting board, which should be covered with a kitchen towel and have a sheet of waxed or parchment paper over the towel, which keeps the crepe from sticking to the towel. The crepe should be filled immediately. Repeat as needed until the filling is completely used.

You will have to experiment with adjusting the liquidity of the batter and with finding the correct amount of cooking the crepe before banging it out. You will know you have it right when the crepe folds correctly and does not crack when it is filled, folded, and rolled up. Sometimes the first couple crepes are not right. (You will then be forced to fill them with raspberry or strawberry or other jam or cinnamon and sugar and eat them. Such are the wages of failure.) Stir the batter from time to time as you cook the crepes.

Bobbie fills each crepe, adding a correct amount of filling to the *cooked* side of the crepe, rolling the crepe into a pillow by folding the bottom over the filling, bringing the sides over the filling, and then rolling the blintzes until a pillow is made, with the uncooked side on the outside. The pillow is normally about 3 or 4 inches long and 1½ inches or so wide. The amount of filling is ⅓ to ½ cup, but you should adjust the amount to your own comfort level without overfilling the blintze. The crepe should be filled and rolled while it is still hot but not so hot as to burn your fingers.

We then take each filled crepe and put it on a *double* layer of wax paper on a cookie sheet so that the blintzes are not touching. (When frozen, if only a single layer of waxed paper is used, you will have a solid mass that cannot be separated.)

Of course, the blintze may be cooked for immediate eating by sautéing in butter in a nonstick pan or cast-iron skillet until just browned on both sides and hot throughout so that the egg is cooked. Do not overcook. Serve the cooked blintzes with sour cream and salt. Alternatively, the blintzes may be frozen for future use using the indicated double layer of wax paper for separating layers in the freezer. Do not freeze more than 2 layers of blintzes at a time; more layers simply do not freeze well in a home freezer. After the blintzes are frozen, separate them into double-layered plastic bags, and seal them. Blintzes are not as fragile as kreplach, wontons, or pot stickers and do not need protection with a rigid container. If you freeze the blintzes, it is best to defrost them before cooking, but they can be cooked from the frozen state on low heat with a cover to trap heat and cause the interior to defrost. Remove the cover once the defrosting is complete.

There is *no* sugar or cinnamon in my blintzes. I simply do not like sweet blintzes. If you are of a different mind, you can add cinnamon and sugar into the filling to your heart's content.

Blintzes can also be made with meat filling or with fruit mixed with cheese filling. I assume you would have to be careful with the fruit so that it is not too runny, but since I have never made this version, I do not know, and you will need to find another recipe. If you make blintzes with a meat filling, you would not use butter or milk to make the crepes if you do not mix milk with meat. The meat filling would be the same as is used for Meat Kreplach (Chapter 10)—fully cooked, cooled, and mixed with egg as a binder for filling the crepes. Traditionally you would use Chicken Schmaltz (Chapter 2) to cook the meat blintzes, and you would use water in place of the milk for the crepes, but an alternative fat could be a liquid vegetable oil. There are soy and other vegetable milks you could also try. My mother brushed the meat blintzes with schmaltz to bake instead of sautéing.

HAMANTASCHEN

Hamantaschen are a traditional sweet made at the time of Purim. The shape of a hamantasch is always a triangle, reminiscent of the hat of Haman, an evil counselor for the king of Persia who wanted to kill all of the Jews. Fortunately, Queen Esther, a Jew, learned of the plot and informed the king. The king had Haman beheaded, and the Jews were saved. One of the books of the Bible—the book of Esther, also known as the Megillah—is the extended story of this episode of history. To celebrate the victory, the "whole" Megillah is read in the synagogue on Purim. Whenever Haman's name is mentioned, noisemakers are sounded, and a good time is had by all. One purpose of making this pastry is to use all of the flour in the household before Passover, when flour cannot be in the house. Unlike most hamantaschen recipes, this recipe is not a cookie, and it uses yeast dough. The completed hamantaschen are filled like danishes.

Hamantaschen are traditionally filled with a poppy-seed mixture known as *mohn*, which means "poppy" in German. However, in our house, we prefer to use sweet filling such as cherry pie filling or a honey-nut mixture. The cherry pie filling is the same one used in in the Cherry Pie recipe in Chapter 15. The honey-nut filling is below. There are many other filling recipes now available on the internet.

Prepare the fillings ahead of time so that they can be well chilled.

Honey-Nut Filling

INGREDIENTS

½ cup water
2 tablespoons butter
2 tablespoons honey
1 cup pecans, finely chopped
1 lemon, zested and juiced
½ cup raisins
¼ cup sugar
1 tart cooking apple (such as Granny Smith or Honeycrisp), peeled, cored, and grated into shreds
¼ cup strawberry or raspberry jam
1 tablespoon cornstarch
2 tablespoons water

Make a slurry with the cornstarch and 2 tablespoons of water.

Add all of the ingredients except the apple, the jam, and the cornstarch slurry to a pot, and cook at medium heat to combine. When the heated mixture is thoroughly combined and thickened, stir the cornstarch slurry, and add the slurry, the apple, and the jam to the pot. Cook until the mixture heats so that the cornstarch activates and the mixture is thick. Chill thoroughly before using.

Sweet Citrus Dough

INGREDIENTS

1 package of active dry yeast
¼ cup water, warm, not over 105°F
½ cup sugar, split use
1¼ cups milk, lukewarm, not over 105°F
4 tablespoons butter, melted
½ teaspoon salt
2 eggs, beaten
2 oranges or 2 lemons or both, zested
3¾ cups flour, sifted
1 egg yolk, beaten (for brushing the pastries just before baking)

Combine the yeast, water, and 3 tablespoons of sugar to activate the yeast.

In a separate mixing bowl, combine the milk, remaining sugar, butter, salt, eggs, and citrus zest. Stir to mix well. Add the yeast mix and stir. Add the flour gradually, mixing together until a dough is formed. A KitchenAid mixer is ideal for this chore, using the dough hook attachment. Knead until the dough is fully combined and the gluten is fully activated, just as for any yeast dough. Place in a buttered bowl, and cover. Set in a warm place for 2 hours or until the dough has doubled in bulk.

When the dough has doubled in volume, punch it down, and knead for 1 minute by hand on a lightly floured board. Then roll the dough out to no more than ⅛ inch thick on a lightly floured surface. Cut the dough into 3-inch or 4-inch squares, as desired. Use approximately 1 heaping teaspoon of the filling (either the cherry filling or the honey-nut filling or other filling as desired) for the 3-inch square. For the 4-inch square of dough, use 1 heaping tablespoon.

Dampen 2 adjacent edges of the square with water or an egg wash, and fold into a triangle, pressing the edges firmly to seal. Place the filled hamantaschen on a baking tray lined with parchment paper, with space between for the dough to rise. Cover with a clean towel as each hamantaschen is prepared.

When the tray is filled, cut a hole in the center of the top of each of the hamantaschen so that you will be able to see a little bit of the filling. Cover with a warm, moist towel, and allow the pastries to rise for about 30 minutes.

Preheat the oven to 350° F. When the pastries have risen, brush the tops of the pastry gently with egg yolk that has been beaten with a touch of water.

Bake the pastries for 20 minutes until they are delicately browned on top. Remove and cool. Continue until all of the dough and filling has been used. These pastries freeze well. Thaw before eating and serve at room temperature or lightly warmed.

Osso Buco Alla Milanese, p. 205

Chapter 11: *Main Course*

FOWL

Before cooking or freezing, it is necessary to clean and prepare the chicken for cooking. What this means—for example, in the case of thighs—is to remove excess skin and fat, which can be used to make Chicken Schmaltz (Chapter 2). Even more importantly, in the case of whole chickens and other fowl, the cavity needs to be thoroughly cleaned and remaining bits of innards (such as in the backbone indentations near the tail) pried out and discarded. The cavity then should be thoroughly washed and drained. This is not the time to be squeamish; the chicken will not hurt you. Interestingly, I had never seen this process shown or discussed on any television cooking show until I saw Martha Stewart perform this step, although I do remember a colloquy between Julia Child and Jacques Pépin on whether it was even necessary to wash the chicken before cooking. If you check fast-food fried chicken or roasted chicken from grocery stores, you will see this step has been omitted. It is not an issue of germs or bacteria, because the cooking heat takes care of that—it is both a flavor issue and essential to the process of making a bird kosher (for example, by removing blood remaining in the cavity.

An issue in the case of the modern chicken and other birds is the risk of spread of bacterial infection such as salmonella in the washing process. I personally see no way around the problem other than being careful in washing and cleaning surrounding surfaces with a Clorox-and-water mixture. The purpose is to remove the undesirable materials—not the germs that are killed by proper cooking. Just be careful to avoid cross contamination. Cooking does kill bacteria—just remember that you should never serve rare or medium-rare chicken or turkey. While many think this is not a problem with duck and so cook duck breasts to medium rare, the salmonella issue exists also for duck. Thus, simply for food safety, even aside from the rules of kashruth, one should never eat fowl if it is undercooked; that is, if there is the appearance of blood and if juices do not run clear.

ROASTED DECONSTRUCTED TURKEY, STUFFING, AND TURKEY STOCK

For many years when we cooked a turkey, it was done in the traditional manner as a whole turkey. Invariably, either the breast meat was overcooked, or the bird was otherwise not properly satisfactory. Unlike for a chicken (which, if one follows the recipe in Julia Child's *The Way to Cook*, you start the bird with its breast down, turning the bird every 10 to 15 minutes and finishing it with the breast up so that the whole bird is perfectly cooked), it is not practical or safe to try to flip a hot 15-to-20-plus-pound turkey, particularly if it is stuffed. It is now common wisdom that it is not wise to stuff a turkey because it is simply not possible to cook the turkey so that the meat is not overcooked if the stuffing is heated to an appropriately safe temperature. Finally, even if you stuff the bird, there is never enough stuffing, so you still need to make a separate pan of dressing.

These problems are solvable! Simply make a stuffed but deconstructed turkey, as described below. (You can, of course, start with purchased turkey thighs, breasts, etc.) A significant advantage of the process is that although the total preparation and cooking process may take place over a couple of days, the work can mostly be completed before the day of the feast, thereby reducing the time spent cooking on Thanksgiving. The actual cooking process of the deconstructed turkey is substantially faster than with a whole bird (less than 2½ hours in the oven as compared to 4½ or more hours for a 20-plus-pound bird). And there is the advantage of plenty of stuffing and wonderful turkey stock for sauces and soups! Sometimes I buy two 20-plus-pound turkeys, deconstruct both turkeys, and only use the dark meat for the initial roasting process, leaving the wings for barbecue or grilling and the breast for separately roasting inside in the oven or outside on the grill. This entire process works equally well for a 12-to-15-pound bird.

The process is simple to start and not difficult to execute; it just has several discrete steps. The real work is up front, the day or so before the bird is cooked. The defrosting process is best if the frozen bird is in the refrigerator for the requisite 2 to 4 days, depending on the size of the bird. I buy frozen birds on Friday or Saturday before Thanksgiving and put them in the refrigerator in a pan to catch any liquid as the bird thaws. The bird will be almost fully defrosted by the following Wednesday and can be worked with by running water through it. I commend the many books, including those by Jacques Pépin and Julia Child, and videos that illustrate the process of cutting up (dissecting) a bird. The only difference between a chicken and a turkey is size. The stock is made before the day of the feast and put in the refrigerator, ready to make sauce—with much leftover to freeze and to make soup on your own schedule.

Deconstructing the Turkey

First you deconstruct the turkey as you would a chicken. You remove the insides of the turkey (all the bags and giblets). If there is a bag of "gravy" inside the bird, that gets tossed. Peel away the fat attached to the skin and in the tail opening of the bird and other loose fat, and reserve it to render (see the following section for steps).

Remove the leg quarters just as you would for a chicken but with somewhat more physical effort because the turkey weighs 3 to 5 times more than the chicken. With a 20-plus-pound turkey, it is just somewhat more physically awkward to maneuver the bird and to push the leg quarter back and out to break the tendon.

Next, remove the wonderful "scallop" from the backbone, next to where the thigh joins the backbone. Then break the leg quarter back, exposing the connection of the thigh to the backbone (in essence, the hip). You have to cut through the tendon with a knife and then carefully slice off the leg quarter, keeping the knife edge against the carcass bone (unlike the chicken leg quarter, which can simply be pulled off, as Jacques Pépin has demonstrated so many times). Put it aside and repeat on the other side of the turkey.

Then you remove the wings, 1 at a time, leaving the breast and carcass. Remove the wishbone. Then completely remove the backbone with a knife and/or poultry shears. This leaves only the breast meat on the bone. It is then simple, just as with a chicken, to remove the breast meat from the bone, slicing on each side of the breastbone, keeping the knife edge against the bone. You wind up with 2 boneless breast halves. Do not remove the skin from the breast meat! When Julia Child and Jacques Pépin performed this process on a TV show, they also knocked off the tips of the legs on each of the leg quarters so that the meat would pull back as it cooked. I do not recommend this because that bone is very hard, and you are likely to ruin a knife; also, such a presentation is totally unnecessary for a wonderful finished product, although it does make it somewhat easier to extract the tough tendons from the fully cooked leg. You may, of course, run a sharp knife around the leg at the end knob so that the meat pulls back as the leg roasts. Remove the wing tips—they are useless for eating but have great flavor and are best used for the stock.

You are left with 2 wings, 2 leg quarters, and 2 breast halves, along with the carcass of the turkey and the giblets. Wash and dry all parts.

Preparing the Stock

INGREDIENTS

turkey carcass—bones, neck, gizzard, heart, wing tips, and tail, *but not the liver*
2-3 celery stalks
2-3 carrots
2 onions
2 bay leaves
1 teaspoon whole black peppercorns (or ground)
1-2 teaspoons dried thyme, or several fresh sprigs
3 or so cloves garlic, smashed lightly and peeled
2 tablespoons or so olive oil
leek leaves (optional)

Thoroughly clean the carcass, removing any remaining bits of organ in the backbone. Wash and dry carefully. Lightly oil the giblets—neck, gizzard, heart, wing tips, tail, any spare skin, and the carcass (breastbone, wishbone, and backbone, rinsed well with water), *but toss the liver.* Put all these parts in a roasting pan. Roast these bones and parts in a 425°F oven, turning from time to time until thoroughly browned. This process will take about 1 hour, and the goal is to thoroughly brown the bones and parts for flavor.

Vegetables should be roasted at the same time. Clean and peel the celery, onion, and carrots, and cut them into chunks. Using a separate pan, lightly oil the vegetables with olive oil, and roast them until browned. Every 15 or 20 minutes, stir and turn over the materials in the oven so that everything browns evenly.

When the vegetables and the turkey parts are all nicely browned, place them in a stockpot together with the bay leaves, pepper, thyme, garlic, and leek leaves, if you have them. Deglaze the roasting pan with water and add this water to the stockpot with more water to cover the ingredients. (As an additional advantage, you then reuse the same pan for the turkey the next day, saving a pan from washing.)

Do not add salt at this stage because you will want to salt to taste when the stock is being used in its final end use as sauce or soup. This produces a wonderful stock for gravy and soup. Simmer for at least 2 to 4 hours as with any stock, and then cool and refrigerate.

After the stock is fully cooled in the refrigerator, remove the now congealed turkey fat, and reserve it to be combined with the turkey schmaltz previously rendered (see the next section). The turkey stock should be strained (discarding the fully used solids) and reserved for use in making gravy and soups. See, for example, the recipe for Mushroom Barley Soup in Chapter 6. Any meat, including the giblet meat from the heart or the gizzard and the meat from the neck, has great flavor and can be chopped finely and put into the stuffing or reserved for leftovers—or your dog will love these overcooked items if you carefully remove the bones. Waste not, want not!

Preparing the Turkey Schmaltz

The fat that is removed and reserved before the turkey is deconstructed should be made into turkey schmaltz, as you would Chicken Schmaltz (Chapter 2). The process is the same except that I do not put onion in the turkey schmaltz, although there is no reason not to do so if you want that taste. This turkey schmaltz should be strained into a jar when the fat is fully rendered and lightly golden. Turkey schmaltz seems more sensitive to heat than chicken schmaltz, so be careful to not overcook it.

Combine the schmaltz with the fat lifted off of the broth. Seal only after it is cool and refrigerate or freeze for future use. This fat is delicious to cook the vegetables, to flavor and make stuffing when you do not have a turkey available to make stuffing with, and to flavor the roux for a sauce. Remember, fat carries flavor, and rendered turkey or chicken fat has no more calories than butter, olive oil, or any other fat.

Important note: Take care to not seal hot items; you do not want to create a vacuum for the potential growth of botulism, which can be deadly. Botulism grows and produces a deadly poison in the absence of oxygen.

Cooking the Turkey

INGREDIENTS

Rub

```
salt
pepper
desired herbs (a mix of thyme, sage, oregano, rosemary, lemon
peel, freshly made garlic paste of 8-12 cloves, etc.)
olive oil
```

Roasting

```
stuffing (see recipe in next section)
prepared rub
deconstructed turkey parts: legs, thighs, breasts, wings
up to 10 or so carrots, cleaned and peeled
2 onions, peeled and quartered
several stalks of celery
several parsnips, if desired
```

For the rub, proportions are approximate and variable to your choice. Use several teaspoons of each of the herbs you choose to make a loose, crumbly, finely mashed mixture. You need at least ½ cup or more of rub mixture. If you add the rub the night before, the turkey will be even more deeply flavored since the salt will draw the flavor through the meat. I use a mortar and pestle (which I regard as a really valuable tool even in this mechanized world) to grind all of the seasonings to a paste but reserve the olive oil to add just before cooking. Rub the meat thoroughly with the spice mixture, and rest it uncovered in the refrigerator overnight, skin side up to dry the skin.

Unlike cooking a whole bird, where the risk of undercooking the stuffing may be significant if you do not overcook the bird, the stuffing in this process is cooked thoroughly at the same time as the rest of the bird, and the bird is not overcooked. Simply prepare the stuffing as you prefer. A wonderful and simple stuffing is described in the next section.

Mound the stuffing fairly evenly on a roasting pan, leaving space at the edges for vegetables. Then layer the desired amount of leg quarters, wings, and deboned breasts, all skin side up, which have been rested overnight. Rub olive oil on the meat just before cooking on top of the mounded stuffing. Using cotton twine made for cooking, tie the breasts into an even cylinder with any small scraps of turkey stuffed inside to promote even cooking. Freeze any unused portions of turkey for future use.

If desired—and you should—put the onions, carrots, celery, and parsnips, lightly oiled and seasoned with the same rub, around the edges of the roasting pan so that you have roasted vegetables done at the same time as the bird. I know that some chefs like to use roasted vegetables that are not cooked as long as the meat, but in our house we like root vegetables to be well roasted. If you prefer less done vegetables, add them after the bird has cooked for 1 hour.

Insert the thermocouple from a Polder or other oven-safe thermometer so that the reading portion of the thermometer is outside of the oven and can be set to the desired temperature. Actually, if you have 2 units, you can keep track separately of white and dark meat. Since the thermocouple is in the meat, you can cook to the exact desired temperature (160°F for the breast, and 165–170°F for the dark meat). Our parents simply did not have this kind of fail-safe technology.

Even for a very large bird (20 to 25 pounds), the cooking process will take less than 2½ hours. The bird and the stuffing will be perfectly cooked, and the meat will be perfectly juicy. Remove the bird from the oven, move it to a separate platter, cover it with foil, and let it rest. If some pieces of turkey cook faster, then remove those as the proper temperature is reached, and cover them with foil until the whole bird is done perfectly. If for some reason the skin is not crispy, that can be solved with a couple of carefully monitored minutes under the broiler. Rest the meat 15 to 20 minutes before slicing and serving.

Making the Stuffing

The stuffing we use is very simple. Many people make exotic stuffing with chestnuts, sausage, seafood, etc., and if that is your choice, then knock yourself out (although the seafood would not be kosher, and you would need to use nonpork sausage). Our family finds that the commercial Pepperidge Farm cornbread mixed with traditional white-bread stuffing (slightly modified), is simply absolutely delicious. For some reason the manufacturer of Pepperidge Farm stuffing has not seen fit to obtain a kosher labeling, although a careful reading of ingredients suggests the mix should be pareve since none are per se *trayf* (not satisfying the requirements of Jewish law), and none contain any milk product. There are kosher-labeled stuffing mixes on the market, and you can easily make a fully homemade kosher dressing.

INGREDIENTS

```
2 (14-ounce) packages of stuffing mix
1 quart chicken broth (boxed chicken broth works well)
1-2 large onions, chopped
2-3 cloves garlic, chopped
2-3 celery stalks, chopped
2-3 tablespoons olive oil
any meats from the giblets, chopped (optional—use after they are
removed from the stock, but do not use the liver)
```

Sauté the vegetables in the olive oil merely to sweat but not brown. Mix the sautéed vegetables and stuffing mix with chicken broth (and giblets, if you are using them). Boxed low-salt broth or stock is fine for this use, particularly since, with the bird roasted on top, the juices of the bird soak into the stuffing. Despite what the package instructions say, no added oil or fat is necessary because the turkey will render sufficient fat as it cooks. If you cook this mix separately as a dressing rather than under the meat, you need some fat: alternatives include, for example, olive oil or some of the rendered turkey fat. It is unnecessary to add egg as a binder before cooking. The stuffing should be assembled immediately before cooking the bird to avoid risk of spoilage.

Making the Sauce

INGREDIENTS

These measurements indicate the correct proportions of flour, fat, and liquid and are intended to be scaled up as needed.

½ cup turkey schmaltz (or olive oil)
½ cup flour
8 cups stock
salt to taste
pepper to taste

The gravy is also very simple since the stock is already made; it is primarily a basic turkey-flavored velouté. The formula is simple: 1 tablespoon each of flour and fat to 1 cup liquid.

Merely mix some turkey schmaltz (or, if desired, olive oil) together with flour to make a roux in the desired quantity. Remember, fat is fat, and the fats for equal quantities have the same calories. I use turkey schmaltz because it is easily available and adds a wonderfully rich turkey flavor to the sauce.

Lightly brown the roux on the stove top over low heat for a couple of minutes to a very light tan stage for flavor and to cook the flour—not as heavily cooked as for a Cajun roux. Stir the cooking roux constantly to cook evenly and avoid excessive browning. Then whisk the stock slowly into the roux, continuing to whisk so that there are no lumps, until the sauce simmers and thickens. This is not a time that you can leave the stove. Add salt and pepper to taste.

It is a good idea to make plenty of sauce because if there is any leftover turkey (and I make enough to ensure leftovers), you can then slice the turkey and put it and any unused giblets (other than the liver) in a CorningWare or other freezer dish with sauce, carrots, etc. for a future meal. So prepared, the assembly freezes perfectly. This is not a leftover that we regard as a "leftover" but is a meal that is highly prized at our house and a very easy worknight meal. Cook some rice, prepare a salad, heat the turkey, and in less than 30 minutes, leftovers become a feast. If you have leftover sweet potato casserole or stuffing, that is even better.

Serving the Turkey

Serve the turkey with all of the traditional accompaniments, including Cranberry Sauce (Chapter 14), Sweet Potato Soufflé (Chapter 14), and the desired vegetables. I know that green bean casserole is classic in many parts of the South, but since it contains milk, it is not something we serve at our house as an accompaniment at the Thanksgiving meal. If you want green beans, either sauté those lightly with garlic and olive oil—perhaps adding reconstituted porcini mushrooms and liquid, boiling to evaporate to create a mushroom sauce—or grill or steam them to serve as part of a salad of assorted vegetables. We frequently serve vegetables (cauliflower, carrots, onion, zucchini, eggplant, etc.) flavored with garlic powder and salt, then lightly coated with olive oil before grilling or roasting. Serve the vegetables either hot or, if served cold or at room temperature, with an aioli, mustard mayonnaise, or Pink Salad Dressing (Chapter 8). If you grill the vegetables ahead of time to serve cold or at room temperature, there is that much less work on the day of the feast.

Finally, Thanksgiving dessert in our house includes Pecan Pie (Chapter 15), Apple Pie (Chapter 15), or, more recently, a Coconut-Lemon-Custard Cherry Pie (Chapter 15). If you do not eat milk after meat, the dessert must be pareve—so, for example, make the crust with Crisco vegetable shortening rather than butter and omit added butter to the apple pie filling. There is no need to be deprived to keep kosher.

TAGINE

A tagine is classically made in a type of Moroccan dish with a cone-shaped lid called a tagine. While I think my version is outstanding, under no circumstances should it be deemed to be authentic because I do many things that are simply not authentic, including browning the meat, which, in my view, adds significant flavor to the final product and renders fat that can be discarded. In addition, I simply do not bother with cooking in a tagine, which I regard as an unnecessary special-purpose dish. I instead use a large metal (aluminum-clad with a stainless steel interior) casserole pan with a domed lid that is of sufficient size to contain all of the ingredients.

The tagine is a process, and its flavor profile essentially depends on the herbs and spices used in it together with the preserved lemon and variety of dried fruits. It can be made with chicken, lamb, goat, or beef, and each meat changes the result. Since this dish includes preserved lemons (and optional olives), when you are adding salt, remember that the final dish will have the lemons that are preserved in salt and optional olives that are also salty; therefore, do not oversalt the dish.

INGREDIENTS

about 4 pounds chicken thighs, bone-in goat (preferably shank), lamb shoulder (boned and fat removed), or beef chuck

olive oil to brown the meat

3 tablespoons ginger, grated

3-4 cloves garlic

3 shallots, minced

2 chiles (jalapeños or other green chiles, if desired)

½ cup cilantro, chopped, plus extra for garnish

1 teaspoon salt

1 tablespoon Tagine Spice Mixture (Chapter 2), or to taste

1 tablespoon ground turmeric

1 tablespoon palm or brown sugar

1 onion, chopped

2-3 carrots, chopped or shredded

2-4 cups Chicken Stock (Chapter 6)

large pinch saffron

1 bay leaf

2-3 preserved lemons, rind only

1 cup olives of your choice (optional)

1 can chickpeas, drained and washed (optional)

1-2 cups dried fruit such as dates, raisins, or apricots (optional)

pepper

Make a spice paste of ginger, garlic, shallots, fresh chiles, cilantro, and salt. If less heat from the chiles is desired, remove the ribs and seeds before cooking. While I like a certain amount of heat, many do not, particularly including children, so I suggest going for flavor and omitting the seeds and ribs of the chiles.

Brown the meat or chicken in olive oil and remove it from the pan. Drain excess oil. In the empty pan, off heat, mix together the tagine spice mixture, a tablespoon of olive oil if needed, and turmeric. Then add the ginger paste along with the sugar. Add onion and carrots. Add chicken stock to barely cover. Add chopped olives, if using, and a large pinch of saffron. Add bay leaf. Add chickpeas, if desired. If using canned chickpeas, drain and rinse before adding. Add back the chicken.

Simmer until the chicken or meat is cooked. 10 minutes before serving, add diced preserved lemon rind, disposing of the flesh of the lemon. Add dried fruit such as dates, raisins, or apricots 10 minutes before serving. Add chopped fresh cilantro just before serving. (Unlike parsley, the small stems of cilantro are flavorful and are not tough. They should be added, finely chopped.)

Serve with rice (basmati or other naturally flavored is best).

INDIAN-STYLE GRILLED CHICKEN

This recipe is not truly Indian, in the sense that I suspect no Indian chef has actually made anything exactly like this recipe, just as I suspect no Italian *nonna* ever made the Mushroom-Spinach Lasagna in Chapter 12. However, it has Indian flavors accessible to the home cook while meeting the laws of kashruth relating to mixing milk and meat. It is certainly a rip-off of the tandoori chicken commonly served in Indian restaurants. As with other variants (for example, Bouillabaisse a La Juive in Chapter 6), this recipe is intended to be includable in a kosher kitchen but equally attractive to the non-Jewish cook. It certainly meets the standard of *Deep Flavors*. Therefore, unlike a traditional tandoori chicken, which is marinated in regular milk yogurt, this chicken is not marinated in a milk-based yogurt but rather in a coconut- or almond-based nondairy yogurt, although the chicken is very good even without the yogurt, if that is not available. As with most grilled items, this recipe is very simple to execute, even as it tracks the Indian flavors that one would expect in an Indian restaurant.

The tandoori and garam masala—as well as other Indian spice mixtures or masalas—are available for purchase at ethnic Indian food stores, Penzeys's website, and, increasingly, at your local grocery store or online from American spice companies that are certified kosher. There are a number of recipes just for garam masala that are regional variants based on the source in India. I have also included the recipe I use in Chapter 2.

INGREDIENTS

This recipe is easily multiplied.

8 chicken thighs (bone in and skin on—these add flavor and protect the meat during grilling)

about 1 cup of coconut or almond yogurt (preferably unsweetened and containing no milk products)

1 tablespoon or more tandoori masala (or another masala as desired)

1 tablespoon or more Garam Masala (Chapter 2)

2 tablespoons or more fresh ginger, finely minced or ground

3 or more cloves garlic, finely minced or mashed to a paste

1 teaspoon ground peppercorns

salt to taste

½ cup or so cilantro, finely chopped or ground

Using a mortar and pestle (or, if you do not have a mortar and pestle, use a blender or food processor), make a paste of all of the ingredients except the chicken and yogurt. Use kosher salt to facilitate the grinding. Grind to a fine paste, and then add the spice mixture to the yogurt. Spread the yogurt-spice paste over the chicken, and let it sit for up to ½ an hour, covered.

When moving to the grill, it is best to have a section of the grill that you turn off as you start to put the chicken on the grill so that you will have an area where you can cook the chicken over indirect heat to avoid flare-ups and burning. Start the chicken skin side down, flipping as necessary and moving to cooler sections until the chicken is thoroughly cooked to at least 165–170°F internal temperature next to the bone. Move to indirect cooking as needed. I find that a Thermapen or similar instant-read thermometer is essential to obtain a perfectly cooked grilled product.

I serve this chicken with Lemon Coconut Rice (Chapter 9), or if I am serving Indian-Style Lentils (Chapter 14), I frequently just serve with plain white basmati rice. Leftover chicken makes a great snack or lunch.

For a vegetable, I suggest Pan-Roasted Cauliflower (Chapter 14), with the variation that before roasting, when rubbing on olive oil and garlic powder, add a sprinkle of Garam Masala

(Chapter 2) and/or sweet curry powder over the cauliflower. Squeeze on lemon juice about 5 minutes before removing from the oven and serving. (Sweet curry powder is the very yellow curry powder mixture we are all familiar with. I think the mixture sold at Penzeys is superior to what is available in regular groceries, but it is not kosher.)

MUSTARD GRILLED OR BAKED CHICKEN

This is a most simple and quick, yet easily variable, recipe—whether using the oven or the grill. It is most delicious as a fabulous second no-effort meal of cold leftovers or for a picnic if you double the amount cooked. While the concept of grilled or baked chicken may seem very mundane, it can be much more. These concepts can be adapted to a gas or charcoal grill or baking in an oven. This is perfect for a meal with a little advance preparation and short final cooking time. Much of the minimal preparation can be done in the morning for the evening meal.

There is no ingredient list because this is meant to be an infinitely variable, no-holds-barred recipe with ideas for your use and discretion.

I use exclusively chicken thighs, but you could use breasts if you insist. Leave the skins on the thighs, as they add flavor and protect the thighs from burning as the chicken is grilled. The fat in the thighs and in the skin will render during the cooking process. If you use the oven, it is best if you do not mix white meat and dark meat parts in the same baking dish, since their cooking times are different. On an outside grill, timing cooking for the different parts is easy.

Mix a rub of mustard, garlic powder or fresh garlic paste, dried herbs (thyme, oregano, rosemary, etc.) as desired, salt, and pepper for basting and marinating the chicken. I generally use plain dijon mustard, but a whole-grain German-style mustard or a whole-grain dijon mustard works well in this process. Remember, flavor is the goal. Add dried herbs as suggested—or for an exotic twist, use Middle Eastern, Chinese, or Indian flavors (ginger, soy, sesame oil, hoisin sauce, five-spice powder, cumin, various chiles, garam masala and/or other masala blends, lemon or lime or other citrus, mint, cilantro, etc. appropriate to the selected regional variation) as desired.

Add to the rub the grated zest from a lemon or lime, which will be juiced just before cooking to avoid the acid precooking the meat. For an Indian character, a nondairy yogurt made from coconut is an excellent addition to the marinade. Put the rub and the chicken into a covered bowl or plastic bag that can be sealed. Mix well to cover the chicken and refrigerate. No more than 30 minutes or so before cooking the chicken, squeeze on fresh lemon or lime juice (and not the bottled stuff). Mix again.

If you are baking the chicken in your oven, fill a baking dish with the chicken. Unlike instructions for many sautéing recipes, it is not necessary that there be spaces between the pieces of chicken. The chicken should be placed skin side up so that it browns and crisps well. Cook in a 350°F oven for 30 to 40 minutes or until the chicken tests 160°F for the breast (165–170°F for dark meat) and the skin is browned and crispy. Remove the chicken from the baking dish. Separate the pan drippings, which will consist of fat and juices. Remove and discard the rendered fat. The juices can be placed over the chicken or over rice that has been cooked to be served with the chicken.

If you are grilling the chicken instead, grill until the chicken is fully cooked. Note that as you commence the cooking process, the chicken may flame up, and you have to be careful to flip the pieces and to move the chicken to cooler portions of the grill. If you are using a grill with multiple burners, you can start the chicken skin side down on the flame portion of the grill until you have great grill marks or until dripping fat causes flare-ups. Then flip and move the chicken to the cooler side of the grill where the flame is turned off, close the lid, and let it "roast" in that manner until it is done, checking and turning from time to time. Done equals 160°F for white meat and 170°F for thighs and legs; a Thermapen is an essential tool.

The chicken is delicious served with plain basmati rice with the pan juices served over it or fresh herbs fluffed in, perhaps with a squeeze of fresh citrus. Cook a vegetable, and you have a wonderful meal.

CHICKEN AND DUMPLINGS

This recipe is based on the version Lisa, my daughter, makes with some changes to also reflect how we make it at home. The original recipe from which this is derived was from *The Fannie Farmer Cookbook,* and that version was the first recipe Lisa ever made by herself when she was eight years old. Though she has updated it with her flavor and meat-to-vegetable proportion preferences over the years, I believe she has kept it true to the soul of the dish. It continues to be one of our family's favorite comfort foods. This version successfully translates the recipe to a dish that does not violate the prohibition against mixing milk and meat. This is one style of chicken and dumplings in which the dumplings are in the nature of poached drop biscuits, almost like a flour-based matzo ball. There is another tradition in which the dumplings are rolled like pasta.

The meal is better when fresh herbs are used, although certainly that first effort more than twenty-five years ago was made with dried herbs. That should not stop you from preparing the recipe if fresh herbs are not available, but it is a plus if you do have them. Remember this rule of thumb: use ⅓ the amount of dried herbs as fresh.

The dish goes through a few stages over time, making it wonderful for leftovers. The first day, the meal is more of a soup, but by the second day, the dumplings have begun to disintegrate, resulting in a hearty stew. And lastly, while the recipe makes enough to feed a crowd, and freezing leftovers is always an option, Lisa frequently uses the leftover stew as a perfect base for Chicken Potpie (Chapter 11)—just add peas and sautéed mushrooms (and even better if you add reconstituted dried porcinis, together with the soaking liquid) to transform the dish once again. Depending on the size of your pot (or crowd), this recipe is easily doubled.

INGREDIENTS

Soup

8 chicken thighs (about 4 pounds)

7-9 carrots, cut into bite-sized chunks or larger (Larger carrot pieces will become tender but retain a bit more chew and flavor. They can easily be cut into smaller pieces in the bowl.)

2-3 celery ribs, finely chopped

2 large onions, chopped

olive oil, as needed

3-5 large cloves garlic (up to a full head), smashed and chopped

8-10 cups unsalted chicken broth

2 teaspoons dried thyme

2 bay leaves

1½ teaspoons dried rosemary, crumbled or chopped

2 teaspoons salt (taste after you add 1 teaspoon, and adjust after the chicken is done but before adding the dumplings—you can always add more, but you cannot remove excess salt)

½ teaspoon freshly ground pepper

Dumplings (You may wish to multiply by 1.5 because they usually disappear before everything else)

```
2 cups flour (white, unbleached—Lisa uses a mixture of unbleached
and whole wheat flour)
3 teaspoons baking powder
1 teaspoon salt
2 tablespoons fresh parsley, minced (dried parsley is inevitably
tasteless and should not be taking space in your kitchen)
4 tablespoons Crisco vegetable shortening, solid
¾–1 cup water
```

Making the Soup

Trim the excess fat from the chicken thighs. Using bone-in, skin-on thighs adds much flavor. The skin can be removed before finishing with the dumplings or just before serving. Sauté the whole thighs, starting skin side down to caramelize the meat and render the fat. After sautéing the whole thighs, remove them from the pot, and then drain the rendered fat. This drained fat is chicken schmaltz that can be reserved and stored for future use.

Add the carrots, celery, and onion to the empty pot with a small amount of olive oil, if needed. Sauté the vegetables for 3 to 5 minutes over medium heat. Then add the garlic, and sauté for another minute. Deglaze with the broth. Add the herbs, salt, chicken, and sufficient additional broth or water to cover everything generously, with room for the dumplings. Bring to a boil, and then turn the heat down to a bare simmer for about 45 minutes (until the chicken is almost fork tender). While it is simmering gently, make the dumpling dough, and chill the mixture in the refrigerator until ready.

Making the Dumplings

Combine the dry ingredients and parsley. Cut in shortening until it looks like coarse meal. Stir in ¾ cup of water with a fork—add additional liquid if the dough will not hold together. Mix the dumpling dough like pie or biscuit dough—that is, as little as possible to get it to come together, since the more you stir, the tougher and denser the dumplings will be.

Once the chicken is nearly fork tender, skim off and discard any additional rendered fat. At this time, you may wish to remove the meat from the bones. Return the meat to the pot.

Then gently drop dumplings spoonful by spoonful into pot. Cover and simmer for 20 minutes without lifting the lid. Enjoy!

MEAT POTPIE (CHICKEN, TURKEY, OR BEEF)

The recipes for chicken, turkey, or beef potpie are substantially identical to each other except for the stock that is used to make the velouté (sauce) that goes into the potpie and the meat that is the principal protein. Obviously, chicken and chicken stock go into chicken potpie, turkey and turkey stock go into turkey potpie, and beef and beef stock go into beef potpie. However, the resulting tastes are quite different and obscure the similarities in process and congruity of other ingredients. Homemade stocks are, of course, best. If you do not have turkey stock, you can substitute chicken stock.

These recipes are some of the most serious comfort foods imaginable, and although there are many recipes extant, I like my recipes the best—the flavor is enhanced because I use mushrooms that have been caramelized, and I also use dried porcini, chanterelle, and/ or trumpet mushrooms and their reconstituting liquid. As the reader will note, I am very fond of wild European mushrooms since they add an incredible flavor profile and intensity otherwise unattainable. (I refer to these mushrooms as European even though they—for example, porcinis, also known as cèpes—are found not only in Italy and elsewhere in Europe but also in widely disparate regions of the world, even including China.) Meat potpies are an outstanding use for leftover meat.

INGREDIENTS

This recipe fits in a 10x10-inch baking pan.

Bobbie's Piecrust (Chapter 15)

½ cup onion, diced

1 cup carrot, finely minced or shredded

1 celery stalk, finely minced

½–1 cup white portion of leek, minced (optional)

olive oil (or turkey schmaltz)

2 cloves garlic, minced

1 cup fresh mushrooms, caramelized and diced (button, portobello, or cremini, but not shiitake)

salt

pepper

1½ teaspoons dried thyme, split use

1–2 ounces dried porcini, trumpet, or chanterelle mushrooms, reconstituted in 1 cup hot water, reserving the liquid for the sauce

2–4 cups stock (chicken, turkey, or beef, respectively)

unbleached flour, as needed for the sauce

1–2 cups of the respective meat: chicken or turkey (preferably dark meat, precooked) or beef chuck or shoulder (cooked as discussed below)

1 cup frozen english peas

egg for egg wash

Preheat the oven to 400°F.

The recipes (or concepts, really) all start the same. The 10x10-inch baking pan should have a bottom crust of Bobbie's Piecrust laid in and prebaked.

First, you cook what the French would refer to as mirepoix (and the Italians would refer to as *sofrito*—with the addition of garlic). Sauté the onion, carrot, celery, and leek (if using) in olive oil until they are transparent and partially cooked. The carrots should, depending upon how small you dice them, become softened quickly. Add the garlic and cook for another 30 seconds or so until you can smell the garlic. Add a cup of fresh, caramelized, diced mushrooms. Add salt, pepper, and about ½ teaspoon of thyme to taste.

Soak dried porcini, chanterelle, and/or trumpet mushrooms in water to reconstitute them, and when they are softened, lift the reconstituted mushrooms out of the water, and chop them. Reserve the water. Add the mushrooms to the other vegetables and cook briefly.

Make the velouté sauce, which is like a béchamel but with meat stock instead of milk and olive oil or schmaltz instead of butter for the roux. The sauce is simple: for 4 cups of sauce, cook 4 tablespoons of fat with 4 tablespoons of flour until the mixture barely turns tan, and then slowly whisk in 4 cups of liquid, carefully avoiding lumps. The liquid should be a combination of the mushroom-reconstituting liquid plus the appropriate meat stock. When the sauce is fully heated, it will magically thicken. If you do not have turkey stock for a turkey pie (or even if you do), use turkey schmaltz (rendered fat) for the roux to enhance the turkey flavor. Since this is a meat pie, do not use any milk product. When using the mushroom stock, carefully drain any sand from the mushroom-reconstituting liquid that inevitably exists in dried mushrooms. Add 1 teaspoon thyme plus salt and pepper to taste.

For the chicken potpie, use poached or roasted chicken thighs (not breasts) and dice them. Chicken breasts tend to overcook, and the dark meat stays unctuous for a far longer period in the cooking process. Similarly, with turkey, use roasted and diced dark meat. (If white meat is what you have, you can use that also.) Add the meat and thickened sauce to the vegetables.

For the beef, use nonfatty beef chuck that you have cut into pieces. For beef, the sizes of the meat cubes should be small bite-sized cubes, no larger than ¾ an inch; otherwise they will take too long to cook and would require a knife to eat. If the beef is uncooked, it should first be browned in olive oil—even better is using leftover chuck roast or brisket. If you are using raw beef, after you brown the beef, add Beef Stock (Chapter 6), and simmer it for about 30 to 45 minutes until the beef is cooked and tender. Then add the stock to the roux to thicken it. Finally, add the meat and thickened sauce to the vegetables. Since the beef is in very small pieces, it should not take too long to cook.

When you add the velouté sauce and the meat to the cooked vegetables, if you are making the potpie immediately, add frozen small english peas. You should not add and cook the peas until you cook the pie, because they will overcook. If you are deferring cooking the pie, cool the pie filling without the peas, and then reheat in a microwave to bubbling immediately before adding the frozen peas. Taste the filling for seasoning before adding to the pan. At this point (when ready to bake), you should cover the potpie filling with more of Bobbie's Piecrust. Alternatively, pareve frozen puff pastry made without butter would be a time saver.

Cut holes into the top of the pie so that steam escapes. Coat with an egg wash to facilitate browning. Cook at 400°F until the crust is cooked and lightly browned (about 30 to 40 minutes). At this time the pie will be bubbling, and the filling will be done.

Serve and enjoy. In our house, even if the filling is only partially eaten, the crust will be demolished. For the next serving, cover with fresh crust and rebake.

MEAT

BRAISED BRISKET

Brisket is a traditional food for the Jewish holidays. Brisket starts as an inherently tough and inexpensive cut of meat that requires proper cooking and proper slicing to make it the centerpiece on the table that belies its humble origins. That includes a long, slow cooking at a low temperature, such as in a braise, and even then, it must be sliced across the grain to avoid long stringy portions.

I have seen numerous recipes over the years. However, I have resolved on using a high-temperature start because the flavor is outstanding. I originally got the idea for a high-temperature start from Barbara Kafka's book *Roasting: A Simple Art*, although this recipe is not the same as her recipe at all, beyond the high-temperature start. For example, she adds tomato; I do not. Because tradition plays an important role, I try to maintain a flavor profile similar to what I remember my mom making. That does not mean that as a naturalized Texan, I do not also make and love brisket smoked at a low temperature (225–250°F) in a smoker using pecan, hickory, or oak logs as a fuel with a total cooking time of at least ten to twelve hours (a far better barbecue than versions cooked in other parts of the US).

The beef brisket is the same cut of meat from which pork bacon is made. It is also the same cut of meat that constitutes a veal breast from a calf. The whole brisket consists of two very different muscle layers separated by a fat layer: the first (or flat) cut and the point (also referred to as the "deckle") cut. The point cut has a significant amount of fat marbling and connective cartilaginous tissue, which is not fat. That cartilaginous tissue adds moisture and unctuousness when properly cooked. Since the muscle fibers in the two muscles run in different directions, the cuts need to be separated so that the meat in each muscle group can be sliced across the grain, or you will be chewing tough strings of meat no matter how long you cook it. This must be done either before or after cooking, but in any event before carving.

While my wife and daughter are not particularly fond of the point cut, this is my favorite part of the brisket—it is a matter of taste. I suppose one could just use a first or flat cut in the process that I am going to describe, but it should contain a layer of surface fat for cooking. Unfortunately, that fat layer is frequently trimmed off by grocery stores before sale. I think this produces a dry brisket, although *America's Test Kitchen* describes a process that they claim produces a moist end product by resting the meat in the braising liquid overnight. I am not convinced.

INGREDIENTS

1 beef brisket—whole packer trim, point cut, or flat cut, your choice

1-2 tablespoons flavorless vegetable oil or olive oil

2 whole onions

6-10 large carrots

2-3 celery stalks

4-6 parsnips

3-4 bay leaves (dried or fresh)

2 teaspoons or so thyme

salt

pepper

4-6 cloves garlic, peeled

1 bottle dry red wine, inexpensive but drinkable (which my mom certainly did not use)

1 quart unsalted beef stock, preferably homemade, plus water as needed

I start with a whole "packer trim" brisket, which is easily available in Texas since that is the cut used for smoking—but you can, as many do, use only the first cut. The whole brisket will weigh 10 to 12 (or as much as 18) pounds, and if you are lucky, you will have leftovers. The first cut will weigh 6 to 8 pounds. The brisket has a significant amount of waste fat all over it, but it can be purchased on sale for a low price per pound. However, the price is not why you should purchase this untrimmed brisket. While I trim the excess fat from the top and from the middle between the 2 layers before cooking in a braise (but not before cooking by smoking), I leave on at least a ¼ inch of the fat at the start of the process to help keep the meat moist and flavorful while it cooks. Whenever you separate the layers, do so by carefully separating the 2 layers (the flat and the point cuts) using a boning or short chef's knife (or combination). Take care to separate layers at the fat between the 2 cuts, not rushing the process or cutting into the meat muscle. A sharp knife is critical. Separating the layers before cooking makes the rest of the process easier, and it has the advantage that this separation process is not done while the meat is hot. Early separation also facilitates the rendering of fat and the exposure and browning of more surfaces during both the high-heat process and the braising process.

What Ms. Kafka suggested (and I thought dubious at first but have found works to great success) was to start the roasting process at 500°F to caramelize the meat and vegetables. You can brown the meat on the stove top, but this process produces a great mess of splattered fat without the deep rendering produced by the high and even oven heat. Preheat the oven to 500°F, because if you try to heat the oven with the meat in it, this process will not work: the oven simply will not heat fast enough. I do not use the convection setting for this process.

Lightly oil the metal roasting pan to be used to cook the brisket with no more than 1 to 2 tablespoons of a flavorless vegetable oil or olive oil. Lay the brisket pieces (flat cut and deckle) fat side down. Do not use a Pyrex or other Pyroceram baking dish for this process, as it could break. Do not use a lightweight metal pan for this process. I use a heavy anodized aluminum roasting pan, and there are many excellent roasting pans.

Use a second large roasting pan for the vegetables: carrots, celery, parsnips, and onions. Cut the onion into halves or quarters. The rest of the vegetables are cut into reasonable lengths or 3 to 5 inches. Salt, pepper, and coat the vegetables very lightly with olive oil, spreading the oil all over the surface of the vegetables. We like to eat the cooked carrots with the brisket despite the fact that many chefs sneer at these "overcooked" vegetables. They suggest the use of freshly cooked vegetables, but these will never have the flavor acquired in a long braise. These carrots and other root vegetables may not be beautiful after the long braise, but they have an incredible flavor. Peel several cloves of garlic to add later; do not roast the garlic at this stage, as it would burn and become bitter.

Depending on the size of your brisket, you may need to brown each cut separately, letting the first browned cut rest on a half sheet pan while the second cut browns.

When the oven is fully preheated, place the pan with the brisket on the lower rack and the pan with the vegetables on an upper rack. Set the timer for 15 minutes. After 15 minutes, stir and turn the vegetables over. Carefully (because it is really hot) turn the brisket fat side up. Return the vegetables and the brisket to the oven for 30 more minutes at 500°F.

At the end of a total of 45 minutes, the brisket will be externally browned but not cooked. Remove the brisket and the vegetables from the oven and lower the oven temperature to 350°F. Put the brisket in the second pan on top of the vegetables, and carefully pour off and dispose of the rendered fat (there will be a generous quantity). Do not pour the fat into the sink, as it will congeal and cause a stoppage. You can pour the rendered fat into a large Pyrex measuring cup to cool. Then pour the cooled fat into a glass jar for ultimate disposal in the trash. (Empty pickle jars are perfect for this purpose.) Although I am sure there may be a use for that fat (such as roasting potatoes) and notwithstanding my general philosophy—waste not, want not—I do not use this rendered beef fat.

Return the brisket to its own roasting pan, fat side up, and place all of the roasted vegetables with the halved garlic cloves around the brisket. Salt and pepper the brisket, which was not previously done. Pour in a bottle of dry red wine. Pour in a good-quality low-sodium beef stock, preferably homemade, to about ¾ of the height of the brisket. Add water if necessary, but do not cover the meat: the meat should braise, not boil. Add bay leaves, dried thyme, salt, and pepper. Tightly cover the roasting pan with foil and place it in the 350°F oven for 1½ hours. Then reduce the oven to 250°F for about 2½ hours or until the brisket is tender. When it is tender, carefully (as it will be heavy and filled with hot liquid) remove the pan from the oven.

It is a good idea to prepare the brisket to this stage in advance of when you plan to serve it. After the requisite 3-to-4-hour roasting or braising process needed in order to tenderize the meat, cool the meat for an hour, and then place it into the refrigerator. This resting improves the final product. The cooling can be accelerated by placing the pan carefully on ice in a large sink. After the meat has fully cooled in the refrigerator (at least 24 hours), carefully remove the congealed fat layer. Reheat gently just until warmed—the meat is fully cooked already. At this stage, the brisket can be frozen for future use or reheated and served. If desired before freezing, you can portion the meat, vegetables, and gravy into smaller containers. Trim excess fat off the meat when you carve it for serving. I cannot overemphasize—carve across the grain to serve, and it will be tender and delicious.

Serve the brisket with kishke (a nonvegetarian variety), which can be purchased from the freezer case in a grocery store in a Jewish area of your city; otherwise, it may be difficult to locate. Kasha or *Kasha Varnishkes* (Chapter 9) are outstanding side dishes to serve with brisket. Particularly at Passover, we serve the brisket with Potato Kugel (Chapter 14) because potato is not a grain proscribed for that holiday. It is also traditional to serve potato latkes with applesauce (but not with sour cream, since that is a milk product) with brisket. Since we do not mix milk and meat, I generally do not serve mashed potatoes with brisket, because I make mashed potatoes with milk, but there are recipes without milk product.

This process of cooking brisket is a Jewish version of the French pot-au-feu; other cuisines have other variants of this process. Lisa recently gave me a variant using spices such as cumin, chili powder, bay leaf, chipotle, another dried chili powder, liquid smoke (about 1 teaspoon), thyme, oregano, garlic, and onion that has a southwestern or Mexican flavor profile. (I would also add cilantro, but Lisa does not like cilantro.) Her flavor ideas can be used with the techniques in this recipe. Lisa's version of cooked brisket would be great served shredded in a soft flour or corn tortilla taco with garnishes of your choice: lime, Pickled Jalapeños (Chapter 7), Guacamole (Chapter 5), grilled (or pan-sautéed) onions, shredded purple or green cabbage, pico de gallo, and my special Refried Beans (Chapter 14), but just not at Rosh Hashanah or Yom Kippur and certainly not Passover.

OSSO BUCO ALLA MILANESE

There are recipes for osso buco made with veal shanks, lamb shanks, beef shanks, and even turkey legs, but traditionally and originally, the Italians made osso buco with veal shanks. The term means "hole in the bone," a reference to the wonderful marrow that is a part of the experience of this dish. This recipe is another perfect example of the utilization of a tough and otherwise inedible cut of meat made delectable and delicious by properly cooking slowly in a braise over an extended period of time in a highly flavored broth. It is like nothing else you will ever eat, and I know of no one who has ever tried osso buco and did not fall in love with it.

When cooked, not only is the meat delectable, but the center of the shank bone releases the marrow that has become cooked and very soft and delicious.

In Milan, Italy, osso buco is traditionally, but not always, served with a gremolata (a quick fresh sauce of chopped fresh parsley, garlic, lemon zest, and anchovies) and served over a bed of saffron risotto, but that is a step I do not take. Meat with fish on the same plate is regarded as not kosher. If you are observant in this regard, omit the anchovies. There are questions as to whether veal can be kosher if the conditions in which it is raised are inhumane— particularly Provimi veal, which is young, milk-fed veal or veal fed a special diet so that it has not started to mature to beef.

Sometimes it may be difficult to find properly cut veal shanks. Properly cut veal shanks should be about 12 ounces each and about 2 inches thick. You should look for a high proportion of meat to bone. Center cut is best. While the average grocery store may not carry veal shanks, you can generally find this cut from specialty meat butchers in most major American cities. It is also available at specialty or high-end supermarkets such as Central Market in Texas, or your butcher at other major markets may be willing to order veal shanks for you as needed to cook osso buco. It never hurts to ask. This is a feast dish and, unlike brisket, not inexpensive.

This recipe is for eight to ten meaty center-cut veal shanks. This amount requires a large pot—nine to twelve quarts—or you can use a large roasting pan. If you do not have a pot or pan sufficiently large, you can certainly cut the size of the recipe down to fit your pot. There is nothing particularly precise about the recipe, in that the proportions are approximate. You just want to make sure you do not overspice or oversalt the recipe. Always taste for seasoning. And leftovers do not suffer from time in the refrigerator or freezer.

INGREDIENTS

8-10 veal shank pieces, center cut, 2 inches thick
½-1 cup all-purpose flour
olive oil for browning the vegetables and meat
1-2 onions, finely diced
1-2 celery stalks, finely diced
2-3 carrots, finely diced
2 tablespoons or so tomato paste

3-4 cloves garlic, finely minced

2 cups dry white wine

2 teaspoons dried thyme

1 teaspoon dried rosemary

2 bay leaves

1 teaspoon salt, or to taste

½ teaspoon freshly ground pepper, or to taste

2 oranges, zested

1 lemon, zested

1 (28-ounce) can whole peeled tomatoes, canned in juice, not sauce

4-8 cups chicken stock to cover the shanks

Preheat oven to 325°F.

Dredge the veal shanks well in the flour, shaking the meat to dislodge any excess flour. Add a couple tablespoons of olive oil to the pan, and heat. Brown the shanks well in batches, being careful not to burn them or the fond in the pot. This is not a time to be multitasking. Moderate the flame or burner and add additional oil as necessary. Remove and reserve the browned meat. It will take 5 to 10 minutes to brown each group of shanks, turning so that each side is browned.

Add the onions, celery, and carrots to the empty pot with more oil as needed. Scrape up the fond. Add the tomato paste, and cook for 30 seconds to 1 minute, stirring in well. Add and stir the garlic. After about 30 seconds, add the wine, and deglaze the pan, scraping up any remaining fond. Add the herbs, salt, pepper, citrus zest, and canned tomatoes and juice. Break up the tomatoes as you add them to the pot. Take care to not oversalt. As with other braises, adjust for more salt, if necessary, after the meat is cooked and the sauce is reduced for serving. Add back the meat. Add chicken stock to barely cover. Put the lid on the pan and bring it to simmer.

Once it is simmering, immediately put the pot into a 325°F oven for 2 to 3 hours until tender. As you check the progress from time to time, add liquid as needed. When the veal is tender, remove and reserve the veal and vegetables. Discard the bay leaves and the zest. Skim the sauce to remove fat, or if you have time overnight, refrigerate everything. Before reheating, lift off and discard the congealed fat.

Reduce the sauce to concentrate flavor. Do not add more salt until the sauce is reduced. As it reduces it will take on a slight viscosity. When the sauce is reduced, perhaps by ⅓ to ½, taste and adjust for salt.

Serve over polenta or pasta. If you are serving the osso buco with pasta, undercook the pasta so that is not yet even al dente. Then cook the pasta with the sauce for a couple of minutes so that the pasta can absorb the sauce, the sauce can further reduce, and the pasta becomes al dente. If you need more liquid, add some pasta-cooking water. The meal is ready for service.

A fresh vegetable (broccoli, broccolini, broccoli rabe, brussels sprouts, snow or sugar snap peas, string beans, haricot verts, etc.) sautéed with garlic is an excellent accompaniment.

SMOKED BRISKET, CHICKEN, AND OTHER MEATS

Smoked brisket is very different than an oven-braised brisket. It requires a smoker and a very long (8 to 12 hours) and low-temperature process to tenderize the brisket. You need to use a whole brisket—flat cut and point cut—with all of the fat, which can be trimmed before cooking but not completely removed until after cooking. The night before cooking the brisket, rub the whole brisket with a barbecue rub (a dry rub). You can assemble your own favorite kosher dry spice rub or use a commercial rub. A visit to the various Texas barbecue restaurants shows considerable variations in the rubs. I personally use Angelo's Bar-B-Que rub, which I have seen in grocery stores outside of Texas. Angelo's rub is very spicy and probably consists of at least salt, pepper, cayenne, and garlic powder. You could use other mixtures such as garlic powder, celery salt or powder, salt, pepper, and perhaps dry herbs of whatever nature desired for the final product. Variations exist depending on who is cooking; for example, at Louie Mueller Barbecue in Taylor, Texas, the rub is simply a 50-50 or 60-40 mixture of salt and cracked black pepper.

For chicken or turkey, a spicy rub is good, as is a non-spicy garlic powder, dry herb (thyme, oregano, and rosemary mix), salt, and pepper rub. Do not ever use a basting or marinating sauce!

Smoking in a smoker with an offset firebox requires real wood logs. If you are using a smoker with an offset firebox, you would use aged pecan, hickory, oak, or similar hardwood (but not mesquite, which burns too fast, and never any evergreen wood such as pine or cedar, which are too resinous). If you are using a new smoker, you should season, as with a cast-iron pot, by rubbing the interior with vegetable oil, then burning logs to create smoke for a number of hours prior to cooking any food. Your smoker should have a drip hole for fat and a hook to hang a can to catch the fat, which you can discard after the cooking is complete.

If you are using such an offset cooker for the first time, you should be aware that it is an art to maintain the temperature-cooking range so that the temperature is no higher than the 250–275°F range (and better in the 225–250°F range). Using logs such as described produces a thick smoke. Most pit masters have concluded, and I agree, that after 3 to 4 hours, the brisket should be removed from the smoker or covered tightly in foil to avoid too heavy of a smoke flavor. At that time it should be immediately placed in a roasting pan with a rack, tightly covered with foil, and placed on an oven rack with very little water—not enough to touch the meat—in a 250°F oven for another several hours. Fat will continue to render during this process, and at the end of that time, the meat should be moist and tender. You can separate the liquid from the fat and use the liquid in the sauce to add more smoky flavor if you desire. This also allows you to use the smoker for meats with a shorter cooking time such as prime rib, turkey, or chicken while you wait for the brisket to finish cooking. The smoke-box temperature should continue to be no more than 250°F.

The brisket that should be smoked in this process is the packer trim whole brisket (both the point and flat cut), lightly trimmed of excess fat; do not separate the cuts until after cooking. Packer trim with just the flat cut is sold from time to time, but this is not what you want for smoking. Final trimming should not occur until after the meat is fully smoked and cooked and ready to serve. During the smoking process in the offset smoker, I always place a pan of hot water just above the connection between the firebox and the smoker itself. This assists in maintaining a moist food product.

A bullet-shaped vertical smoker that uses a combination of charcoal and soaked wood cubes to produce smoke also works. One brand is the Mr. Meat Smoker. I think that after 4 to 6 hours in such a bullet smoker, the heat is too low except on a very hot (100°F) day, and the meat should be removed to a 250°F oven as described above. In such a case, total cooking time would be at least 9 to 10 hours. I have never used a Big Green Egg, but I understand that decent smoked meat can be produced in one. There are other types of equipment that I have never used, including electric smokers that create smoke using compressed sawdust.

If you cook meats other than brisket, such as prime rib, chicken, turkey, or beef short rib, you should invariably use a thermometer stuck into the meat (with the reader outside of the smokebox) so that when the meat reaches the desired temperature (120°F for prime rib or lamb, 160°F for chicken or turkey breast), the meat can be removed to be rested, then served and eaten. For fowl, before removing from the smoker, make sure that the juices from the joints when pricked run clear. You do *not* want to eat undercooked fowl. For meats other than brisket, the time in the smokebox will not be such as to produce an excessively smoked product.

To smoke turkey, you may remove the leg quarter and debone the breast. The breast halves should be seasoned and tied small end to large end to produce an evenly smoked breast loaf. If you smoke the carcass, it can be used to make a wonderful smoked turkey stock (see recipe under Roasted Turkey in Chapter 11). To smoke the whole bird, first remove the wishbone for easier carving. Apply rub to the bird and allow it to rest uncovered in the refrigerator overnight. Smoke with the neck, gizzard, and heart inside the cavity. These giblets, along with the carcass when carved, plus carrots, onion, celery, garlic, bay leaf, peppercorns, thyme, and water to cover, will make a wonderful smoked turkey stock.

If you smoke beef short ribs, after 2 to 3 hours, remove the beef from the smoker, and use the same kitchen-oven process as for the brisket in a 250°F oven. I know some boil the meat first and just smoke to add flavor; that does not produce the best result. I have tried to smoke raw beef sausages in an offset smoker, but the results I achieved are not satisfactory. Perhaps you can be more successful.

Any meat should be rested for 10 to 30 minutes after it is removed from any cooking oven or roasting process to allow the juices to redistribute themselves. If the meat is not rested, the juices will just drain out when the meat is carved, resulting in dry meat. This is just as true for a brisket, even though the roasting temperature is low.

Texas barbecue is not made using a sauce before or during cooking, but certainly you can serve it with a good barbecue sauce on the side. See my Barbecue Sauce recipe in Chapter 2. I use barbecue sauce when I make a sandwich with the meat, but rarely otherwise. It is a matter of taste.

Potato Salad (Chapter 8) and Coleslaw (Chapter 8) are traditional side dishes.

When I was starting to draft this recipe, a dish my mother made when I was young and that I have made many times, I looked on the internet to see if there were any other recipes for stuffed veal breast, and I was surprised that there are many—primarily Italian, although other cuisines apparently include stuffed veal breasts. Many of the recipes were for boneless veal breasts, and none called for the whole breast, which is the recipe that is in this book. The bones add great flavor. I was surprised to see the number of recipes because I do not recall seeing a recipe for stuffed veal breast, or any veal breast, in any of the cookbooks that I own, and I have never seen it on a restaurant menu. I have talked to many friends and relatives who remember their mothers or grandmothers making this dish but have not eaten it for many years. Properly cooked, this is a festive meat fit for any holiday table.

INGREDIENTS

A whole veal breast will serve 10 people generously.

```
1 whole bone-in veal breast
2 onions
2-3 celery stalks, divided use
12 (or more) carrots
2-3 teaspoons dried thyme, split use
several cloves garlic, peeled
2-3 bay leaves
1 bottle dry white wine
2 quarts low-sodium chicken broth, divided use
salt
pepper
```

Stuffing

```
2 (14-ounce) packages of stuffing mix
1 quart chicken broth (boxed chicken broth works well)
1-2 large onions, chopped
2-3 cloves garlic, chopped
2-3 celery stalks, chopped
2-3 tablespoons olive oil
```

Veal breast can be a difficult cut of meat to find, but you can find a purveyor if you persist. In Dallas, Central Market has carried veal breast and will order it upon request. You may have to order it as much as a month in advance. You should have that relationship with your butcher, although you may be unlikely to find a willingness at most mass merchants and regular grocery stores to special order meat. You may have to go to a specialty butcher or an ethnic market such as a German or Russian market that sells specialty meats, and a kosher butcher should be able to order it. I assure you that veal breast is a cut of meat that, when properly cooked, is worth whatever the effort or cost.

Veal breast is the same cut of meat as bacon from a pig or brisket from a cow, so this recipe is essentially a long, slow braise. Based upon the recipes available on the internet (and based on my own market search in Dallas), it is sometimes available boned, but I do not buy it this way. I buy the full primal cut with all of the bones. Frequently, when I buy the veal breast, it is frozen. You should buy it in advance of when you intend to use it, and then thaw it gently in the refrigerator for 3 days. As with any other meat, a slow refrigerator thaw produces less damage to the meat's cell walls.

Preparing the Veal Pocket

After the veal has thawed in the refrigerator, remove it from the plastic in which it is sealed. The last 3 or 4 bones of the breast (the small end) do not work for a pocket, and the whole breast will probably not fit your oven. Before starting to cut the pocket, just cut off that small end so that the larger end fits your roasting pan. Reserve the small cut end.

You will then need to create the pocket. Carefully, using a boning knife or short chef's knife, insert the blade between the bones and the meat, cutting gently against the bones to make a pocket the full depth of the bones. Take your time (maybe 10 minutes), and this will not be a difficult process. Take care not to ruin the integrity of the pocket by making extra holes in the sides or back of the pocket.

When making the pocket for the veal, carefully remove any excess fat that you run into inside the pocket and any excess fat around the exterior of the veal breast. As with a brisket, since it is the same cut, the veal breast has a certain amount of fat in it, much of which renders as it cooks and can be removed before service.

A whole veal breast will weigh around 12 to 15 pounds and will be around 27 inches long. It simply does not fit into a normal roasting pan unless you cut off the 3 or 4 ribs at the small end that will not be stuffed. That is okay, because when you prepare the stuffing, you will prepare more than enough stuffing to go into the pocket that you make, and the remainder of the stuffing is put into a baking dish and cooked separately as a side dish.

Preparing the Stuffing

The stuffing is exactly the same stuffing that I make for turkey except there are no giblets. See the Roasted Turkey recipe earlier in Chapter 11 for instructions. Because the veal breast has fat that will render, I do not add any more oil than the tablespoon or so necessary to cook the onion, garlic, and celery.

Salt and pepper the inside of the veal breast. Then place the stuffing into the pocket you have made. Do not overstuff the veal. The stuffing will expand and will protrude somewhat during cooking. I once made this dish for Passover using a matzo meal stuffing, and it was okay, but I am not a huge matzo meal fan. You can substitute your favorite stuffing.

Roasting

Peel a couple onions, several cloves of garlic, a couple celery stalks, and at least a dozen carrots. Lay these vegetables in the bottom of your roasting pan. Lay the stuffed veal breast on top of this bed of vegetables. Add 2 or 3 bay leaves and 1 to 2 teaspoons of the thyme to the pan. Put the portion of the veal breast that was cut off and does not have stuffing underneath the smaller end of the stuffed veal breast. Add a bottle of dry white wine and about a quart of chicken stock, but do not completely cover the meat. Salt and pepper the surface of the veal breast and rub in the remaining teaspoon of dried thyme. Cover tightly with foil. Heat briefly on the stove top to jump-start the cooking and move to the oven when hot. Roast in a 350°F oven until the veal breast is very tender. This will take about 3 to 4 hours. For the last ½ hour, uncover the pan, and increase the oven to 400°F to brown and crisp the top.

Remove the pan from the oven and allow the meat to rest. After the veal is cooked and the meat and vegetables are removed from the roasting pan, remove the sauce to a defatting container. Allow the sauce to settle, pour out and retain the liquid, and leave behind the fat to dispose of. I do not thicken this sauce, although you could, if desired, thicken it with cornstarch slurry (or, at Passover, with potato starch) so that it is slightly viscous.

After the veal is cooked, it will be very tender, and the connective tissue at the end of the bone that was closest to the spine of the animal will be softened and delectable. The veal should be sliced between the bones into serving portions. Your guests may not want a whole bone and all of the meat and stuffing attached, so you can cut it into portion sizes as desired. Leftovers are delicious.

You do not need any additional spices beyond the indicated herbs and that which the stuffing will supply because this is a very mild and delicious meat with a flavor that you do not want to overpower.

"OVEN" STEAK

Following is a wonderful recipe for steak cooked in the oven that is almost as good as steak cooked on a grill. I reserve it for times when the grill is not available or when I do not wish to stand in the cold as a martyr for the steak. I rub the steak with olive oil, salt, pepper, and garlic powder. While I use the loin (a cut that is generally not kosher in the US), this technique works perfectly with a rib eye steak. While it may seem problematic that the cited temperatures leave the steak medium rare, that is not the case. My rabbi explained that once the meat is koshered, if you prepare the steak (or other meat) to medium rare, the meat is still kosher to eat since sufficient blood has been removed before cooking commenced.

I use steak that is at least 2 inches thick, and boneless steaks are best for this process. Preheat the oven to 275°F. Prepare a pan with a grill rack or grate over it. Lay the grill rack over the pan so the steak is off the bottom of the pan. Place the steak on that assembly. Insert an oven-safe temperature probe into the side of the steak and set the probe to 95°F (for medium rare). Cook the steak in the preheated oven until the temperature gauge buzzes. Immediately remove the steak from the oven and take out the temperature probe.

On a heavy-duty pan—and cast iron is perfect here—heated at high heat, place a tablespoon of peanut oil (because it has a high smoke point) or other vegetable oil. Olive oil has too low a smoke point and would burn. Place the steak on the pan, and cook while standing at the stove, turning the steak until each side and edge is caramelized. This takes very few minutes. Remove the steak, and let it rest, lightly covered with some aluminum foil, for 10 minutes. The steak should be cooked to a perfect medium rare throughout.

This process seems counterintuitive, but the resulting steak will be a juicy deep pink edge to edge, surface to surface, with no overcooked gray meat. Serve with Pan-Roasted Potatoes

(Chapter 14) and caramelized mushrooms and onions for a great steakhouse meal at home for a fraction of the cost.

TASHREEB (IRAQI-STYLE LAMB, CHICKEN, OR GOAT STEW)

Tashreeb is an Iraqi stew, and this is merely a variant, inasmuch as the original stew calls for lamb tripe and feet, ingredients not generally palatable to Americans—including me. I make this delicious dish with either goat (cabrito), boned lamb shoulder, or occasionally chicken. The goat (or cabrito) can be obtained either in a halal meat store or a Mexican grocery and is certainly available kosher online. I prefer for this purpose to use the shank of the goat, having the butcher cut the meatiest portion of the shank so that there is a lot of meat in proportion to the bone.

The process is like most stews; it is the spicing and the additives that make this dish unique and delicious. This is excellent if you also vary from the original by adding dried fruit—either raisins or apricots or both. Serve with basmati rice, which is a wonderful foil for the flavorful sauce this dish makes.

INGREDIENTS

5-7 pounds of meat (goat, lamb, or chicken)

¼ cup oil as needed for browning (ghee is also traditional, but since ghee is a milk product, I use olive oil)

1 head of garlic, peeled (the original recipe called for unpeeled garlic, but that makes it hard to eat)

1-2 large onions, finally chopped

chicken stock as needed to cover the meat, perhaps a quart

2 dried limes (*noomi basra* or *limoo amani*) or the thickly peeled rind or zest of a lemon or lime

several tomatoes, chopped and peeled, or 1 (28-ounce) can whole tomatoes, packed in juice, not sauce (Muir Glen or San Marzano work well)

1-2 tablespoons Baharat (Chapter 2)

1-2 (16-ounce) cans chickpeas, drained and rinsed (alternatively, you could rinse and soak raw chickpeas overnight before proceeding, but plain, canned beans are generally excellent)

freshly ground black pepper

salt to taste

raisins or apricots

Clean the meat, cut it into large pieces, remove excess fat, and brown the meat well in a heavy saucepan. Chicken should be separated into legs, thighs, etc. Lamb or goat should be in 2-inch chunks. The traditional recipe does not call for browning, but I find that the flavor is worth the effort. Remove the meat after it is well browned, drain any excess fat, and add the onions and garlic to the empty pan. Add a tablespoon of fresh oil as needed, and sauté the onions and garlic over low heat, stirring until transparent.

Deglaze with some chicken stock. Then add the tomatoes, the dried limes (or zest of ½ a lemon), the baharat spice mixture, the pieces of meat and juices that have collected, the chickpeas, and sufficient chicken broth to cover. Add salt, but not so much that it becomes too salty; you can always add salt later. As the stew cooks, skim to remove excess fat. Adjust seasoning as necessary, adding more lime (or lemon zest) to your taste. As with most stews, this stew will improve by sitting in the refrigerator. About 10 minutes before serving, add a liberal quantity of raisins or apricots. Cook for 5 to 10 minutes with the fruit so that the fruit will plump up.

Serve with rice or bread for the juices.

Note: Noomi basra are limes processed in a salt brine and then dried in the sun over several weeks. Dried limes originated in Oman and are common flavor additions in the countries along the Persian Gulf. They are generally cooked and served whole or used powdered as a flavoring—like a spice. In the United States, you should be able to find these flavor bombs in Middle Eastern markets. If you do not have access to these dried limes, use, as an alternative, lemon or lime peel. While the result will be different; it is nevertheless delicious. These noomi basra are different from salt-processed (preserved) lemons used in Moroccan food such as tagines.

JAMBALAYA

Jambalaya is a quintessential Cajun dish, core to that cuisine. This version is a favorite in our house but does not contain any pork products and thus is not "authentic" and, I suppose, should be properly referred to as jambalaya in the Jewish style. Classically, jambalaya is made with ham and other pork products, and even the name implies use of ham. It may include seafood such as clams, crab, shrimp, etc. None of these products are kosher, so this version is made solely with chicken and nonpork smoked sausages. Nevertheless, despite the fact that this is not "authentic," this recipe is delicious and approaches the flavor profile of a standard jambalaya. A classic jambalaya can be quite spicy and included is an option to add that heat. You can cook this dish to the point before you add rice, and freeze it for future use, or you can make a double (or more) recipe, and freeze the extra, adding rice only after defrosting for final cooking and service.

INGREDIENTS

```
5 pounds chicken thighs
olive oil to brown chicken
4 pounds various smoked beef sausages
3 large green bell peppers
2 large sweet onions
4 celery stalks
4-6 large cloves garlic
2 cups dry white wine
2 or more tablespoons Cajun Spice Mixture (Chapter 2)
2-3 bay leaves, fresh or dried
cayenne or Tabasco, to taste (optional)
1 (28-ounce) can whole tomatoes packed in juice
3-4 cups chicken stock or smoked turkey stock
2 teaspoons salt
pepper to taste
2 cups long-grain rice (aromatic such as basmati or nonaromatic
such as Carolina Gold)
½ teaspoon liquid smoke (optional if sausages are not smoked)
```

Clean the chicken thighs, and brown them thoroughly in a 6-quart dutch oven, starting with some olive oil. Remove the chicken to a bowl and drain the rendered fat.

Well-smoked sausages made with beef are used instead of pork products. Slice these sausages into coins and sauté them in the drained dutch oven used to brown the chicken until they are lightly brown and have rendered their fat. Remove the sausages to a separate bowl, and leave some rendered fat to sauté the vegetables—remove some fat if there is too much.

Critical to Cajun cooking and to jambalaya is the "trinity" of vegetables; that is, celery, onion, and bell pepper. Unlike a French mirepoix or the Italian equivalent, *sofrito*, this classic Cajun vegetable mixture does not include carrot.

Add the bell peppers, onions, and celery to the pan, using some of the rendered fat from the sausages for flavor. If you are not constantly watching and stirring, you need to lower the heat; the goal here is sweating and wilting—not browning. Stir until the vegetables have wilted significantly, and then add the garlic. Continue until you can smell the garlic, perhaps 30 seconds, and deglaze with 2 cups of dry white wine. Reduce to about 1 cup, scraping the fond.

Put the chicken and sausage back into the pan. Add 2 or more tablespoons to taste of Cajun spice mixture and 2 to 3 bay leaves (fresh or dried). If you want heat—and this is a traditionally spicy dish—add optional cayenne and/or Tabasco to taste. Add the tomatoes and juice, breaking up the tomatoes. Add chicken stock or smoked turkey stock to barely cover. Simmer for 15 minutes to barely cook the chicken. Take the chicken out of the pot to cool. Shred the meat and discard the skin. Place the bones and the chicken back into the pot. Season with salt to taste, recognizing that you will be adding 2 cups of rice. Each cup of rice requires 1 teaspoon of kosher salt in addition to salt necessary to flavor the chicken. Add 2 cups of rice and cook until the rice is fully cooked. Remove the bones before serving.

TEXAS CHILI (A.K.A "BOWL OF RED")

Chili (also known as a "bowl of red") is an iconic dish in the state of Texas, and chili contests abound. Texas chili is unique in a number of respects. For example, I have seen many recipes for vegetable, chicken, turkey, or other variations of chili. Some of these variations, for example, may use bell peppers as a part of the recipe; Texas chili uses chipotle, ancho, guajillo, and New Mexico chiles, among others, not all of which distinguish themselves by their heat (or intensity of capsaicin). A bell pepper's flavor is different, and bell peppers clearly are not used in real Texas chili. Further, Texas chili is classically made with beef, not pork, and generally not other meats, although I have seen recipes using venison. Classically, beans are not used in Texas chili; indeed, some regard their use as heresy. Nevertheless, I do use beans, which I mash. You may, of course, omit them.

Texas chili is very different from New Mexico green chili, which is made with roasted fresh green chiles—a proper dish in its own right with a very different flavor profile. It is not an imposter but is also not a "bowl of red."

Frequently the word *chili* is differentiated from the word *chile*. The word spelled with *i* at its end references the sauce or the cooked dish and is an Americanized version of the word from Spanish, while *chile* spelled with an *e* at the end references the fruit. I understand that the Americanized version with an *i* is derived from a dish *carne con chili* or *chili con carne*, meaning "meat with chile." It was ultimately shortened to just the word *chili* with an *i*. I follow the noted convention.

There are many chile varieties that include green chiles such as bell peppers (totally sweet with no heat), jalapeños (of which the chipotle is the smoked, dried version), poblanos (of which the ancho is the dried version), serranos, and, going up the scale of spiciness, the habanero and similar ultrahot chiles as well as small but intense chiles such as the Thai bird's eye chile. Many green chiles, if left on the plant long enough, will eventually ripen to a red color and are delicious in both stages. Occasionally, for example, in the fall you will find red jalapeños that are spicy but somewhat sweeter and less grassy in flavor than the green. Spiciness can vary tremendously even within a variety; a chile plant that is stressed by high temperatures and dry soil will contain more of the chemical capsaicin, which causes the chile to taste spicy. Thus, chiles grown in northern United States are likely to be less spicy than their Texas-grown relative, even though they are the same variety. Chile varieties each have their own different flavor profiles (other than spiciness levels), and so several varieties are used to add complexity to the flavor in a pot of chili. Mostly dried chiles are used to prepare Texas chili. Many writers freely suggest substitutions of one type of chile for another; for example, jalapeños and serranos are frequently suggested as substitutes for one another. However, the flavor profiles of these chiles are very different (and I mean flavor, not heat). I like the jalapeño's flavor but not the serrano's. Poblanos and bell peppers are another such erroneous pairing; both are mild to sweet, and both are frequently stuffed, but they have very different flavor profiles. Such flavor differences are the rule, not the exception. If you want to experiment but do not appreciate the heat, simply use only the flesh of the chile, and carefully remove and discard the seeds and ribs inside the chile, and this will excise much of the heat.

With that introduction, this recipe is for my version of the Texas "Bowl of Red" or chili.

INGREDIENTS

This recipe is intended for a 6-quart pot.

3 pounds coarse-ground beef (Not fine-ground as for hamburgers. Use ground chuck with 15–20 percent fat. Note that some use chunks of meat—preferably from chuck roast or shoulder as for any stew—rather than ground meat, and this is perfectly acceptable.)

2 large sweet or yellow onions, finely diced

4 large cloves garlic, finely diced

2 tablespoons chili powder mix, or to taste (Penzeys's regular chili powder is not kosher, but McCormick's chili powder is)

1 tablespoon ancho chile powder (ancho chiles are only moderately spicy and have a raisiny flavor)

1–2 teaspoons chipotle chile powder or 1–2 whole dried chipotles or 1–2 whole chipotle chiles in adobo sauce, depending on the heat you want

3 tablespoons tomato paste (Tomato paste is sold in tubes or in cans. The tubes can be easily resealed for storage in the refrigerator if you do not use the whole tube. Apparently, Italians use lists to denote kosher rather than the American practice of the symbols [hechshers].)

1–2 tablespoons ground cumin (preferably freshly ground from whole, lightly toasted seeds)

1–2 guajillo chiles, stem end removed, seeds shaken out, lightly toasted on a griddle for 1–2 minutes, and cut into small pieces

2 tablespoons oregano

1 tablespoon thyme

2–3 bay leaves

salt and pepper to taste

2 (14-ounce) cans of plain beans with no flavorings (optional—kidney beans or black beans)

2 (28-ounce) cans whole tomatoes, packed in juice, not sauce. It is certainly acceptable to use roasted, peeled, whole fresh tomatoes. Plum tomatoes are preferable because they are meatier and have more tomato pulp and less liquid. You should find a brand that you like and use that consistently. Do not use stewed tomatoes or tomato puree for this purpose. Tomato paste, on the other hand, is an excellent additive to be sautéed just after the garlic and onions; cook it slightly to add flavor and texture to the sauce before adding liquid.

In a 6-quart pot, first sauté the ground beef (or chunks of beef, if that is your option) in olive oil until it is thoroughly browned. Remove the beef from the pot. If there is excessive rendered fat, remove all that is not needed to sauté the vegetables. Add the diced onions and sauté them until sweated but not browned. Add the garlic and cook until the garlic aroma becomes apparent (about 30 seconds). Add the chile powders and cook lightly to bloom the flavors. Add the tomato paste, and sauté lightly with the chile powders and cumin. Add the rest of the spices and herbs.

If you are using beans, drain and rinse the beans; then mash the beans lightly. Add the beans to the pot. (Mashing the beans will thicken the chili slightly.) Add the tomatoes along with the juice, crushing the tomatoes as you add them. Then add the beef back into the pot. Add the bay leaves. Simmer on very low heat for at least 1 hour, stirring occasionally to avoid sticking and burning the chili. If you are using chunks of beef, cook until tender. Of course, cooking in the oven is an option. Like many stews, this is better after resting in the refrigerator overnight.

Chili is excellent served plain, with or without garnish, or over rice or polenta. The polenta's corn flavor works particularly well with chili. Common garnishes include grated cheese (but not if you keep kosher) and finely diced sweet onions (such as Vidalia or Texas 1015). Some add Fritos for a "Frito pie." Chili is frequently served with beer. I particularly like amber Mexican beers such as Dos Equis or Modelo Negra. This is great any time, but especially on a cold winter evening.

LOW-COUNTRY BOIL—KOSHER STYLE

Low-country boil is a dish that originated in the Low Country. The Low Country originally referred to the coastal counties north of Savannah, Georgia, through South Carolina. A variant of this method of cooking seafood is found in many coastal areas, from New England through Louisiana, in the United States. Other names for the preparation include *frogmore stew* or *beaufort stew*, references to the locale origins in South Carolina. As noted, Louisiana has its famous and similar crawfish boil. These recipes are frequently based on boiling (or, for example, in the case of Maryland crabs, steaming) of various seafoods and vegetables, spiced with a spicy mixture. In any event, a low-country boil classically consists of potatoes, corn, sausage, and unpeeled shrimp (and sometimes crab). For these purposes, shrimp, crab, or crawfish are not used since these foods are not kosher. In our house we make low-country boil solely with the potatoes, corn, and smoked beef sausages; even without the seafood, it is delicious. I use several pounds of sausage and potatoes—leftovers are good, and the potatoes are excellent sliced and sautéed in olive oil for breakfast. The sausage can—and should—be used as the filling for omelets.

INGREDIENTS

The ingredient amounts are flexible depending on the number of people to be served.

```
1-2 onions
several cloves garlic
several stalks celery
½ cup or so Old Bay Seasoning
1 tablespoon black peppercorns
water
smoked beef sausages or kosher sausages of your choice
boiling potatoes (Yukon Gold, red bliss, etc.)
corn on the cob
dijon mustard (optional as a condiment)
```

First, the sausages should be cut into coins and sautéed in a heavy-bottom pot before adding any cooking liquid. The fat should be rendered, and the sausage caramelized. Then the sausage is removed from the pot and reserved. Roughly chop the onions and celery; then sauté them briefly with the halved garlic cloves in the rendered fat to sweat the vegetables.

To complete the cooking liquid, add water merely sufficient to cover and cook the potatoes and corn (to be added later). Add Old Bay Seasoning. It is not necessary to add salt. A tablespoon of black peppercorns can also be added to the liquid. Simmer the liquid and vegetables until the flavors are infused—about 15 to 20 minutes.

After the flavors have had time to infuse, add the cleaned, halved or quartered potatoes. Cook for about 20 minutes before anything else is added. The potatoes should be either boiling potatoes (red or white) or Yukon Gold potatoes. Idaho or baking-type potatoes are too starchy and do not work for this recipe.

When the potatoes are almost done, which can be determined by testing with a fork or sharp knife, the corn should be added. Fresh corn in season is best. The corn will need to cook for perhaps 5 minutes. Then the sausages can be added to merely reheat. (The sausages will become dry and unappetizing if left to cook in the water with the potatoes and corn.) At that time, all of the contents of the pot can be drained and placed on a serving dish for service.

A low-country boil is best served with mustard, and I prefer dijon mustard for this purpose—of course, use the mustard of your own choice. Beer of your choice is excellent with this casual meal.

If there are leftovers, and I like to make enough to ensure that there will be, slip the excess back into the cooled liquid and refrigerate. The next day, remove and discard any congealed fat before reheating. The leftovers chopped into bite-sized pieces, heated in olive oil, and cooked with whisked eggs are like the Grill Cleaner's Special served at the Breakfast Club on Tybee Island, Georgia, and make a great breakfast.

JEWISH-STYLE "SUNDAY GRAVY"

Italian food is one of the favorite cuisines here in the United States, and this is in part due, at least initially, to two major factors: (1) the large Italian immigrant population that brought Italian family recipes and Americanized those recipes when they came to the United States to live and (2) the effect of Italy on our troops who fought there in World War II.

There are many recipes for spaghetti sauces based upon tomatoes. There is the very simple vegetarian marinara tomato-based sauce that does not have meat in it, and there is a bolognese sauce classically made with meat, relatively little tomato, and added milk product, although American bolognese frequently has a significant tomato component. Then there is the luxury Italian-American construct of Sunday gravy, a tomato sauce that includes various meats, both for use in the sauce and as a second course, created by these Italian-American immigrants who greatly added to the amalgam that is America, as did other immigrant groups. Of course, Sunday gravy in Italian homes includes meat that is most often pork products cooked in the sauce and is always served with grated parmesan or a *grana padano* cheese—clearly not kosher. These meats can include pork shoulder, pork sausages, and beef rolls stuffed with ground pork or beef (braciola). The addition of the various meats enriches the sauce, and these treats are then reserved for service as a second course after the pasta.

Of course, the addition of either pork products or mixing any milk products with any meat is absolutely forbidden under the laws of the kashruth, but as with many dishes, adjustments can be made to avoid the conflict, and the result is just delicious. For example, beef italian sausage (sweet or hot) and beef short ribs or chuck or shoulder can be used in the same manner, producing a Jewish-style Sunday gravy. You can even make braciola with veal scaloppine stuffed with seasoned ground beef (or beef sausage or other non-trayf stuffing). If you cannot find beef italian sausage, there are recipes available; it is an assembly of ground meat with seasoning mixed in, a process that is absolutely not challenging, made better by an overnight rest in the refrigerator.

The only issue is how large a pot you wish to make. This sauce cooks for a long time but requires little effort or attention as it becomes very rich and delicious. It only makes sense to me to make a large pot, portions of which can be frozen for very easy future meals, and that is what I do. Thus, I use a twelve-quart pot to make the sauce. The sauce freezes beautifully and, when thawed, cannot be distinguished from freshly made sauce.

If you are using short ribs, buy ribs that are not overly fatty, and if your store will not oblige, find another butcher. A number of years ago, I wanted to use beef short ribs. The butchers at the national brand store had closed at five o'clock, and all that was out were a couple packages of very fatty meat. I went to Central Market, where the butcher section is fully manned until the store closes, and they cut exactly what I wanted—beautiful nonfatty ribs—and the price was fifty cents less per pound than the national brand store. (Even national brand stores in the same geographic area differ; in early 2017 my wife went to one store to get chuck ground to specification, and the butcher and store manager both refused to custom grind the beef. She went to a different store, same national brand, about four miles away from the first store on the same day, where the butcher was happy to comply with her request as they had for me many times. It is important to find a butcher with whom you can work.)

INGREDIENTS

3 pounds ground beef chuck (referred to in Texas as chili or rough grind, not the fine grind used for hamburgers or meatloaf, but the terminology can vary depending on where you live)

4 pounds or so beef short ribs, beef chuck, or beef shoulder

olive oil as needed

3 carrots, peeled and grated or diced very finely (brunoise)

2-3 large onions, finely diced

3 tablespoons or so tomato paste

6 cloves garlic, chopped

1 bottle drinkable dry red wine

salt and pepper to taste

4-6 tablespoons dried oregano (I like oregano—add less if you desire)

1½ tablespoons dried thyme

1 tablespoon dried rosemary, crumpled as you add, or a small sprig of fresh

2-3 bay leaves

1 tablespoon fennel seeds

4 (28-ounce) cans whole peeled tomatoes, canned in juice, not sauce

1 pound or more (depending on how many guests you have) hot or sweet beef italian sausage

pasta or polenta (Optional for service. 1 quart of shaped, uncooked pasta serves 3 generously, while 1 cup of uncooked polenta serves 2.)

In a large pot, brown the ground beef well in olive oil as needed. Remove and reserve when well browned.

Remove excess fat from the chuck or shoulder as you cut it up (before browning) if you are using those parts of the cow. Add the beef short ribs, the chuck cut into 2-inch chunks, or the shoulder cut into 2-inch chunks, as desired, and brown well, taking care to not burn the fond, lowering the heat and adding oil as necessary. If you made braciola, brown those also. Remove and reserve the browned meat with the ground beef. Drain and dispose of the excess fat rendered in the browning.

Add fresh olive oil to the now empty pot as needed and add the finely chopped onion and carrot. Sweat but do not brown the vegetables. Scrape up the fond. As the vegetables become translucent (but not browned) and the water evaporates, add the tomato paste, and continue to cook for 30 seconds to 1 minute to partially cook the tomato paste, and then add the chopped garlic. When the garlic becomes fragrant, another 15 to 30 seconds, add the red wine, and deglaze. Allow the wine to reduce by about half. *Note*: Alcohol should be added before other liquids and allowed to reduce first because once those other liquids are added, the alcohol tends not to evaporate, a fact ignored by many writers. Details matter.

Add some salt and pepper, oregano, thyme, rosemary, bay leaves, and fennel seed. Add the meat back to the pot, reserving the braciola until about 1 hour before the first cooking is complete. The first cooking takes about 2 hours, so the braciola should be added about 1 hour in. Add the tomatoes, including the juices in the cans. Break up the tomatoes as you add them.

Bring the sauce to a bare simmer, and cook it covered for at least 2 hours, stirring occasionally and testing the meat for tenderness before removing from the heat. Make sure that the heat is not so high as to burn the sauce. This works very well in a 325°F oven. As the sauce cooks, skim the fat that rises to the surface, or you can wait until after refrigeration.

Add salt and pepper as needed. You will probably need at least 2 to 3 teaspoons of salt for this amount of meat and sauce. Add the salt, stir, and taste carefully; you can always add more salt, but you cannot take it out. Cook at a low simmer until the beef is tender. When the meat is tender, remove from the heat, cool, and then refrigerate at least overnight. Take off the congealed fat after refrigerating overnight.

When reheating the sauce for service, perhaps 10 minutes before the sauce is ready, brown the sausages in a sauté pan. Take a desired amount of the sauce and add it to the sautéed sausages.

If you are serving with pasta, boil pasta in very salted water (1½–2 tablespoons table salt to 4–5 quarts of water). Boil to an undercooked, very al dente stage. Add the very al dente pasta to the sauce and sausages and continue to cook the pasta in the sauce until it and the sausages are perfectly cooked. If necessary, add pasta water to loosen the sauce for more moisture. Adjust salt seasoning if needed just before serving. Serve the pasta with the meat and sausages or reserve the meat for a second course. If serving with polenta, serve on a platter over the cooked polenta.

An excellent accompaniment is french baguettes that have been cut in half and spread liberally with a garlic mash: fresh-peeled garlic cloves (½ bulb) mashed with salt and then stirred with olive oil after the garlic is well mashed. Bake the garlic bread in the oven until it is toasty and hot.

There are many excellent vegetables to serve with this meal, including snow peas or sugar snap peas, spinach, swiss chard, brussels sprouts, broccoli, green beans or the haricot vert variant sautéed with garlic, grilled eggplant, zucchini, or a head of cauliflower or cabbage roasted with olive oil, salt, and a bulb of whole peeled cloves of garlic. The list of simply prepared and delicious vegetables could go on. Bon appétit.

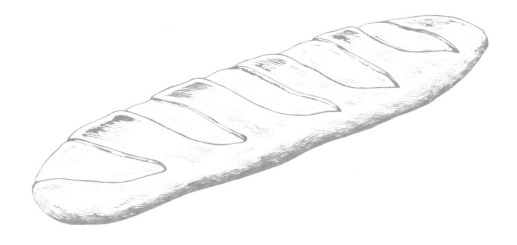

Quesadillas, p. 233

Chapter 12: *Non-Jewish Vegetarian (Nonmeat)*

KEN'S BLUE-RIBBON MUSHROOM-SPINACH LASAGNA

This recipe won the blue ribbon at the Texas State Fair in 2010. It is totally vegetarian and may be the best lasagna you will ever eat (and I am not a vegetarian). There are a number of steps—none of which are complicated—that can be completed over a couple of days or even weeks.

INGREDIENTS

Mushroom mixture

1 cup (2-3 ounces) dried mushrooms (porcini, trumpet, and/or chanterelle)

1½ cups boiling water

3-4 pounds fresh white, brown, or portobello mushrooms, finely chopped

4 tablespoons unsalted butter

5-6 shallots, chopped

4-5 cloves garlic, chopped

1 teaspoon dried thyme

1 teaspoon dried oregano

2 teaspoons salt

1 teaspoon pepper

about 1½ cups water for reconstituting mushrooms, reserved

½-1 cup dry marsala wine

2 cups heavy cream

Béchamel sauce

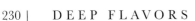

5 tablespoons butter

4 tablespoons all-purpose flour

4 cups (1 quart) whole milk

1-2 teaspoons salt, or to taste

½ teaspoon nutmeg, freshly grated

pepper to taste

For assembly

12-15 lasagna noodles, depending on the size of your pan and the pasta manufacturer

1 pound fresh ricotta

1 egg, slightly beaten

2-3 pounds fresh spinach (it tastes better than frozen)

3 tablespoons unsalted butter

3 cloves garlic, minced

¼ teaspoon nutmeg, freshly grated

2-3 cups mozzarella, shredded (whole milk, packaged, not fresh)

1-2 cups parmigiano-reggiano, grated, or comparable kosher hard cheese

Preheat oven to 350°F.

Make the Mushroom Mixture

Reconstitute the dried mushrooms in 1½ cups boiling water for about 15 minutes. Do not use an Asian mushroom such as shiitake, which has a wrong flavor here. Drain and reserve mushroom stock (lift out mushrooms to drain, leaving the sand in the liquid mushroom stock).

Chop and sauté reconstituted mushrooms and fresh mushrooms in butter until the exuded liquid evaporates and the mushrooms are caramelized. Add shallots and garlic to make a duxelles, cooking until softened. Then add thyme, oregano, salt, and pepper. Add marsala wine and reduce until almost dry. Then add mushroom-reconstituting stock (discarding sand and dregs), and cook to reduce, again until almost dry. The order is important since the alcohol will not evaporate if you add the water too early. Add heavy cream and reduce until you achieve a moist—but not runny—very thick sauce consistency. Correct salt to taste. You may cool and complete the recipe later. See the Mushroom Pie recipe later in Chapter 12 for an additional use of this mixture.

Make the Béchamel Sauce

In a medium saucepan, heat the butter over medium-low heat until melted. Add the flour and stir until smooth. Over medium heat, cook until the mixture turns a light, golden, sandy color, no more than 3 to 4 minutes—this is not a Cajun dish.

Meanwhile, heat the milk in a separate pan until just about to boil. Add the hot milk to the butter mixture 1 cup at a time, whisking continuously until very smooth. Bring to a boil. Then lower heat, and cook for a few minutes, stirring constantly until thickened. Then remove from heat. Season with salt, nutmeg, and pepper, and set aside until ready to use.

Assemble the Lasagna

Soak lasagna noodles in hot water for 15 minutes until barely al dente or as set forth on the package, checking before the full time has passed. If you are using fresh pasta, do not soak, but do make a more liquid béchamel sauce. If you feel compelled to cook the pasta, you should remember that it will cook again when the assembly is baked, so the pasta must be undercooked for assembly.

In a large bowl, combine ricotta cheese with a slightly beaten egg. Set aside.

Sauté the spinach in butter with the garlic and nutmeg. Alternatively, you could use another green, such as swiss chard. Add salt and pepper to taste. Chop lightly on a cutting board after the greens are sautéed, and cool. Use all the exuded liquid with the béchamel as additional liquid when assembling the lasagna.

Remove lasagna noodles from the water bath. Shake water off wet noodles. Coat a 9x13-inch (deep is better) baking dish with béchamel. Place a layer of undercooked lasagna noodles in the bottom of the baking dish. Then spread the noodles with half of the ricotta cheese mixture. Mix the parmesan with the mozzarella and spread ½ the mozzarella mixture over the ricotta layer. Spread ½ the spinach mixture over the cheeses, and ladle béchamel sauce over the spinach with some of the exuded liquid from cooking the spinach. Layer with more lasagna and add a layer of the mushroom mixture. Repeat layers until all ingredients are used.

Change the direction of the noodles in alternating layers to help the cooked and sliced lasagna hold its shape. Sprinkle the very top layer with parmesan and mozzarella. Cover with foil—to prevent sticking, either spray the foil with cooking spray, brush with olive oil or butter, or make sure the foil does not touch the cheese. Bake in a preheated oven for 25 minutes. Unless you want a real mess in your oven, you should place a pan on the rack under the lasagna to catch the inevitable overflow. Remove foil and bake an additional 25 minutes until bubbly. Cool for 15 minutes before serving.

Variation

Mix all ingredients (other than lasagna noodles) with a shaped pasta (fusilli, penne, macaroni, etc.) in a baking dish to produce a *pasta funghi e spinaci al forno* or oven-baked mushroom-spinach pasta.

MUSHROOM PIE

INGREDIENTS

```
1 batch of mushroom mixture from Ken's Blue-Ribbon Mushroom-
Spinach Lasagna (Chapter 12)
1 batch of Bobbie's Piecrust (Chapter 15, but see notes below first
for variation)
12-16 ounces gruyère cheese, grated
1 egg
milk
```

This mushroom pie is easy to make once you have the mushroom mixture for the filling and is one of the most delectable foods you will ever put in your mouth. The mushroom mixture should be chilled (or at room temperature) before you put it into the pie shell. The process is simple.

First make pie dough, preferably using a 50-50 mixture of unsalted butter and solid Crisco shortening. Bobbie's Piecrust is my wife's recipe (with the fat modified), which she never makes in a blender or food processor. See the recipe in Chapter 15. The result using a machine is simply not as flaky and delicious as when the fat is cut into the flour by hand.

Prebake the bottom portion of the shell. Then grate in a liberal quantity of gruyère cheese as a bottom layer. Needless to say, authentic swiss gruyère—of which there are a number, some aged longer than others—is preferable except as needed for a kosher result; I like all that I have eaten. Other easy-to-melt cheeses such as mozzarella are too mild. Cheddar has the wrong flavor. Although I have not tried it in this context, raclette might work, as might brie. Spread a sufficient quantity of the mushroom mixture in the shell over the gruyère layer, and cover with a top crust. Brush the crust with a milk-egg mixture to facilitate browning. Cut a couple of slits in the top crust to release steam.

Bake the pie at 350°F until it is nicely brown and heated through, about 30 to 40 minutes. You do not need to worry about whether the insides are cooked—merely whether they are hot so that the cheese is melted, as it will be when the crust is browned—since the filling is already in a cooked and ready-to-eat stage. Serve promptly.

QUESADILLAS

Quesadillas are the simple and delicious Mexican iteration of an ordinary cheese sandwich but are frequently much enhanced. Quesadillas are traditionally filled with cheese plus other optional ingredients. In our house, since we do not mix milk or cheese with meat, nor use trayf seafood such as shellfish, shrimp, etc., these quesadillas are all vegetarian.

The basic quesadilla is simple. Put cheese between 2 tortillas, and heat to melt the cheese in a cast-iron pan or other griddle. Better yet, spread a flour tortilla (or corn tortilla, if you desire) with a moderate amount of Refried Beans (Chapter 14). Then, layer on American cheese, using a real cheese and not Velveeta or some other faux cheese; a young cheddar, monterey jack, colby, or similar melting cheese is also delicious here. Add some chopped cilantro, if desired. Cover with another equally sized tortilla and cook.

Alternatively, you could fill the quesadilla with additional ingredients. Ideas include simply sautéed and caramelized onions, perhaps combined with caramelized mushrooms, or sautéed and caramelized onions and mushrooms combined with roasted and peeled poblano pepper strips. Additionally, you could flavor those vegetables with cumin, oregano, thyme, and/or one or more of various chile powders to taste (such as a mixed commercial version such as McCormick or pure ancho or chipotle powder, remembering that some chile powders, such as chipotle, are quite spicy, and while poblanos are not really hot, they are certainly not bell peppers). Or you could add Pickled Jalapeños (Chapter 7), particularly some pickled with carrots and onions. Care should be taken not to overfill the quesadilla, or it will not hold together.

A completely different and delicious "fusion" cuisine idea is to simply fill the flour tortillas with a good European melting cheese such as brie or gruyère cheese, with a slathering of pesto on the tortillas. Yum!

A quesadilla is best cooked on a cast-iron skillet, comal, or a nonstick sauté pan. Since the quesadilla is vegetarian, sometimes I will use a very small amount of butter as an alternative to a very small amount of olive oil to barely grease the pan—not so much that the quesadilla will be greasy. You can cook the quesadilla with no oil, being careful not to burn the quesadilla. Because it is thin (depending, of course, on your fillings), it will cook rapidly; it should be flipped once or twice to cook both sides and heat and melt the inside evenly.

Quarter the quesadilla for serving. Serve the Mexican-flavored quesadilla with sour cream, Guacamole (Chapter 5), Pickled Jalapeños (Chapter 7), pico de gallo, chopped cilantro, or other sides to your desire. The cheese-pesto quesadilla is complete as is.

QUESO FUNDIDO

Queso fundido is a dish classically made with chorizo (the uncooked Mexican variety and not Spanish chorizo) as an ingredient. Sometimes in restaurants it is flamed with tequila and called *queso flameado*.

Mexican chorizo is a spicy, fresh, not cured sausage, very different from Spanish chorizo. It is most often made with pork, but it is available made with beef and is available kosher over the internet. I use the beef version as part of an omelet filling (sautéed with some of this mixture but without the cheese), frequently adding tomato, which meshes well with eggs. The chorizo generally available tends to be very fatty, so it should be well sautéed and the oil drained before further use such as by adding other ingredients to the mixture.

Because we do not mix milk with meat, we make a vegetarian variant of *queso fundido* (which, translated, simply means "processed or melted cheese"). This recipe is simple to make and much more complex than the translation implies or than many of the published recipes with the name. It is delicious with deep flavor and is a wholesome meal, ideal for any vegetarian in your life. You can think of this as a sort of Mexican welsh rarebit.

The proportions are flexible to your taste. If desired—and you should—add an ounce or two of dried porcini or chanterelle mushrooms, but not shiitake. A couple of seeded, soaked, and diced guajillo and/or ancho chiles (lightly toasted on a dry skillet before soaking) also add great flavor but not too much heat. Poblanos are also generally not particularly spicy. This is a recipe that can easily be made in stages: roast and peel the poblanos on one day and refrigerate them. Then assemble and sauté all vegetables on day two and refrigerate them. Finally, assemble and heat with the cheese for service later in the week.

INGREDIENTS

The proportions are flexible to your taste. Before adding the cheese, the cooked ingredients will make more than 4 pounds of cooked vegetables. I generally reserve half for other uses, so the measurement of cheese will only cover half. If you choose to use the full batch of vegetables, double the amount of cheese. A half batch with cheese will easily make 12 well-filled soft tacos using 8- or 9-inch tortillas.

1-2 ounces dried porcini, chanterelle, or trumpet mushrooms (not shiitake)

1 cup water for reconstituting dried mushrooms—reserved after use

2 large onions, sliced or chopped

2-3 large leeks, with dark-green parts of leaves removed and reserved for future use (wash well and chop white and light-green portions)

2 pounds or so fresh mushrooms, sliced and caramelized in butter unless you intend to add beef chorizo rather than cheese

4-5 poblano chiles, peeled, seeded, roasted, and julienned

4 or so cloves garlic, minced

1-2 dried guajillo or ancho chiles, lightly toasted, seeded, reconstituted just like the mushrooms, and chopped finely

1 can of well-drained whole tomatoes (optional), canned in juice, not sauce (fire-roasted tomatoes are excellent here, and I find that Muir Glen's whole tomatoes are excellent)

½ cup or so cilantro, chopped

½-1 teaspoon cumin

½-1 teaspoon ancho chile powder

1 teaspoon or so commercial chile powder

1 teaspoon thyme

1 teaspoon oregano

½ teaspoon chipotle chile powder or chipotle chile canned in adobo (no more than 1, unless you really want more heat)

¼-½ cup good dark Mexican beer or heavy cream (optional), but no cream if you intend to add chorizo

½-1 cup cilantro, chopped

salt and pepper to taste

1 pound good melting cheese such as monterey jack, colby, longhorn, or similar cheese (see note above for important measurement information)

fresh corn or flour tortillas to make soft tacos

Chop and prep the listed ingredients. Soak the dried mushrooms in a cup of hot water until they are soft. Lift them out of the liquid carefully, leaving any sand and reserving the liquid. Let the reserved soaking liquid rest so that the dirt can settle to the bottom. Repeat the process to reconstitute the dried chiles.

Sauté the sliced or diced onion until it is lightly browned. Add and sweat the carefully cleaned leeks until they soften and wilt. Add fresh mushrooms that have previously been sautéed so that the juices have evaporated, and the mushrooms have acquired wonderful flavor. Chop and add the reconstituted dried mushrooms. Then add 4 to 5 (or so) roasted, skinned, and seeded fresh poblano chile peppers, 2 to 4 (or so) large, minced garlic cloves, and the reconstituted dried chiles. Add any reserved mushroom-soaking liquid but discard the dregs. Add the optional tomatoes. Reduce the liquid until it is thick like syrup.

Add cumin, ancho chile powder, and chili powder, all to your taste. If you use the Penzeys's regular chili powder, remember that it is much spicier than McCormicks, and add proportionally less, tasting for the hotness of the flavor. Ancho and guajillo chiles are relatively mild; if you also use chipotle chile powder, be judicious with the amount (start with no more than $1/2$ teaspoon), as it is very spicy.

Add thyme and oregano. I use regular dried Greek and not Mexican oregano (which is a member of the verbena family and not a member of the mint family, as Greek oregano is). Add salt and pepper to taste.

Add the optional dark Mexican beer (Dos Equis or Modelo Negra), other beer, or heavy cream, as you desire. Reduce the liquid to a saucy consistency. (Drink the balance of the bottle if you are using beer.) For this recipe, I separate half of the vegetable medley to freeze for future use. To the remaining balance, add 1 pound of grated or diced monterey jack, colby, or other good melting cheese, and stir until completely melted. After the cheese is melted, add chopped cilantro, and stir in.

Serve immediately with fresh flour or corn tortillas for soft tacos. You can just spoon the queso fundido into a tortilla, and fold and eat, or spread some avocado spritzed with lime juice or some Guacamole (Chapter 5) on the tortilla before filling. Serve with Pickled Jalapeños (Chapter 7) for those who want them.

Leftovers make a great filling or topping for omelets or even sunny-side up eggs. Just heat in the microwave and spoon either the heated vegetable mixture or the cheese-vegetable mixture on the cooked eggs. Great served with warm corn or flour tortillas, lightly buttered and salted. Or scramble with eggs and serve as filling for soft breakfast tacos.

GRILLED CHEESE SANDWICH

A grilled cheese sandwich is a very comforting and easy meal served with a salad or soup, but it needs to be made correctly. The bread must be a good-quality bread, and the cheese must be a delicious and good-quality cheese. Rye, pumpernickel, or sourdough bread or a quality whole wheat or white sandwich bread, preferably not one of those breads delivered prepackaged to the grocery store, works here. Commercial grocery-store white, whole wheat, or rye breads simply do not bring an independent character to the table and should be avoided. A quality American cheese, cheddar, longhorn, colby, monterey jack, gruyère, brie, raclette, or other delicious cheese that you like and that will melt is good for this purpose, depending on your taste or mood. A long-aged cheddar is difficult to melt and may not be the best choice for this purpose. A simple spread of dijon mustard on the inside of the sandwich adds an interesting flavor kick but is not necessary—or, if you are using brie, a spread of pesto mates perfectly with the cheese.

A wonderful variant is the addition of cream cheese. Spread it on one of the slices of bread, and liberally sprinkle it with lightly sautéed, minced jalapeño peppers (with or without seeds and ribs, depending on the heat level desired). In this case you would use an American, colby, monterey jack, longhorn, or mild cheddar cheese along with the cream cheese. This variant is also wonderful as a Quesadilla (Chapter 12), grilled on a cast-iron skillet.

The process is very simple: Preheat the oven to 350°F. Liberally butter the outside of 2 slices of bread. Layer the desired amount of cheese inside—but not overlapping the edges of the bread—ensuring that the butter is on the outside of the sandwich. In a hot cast-iron pan or nonstick oven-safe pan, cook over high heat on 1 buttered side of the sandwich. Press lightly. Flip the sandwich, being careful not to spill the cheese out of the bread. Immediately put the sandwich pan in the preheated oven. Cook for about 5 to 7 minutes or so until the cheese is thoroughly melted. This process using the oven may seem like overkill, but it enables the cheese to melt without burning the bread and results in both sides of the sandwich being nicely browned and crunchy; it produces a delicious sandwich.

Gravlax, p. 239

Chapter 13: *Fish*

Gravlax is a traditional Scandinavian "preserved" salmon that has a flavor profile and texture much like that of a traditional cold-smoked salmon such as lox or nova (although very different from hot-smoked salmon, which is essentially cooked as it smokes). Gravlax is a great main dish for Yom Kippur break-the-fast.

It is cooked by "curing" and not cold-smoking. The name implies that it is buried to cure as it was in ancient times, but now we have refrigerators, so the physical process is somewhat different than that which may have been the case in years gone by. A major difference from lox or cold-smoked salmon is that it is incredibly easy to make gravlax at home with a serious cost saving over the commercial variants.

No special equipment is needed: simply use glass or a nonreactive (preferably Pyroceram or similar) baking dish to hold the "pickling" or "curing" salmon, with plastic wrap and weights to help the salmon cure in the refrigerator. If you read Julia Child's and Jacques Pépin's cookbooks, they each make both the traditional gravlax described here and a quick gravlax; the quick gravlax has a very short cure period, using very thinly sliced salmon similar to ceviche.

Unlike these esteemed teachers and chefs, this recipe does not add alcohol to the process. This more traditional recipe takes three days and is for a half fillet of a whole-boned salmon (although you could use the whole salmon with both fillets or, if you are cooking for a smaller group, any part of the fillet). All bones, including pin bones, should be removed before curing, but leave the skin. The pin bones can be easily plucked out with needle-nose pliers, although today many stores sell the salmon fillet fully prepped. You should ask the fishmonger to remove the thinner tail end, which would cure more rapidly and become overcured, so that you purchase and pay for only the part of the salmon that is useable. As with all fish, you must start with the absolute freshest possible salmon fillet. Since fish stays freshest at thirty-two degrees Fahrenheit, I always ask the fishmonger to put any fish I buy into a larger bag with ice. If yours will not do this, find a better place to shop for fish. I start the cure as soon as possible after I get the fish home.

The curing mixture is very simple. It is useful to make large quantities (a quart or so at a time) so that you do not have to remix the curing mixture each time that you make gravlax; the mix will not spoil. Once the curing mixture is available, the time of active work involved in assembling the gravlax for the cure process is only perhaps fifteen minutes (until the time comes to actually carve the gravlax).

INGREDIENTS

1 cup sugar
2 cups salt
½ cup dill weed (For freshly chopped dill, use at least 1 cup.
If you add fresh dill to the mixture, it is perishable, and any
unused mixture should be frozen in a sealed container—Ball jars
work well.)
2 teaspoons black pepper, freshly ground

I have seen and read of (but not tasted) alternative herb-and-spice mixtures, each with a different flavor profile to go into the gravlax rub, including, for example, coriander seeds or fresh cilantro and other herbs or spices. There is no magic to the herb-and-spice mixture; it is simply a matter of taste, although dill is traditional. What is critical for a proper cure is the salt-sugar mixture: 2 parts salt to 1 part sugar.

Have available a Pyrex or Pyroceram baking dish into which the salmon will fit flat. Prepare a sheet of plastic wrap long enough to cover the bottom of the baking dish and to wrap over the top of the salmon fillet in 1 piece so that the salmon can be completely encased in plastic wrap.

To prepare the salmon, wash and thoroughly dry it. You will need 2 to 3 cups of the sugar, salt, and dill curing mixture for each full fillet preparation of gravlax. The amounts are approximate. Place a liberal quantity of the curing mixture on the bottom of the baking dish, into which the plastic wrap has already been placed. Lay the salmon on top of the curing mixture, skin side down. Then spread the top of the salmon with the curing mixture so that the salmon is completely covered. Wrap the entire contents with the plastic wrap and fold the sides up so that the plastic wrap encases the salmon. You will probably not be able to make this completely airtight, but that is okay.

Next, place another glass dish on top of the salmon, and place the baking dishes into a refrigerator. Place weights (such as Ball jars filled with water or unopened large cans of food) in the top dish. Turn the salmon each day for 3 days. The salmon texture will tighten, and the fish will exude a significant amount of water.

After 3 days, the salmon will be fully cured and can be removed from the refrigerator to prepare for service. The salmon should be washed to remove the excess salt mixture, then patted dry. The water that has exuded from the salmon should be disposed of, as should the plastic wrap.

The salmon is traditionally carved into almost paper-thin slices parallel to the skin side of the salmon (and not perpendicular to the skin). A sharp, long, bladed carving knife (not serrated) is required for this process. Carving strokes should be long and smooth, using the whole length of the blade in order to achieve the result of paper-thin slices of salmon to be served. You will be amazed at how the texture of the salmon has become firm and sliceable over the 3-day curing period. Every slice moves head to tail. Start about 4 inches from the tail end, and slice toward the tail. As all of the flesh toward the tail is carved to the skin, move the starting point of your slice about another 4 inches closer to the head end of the salmon. Continue to slice toward the tail, moving the starting point of your slice as each part of the salmon is carved to the skin to complete the slicing.

If you live near a delicatessen where salmon is still carved by hand, you should watch the person carving the salmon the next time that you go in, and you will see that the traditional way is to carve almost parallel to the board so that long thin slices can be taken off the salmon. (Unfortunately, much of what is now available is presliced and prepackaged.)

This is a somewhat time-consuming process, but it is well worth the result to do this properly and carefully. It may take about 20 minutes to complete this task and fill the serving tray. As you are cutting the salmon for service, remember you do not want any of the skin on the pieces. You should trim away and discard the dark fatty flesh that is next to the skin; this is strongly flavored and not as delicious as the orange-pink part of the flesh. You should carve only so much of the salmon as you will be using at a time. Uncarved gravlax will stay fresh in the refrigerator for several days, but not longer than that. This is not a dish that is freezable.

Serve the gravlax in the traditional way as you would serve nova or lox; that is, with bagels. Liberally smear a bagel with cream cheese (either a plain cream cheese or cream cheese with vegetables or chives), slices of muenster or American cheese, very thinly sliced sweet onion, and capers. Some people also add tomato, thinly sliced. Cucumber is another frequent accompaniment to nova or gravlax. Scandinavian service offers different condiments, including a dill-and-mustard sauce.

Other than the time lapse that is involved to cure the salmon (and you do need to plan the time from the commencement of the process with when you desire to serve the salmon), and the refrigerator space that is required for that 3-day period, this is perhaps one of the most easy and elegant dishes you can possibly make, and it is one that is sure to please your guests.

A delicious secondary preparation is to use the gravlax to make "lox and eggs." Beat a desired number of eggs with some milk or cream. Sweat but do not brown some diced onion in unsalted butter. Dice some gravlax to taste. Proportions are not critical. Add the gravlax to the onion, and immediately add the eggs. Cook and stir until the eggs are soft scrambled. Serve with a bagel and cream cheese.

HERB GRILLED SALMON

There are multiple recipes for grilled salmon, with many of the recipes extolling the virtues of the grilled surfaces of the fish; that is not what this recipe is about. The flavor does not depend on a marinade or on a browning or "Maillard reaction" or any involved procedure. It is simple but produces a great light herb-smoked flavor. Everyone who tries this process loves the result.

Purchase the desired amount of salmon fillet for cooking. Freshness is absolutely essential, so buy fish on the day you are going to cook it. Do not allow the fishmonger to sell you the tail end of the salmon, as it is too thin; it will not cook evenly with the thicker part and will be overcooked and dry. If the salmon has pin bones in it, before cooking, extract the pin bones with needle-nose pliers or tweezers, or ask the fishmonger to perform this process.

Salt and pepper the salmon, and oil it on both sides with only a teaspoon or so of olive oil. Heat the grill. Next is the simple trick that makes this salmon special. Clip several branches of rosemary or other woody herbs such as oregano, thyme, or basil stems as long as the length of the salmon fillet. (Rosemary is a bushy and attractive perennial, easy to grow as far north as Virginia Beach, but I understand that it is not a perennial on Long Island, New York.) Put the salmon, skin side down, on a grill pan that has holes throughout. Wash the herbs and place the wet herbs on the hot grill. Place the grill pan with the salmon on top of the herbs. Turn the grill down to low and close the lid.

You will have to experiment with your grill because different grills heat differently, but on my grill, it takes about 10 minutes for the fish to be perfectly cooked, which I define to be medium rare. Wild salmon is less fatty and cooks slightly faster than farmed salmon. You can tell when the fish is done because white collagen beads will form on top of the fish, and the fish will become slightly firm; it will give slightly to finger pressure but will not be squishy. You do not flip the fish. It is cooked only from 1 side, but I assure you it will cook all the way through. Remove the fish from the grill, and put it on a plate for serving, leaving the now burned herbs for cleanup when the grill has cooled.

This fish is wonderful served as it is because it has a light smoky herb flavor from the herbs, which will have smoked and blackened during the cooking process. However, the fish is also excellent served with basil pesto on top.

Pasta tossed with a pesto sauce, a wild-mushroom cream sauce, or a tomato-basil cream sauce makes a great side dish. An alternative starch that we cook frequently with this fish is Lemon Coconut Rice (Chapter 9). Cheese Noodle Kugel (Chapter 10) or macaroni and cheese are also wonderful to accompany this salmon. Serve with a fresh salad, and you could not have a better dinner.

Finally, if you have leftovers, this salmon is excellent to make into Salmon Spread (Chapter 5).

Cold poached salmon is luxurious and will wow your guests, but it is easy to prepare. Since it should be made the day before it is to be served, it is an outstanding dish for a dinner party or for a weeknight dinner. As with any fish, it is absolutely critical to use only the freshest fish possible; if you cannot get really fresh fish, make something else. I buy fish the day I am going to cook it. You should learn what day the retailer gets the fish, and shop on those days. The plastic bag with the fish should be placed by the fishmonger into a second bag filled with ice to keep it fresh until you place it in the cooking pot.

The fillet should have any pin bones removed. The fish is cooked with the skin on and served either that way or by flipping the fish when plating it and removing the skin.

There are 2 absolutely essential points in poaching a salmon: (1) use a well-flavored stock or court bouillon, discussed below, and (2) do not overcook the salmon.

To prepare the stock, finely dice 1 onion, 1 leek (or the dark green waste leaves from a couple of leeks), 1 carrot, 1 celery stalk, and 2 garlic cloves with a bay leaf, 1 teaspoon thyme, salt, and a teaspoon of peppercorns. The stock should start with a combination of about 2 cups of dry white wine such as a pinot grigio, sauvignon blanc, or other non-oaky wine combined with about 4 cups of water. If the total liquid is not sufficient when you lower the fish into the stock as set forth below when you actually commence poaching, just add more water. In lieu of water in addition to wine, you could use a homemade fish stock. In fact, I always strain the stock after I use it to freeze for the next time that I poach salmon, adding fresh herbs and liquid from time to time. I do not use this poaching liquid for other purposes because of the distinct salmon flavor, which is stronger than a fish stock made from flounder, sole, or snapper carcasses. The results only get better as the stock is used multiple times. If you do not use a well-flavored stock, naturally the final result will not be as satisfying.

It is best to use a fish poacher unless you are making a smaller portion of salmon. The poacher is an inexpensive stainless steel container. The poacher has a rack that can be used to lower the salmon into the hot liquid and lift out the salmon after it is cooked so that you do not risk breaking the salmon apart to put it on the platter.

Cook the stock or court bouillon at a simmer for about ½ an hour (if it is freshly made), strain, and then bring the stock to a boil. Place the fish on the rack of the poacher, lowering the rack gently into the poacher container. The stock should barely cover the salmon. Add water if needed. Bring the stock back up to a bare simmer. Immediately cover, and lower heat to maintain a bare simmer. Cook for *exactly* 3 minutes and *no more*.

Immediately turn off the heat, and promptly place the container in the refrigerator. I assure you that the salmon will be cooked when it is cold, and you will have a perfectly cooked and moist salmon to serve.

The cooked salmon can be made extremely fancy by encasing it in gelatinized fish stock, and recipes for that can be found in many cookbooks, including Julia Child's *The French Chef Cookbook*. Decoration could be with cucumber to look like scales and halved olives for eyes, "glued" to the fish with the jellied fish stock—but I can assure you, this is not necessary in order to have a spectacularly successful dish. The fillet of salmon, served as such on a platter with minor decorations—including, perhaps, carrots poached with the salmon on the side—makes a spectacular serving, albeit simple. The cooking stock naturally jellies softly when cold. You can brush the cold poached salmon with a layer of the jellied stock, slightly warmed, and then chill so that the stock re-jells; this will make the fish shiny and fresh looking for serving.

The salmon can be served with any manner of vegetables, including, perhaps, a salad of grilled vegetables or cold or hot asparagus. Serve with a couple of homemade dressings for the fish and salad, such as Pink Salad Dressing (Chapter 8) or a homemade dijon mustard aioli (see Mayonnaise recipe in Chapter 8), perhaps made with lime rather than lemon as an alternative flavor. Other excellent accompaniments include any manner of starch, from rice (such as the Lemon Coconut Rice recipe in Chapter 9) to pasta (either a stuffed pasta, such as tortellini or ravioli, or a shaped pasta) dressed with pesto or a lemon cream sauce (both of which have a natural flavor affinity for salmon) to the Italian Potato Salad recipe in Chapter 8 or, even richer, potatoes thinly sliced in a mandoline, layered with sautéed garlic, shallots, and dried, reconstituted porcini mushrooms and baked in a casserole with the mushroom-soaking liquid and heavy cream.

COCONUT-CURRY FISH

You may think that preparing Indian food is daunting and beyond the scope of your capabilities; this is simply not true, particularly now that there are numerous Indian spices and mixtures such as garam masala and other masalas available from your normal grocery with kosher brands. Or you can buy from a spice market such as Penzeys or a local Indian or Asian grocer so that you do not need to assemble multiple spices. However, I do still make my own Garam Masala (Chapter 2). The high-tech industry has brought more than just smartphones, and the growing ethnic diversity enriches us all. The final flavor of the dish will vary depending on the spice mixtures or masalas used; it is easy to change the flavor of the recipe as desired.

INGREDIENTS

peanut oil or other neutral-flavored oil or butter for sautéing

2 large shallots, finely chopped (or ½ a sweet onion, chopped)

2-4 cloves garlic, finely chopped

2 tablespoons ginger, finely chopped

3 pounds fish (Use a white-fleshed fish such as chilean sea bass, black cod—also known as sablefish—red snapper, grouper, cod, haddock, or other similar mild-flavored fish, but not salmon, which does not meld well with these flavors.)

1 can high-quality, unsweetened, full-fat coconut milk

1 tablespoon Garam Masala (Chapter 2)

1 tablespoon sweet (ordinary store-type) curry, or another masala mixture such as tandoori or tikka masala or other Indian spice mix, as desired

1 lemon or lime, zested and juiced

1 cup cilantro, chopped

salt and pepper to taste

Preheat oven to 350°F.

Lightly sauté the shallots, garlic, and ginger in a small amount of butter or vegetable oil until the vegetables have wilted and the aroma is incredible. If you are sautéing in an oven-proof pan, add the fish, the spices, the can of coconut milk, and the citrus zest; otherwise, transfer all of the ingredients except the citrus juice and cilantro to an oven-safe CorningWare or Pyrex dish. Reserve the cilantro and citrus juice to be added a couple minutes before cooking ends.

Place the pan or dish into the oven and cook for 30 minutes or until the fish is just cooked. The cooking time will vary depending on the thickness and variety of the fish; for example, a thin snapper fillet will cook much faster than a thick fillet of black cod or chilean sea bass. Some varieties, such as black cod or chilean sea bass, need to be fully cooked and not medium rare, while you need to be careful not to overcook ordinary cod or snapper.

When the fish is done, and the sauce is bubbling, at the last minute or so of cooking time, stir in the cilantro. Squeeze ½ or more, as desired, of a lemon or lime into the sauce, and stir the sauce carefully.

Serve with basmati rice and a salad or vegetable, and you will have a wonderful Indian-style meal ready in less than an hour.

Note: If you are using a fish such as black cod (also known as sablefish) or chilean sea bass, each of which has an inedible skin, be sure to remove the skin before cooking. Furthermore, many fish species, such as black cod, have a centerline of bones in most fillets, which the fishmonger may not remove. I always trim these bones out myself because I am careful not to remove too much of the flesh, which you will pay for, and at the prices for these fishes, it is expensive. You should carefully trim around these bones and remove the bones before cooking. The skin of a fish such as red snapper is edible and delicious, provided it is carefully scaled. You should check the skin before cooking to ensure that all the scales are removed, because many times the fishmonger will not be particularly careful.

Grilled Vegetables, p. 251

Chapter 14: *Side Dishes*

PAN-ROASTED CAULIFLOWER OR CABBAGE

Roasted cauliflower is a sublime and simple vegetable to prepare. I know many people are not necessarily fond of cauliflower, but as evidence of its delectability, when my grandson was four years old, he did not eat most vegetables, but he would eat half of a head of roasted cauliflower by himself. He called them "trees." The process is simple and must start with very fresh cauliflower.

INGREDIENTS

1 head of cauliflower (or cabbage)
1 head of garlic
salt
pepper
olive oil, as needed
1 lemon

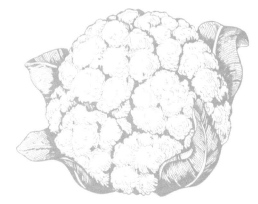

Preheat the oven to 425°F. Trim the stem end of the cauliflower of its excess leaves. Shave off the dried, cut end of the stem. Everything left is now useable. The cauliflower should be cut into florets smaller than a baseball but larger than a golf ball. Large florets are desirable. Cut at the stem of the cauliflower so that the entire floret comes apart from the head. Place the florets in a roasting pan.

Slice the stem into thick chunks and put that into the roasting pan too. Peel an entire head of garlic. Put all of the garlic cloves into the roasting pan. Toss the garlic and the cauliflower with salt, pepper, and olive oil—enough to coat without a large excess of oil. Put the roasting pan into the oven. Check in about 15 minutes to turn the cauliflower and stir the garlic. The cauliflower will be cooked in 30 minutes or so, and some of the surface of most pieces should be nicely browned. The final step is also very simple: cut a lemon in half, and squeeze the lemon juice over the cauliflower, and continue to roast for 3 to 5 minutes, stirring the cauliflower with lemon juice. Serve.

Variations

To roast cabbage, simply quarter the cabbage before coating with olive oil, salt, and pepper, making sure to leave the core intact to hold the cabbage together. Follow the same process as for cauliflower. You can roast cauliflower in the same pan with cabbage, resulting in a subtle and interesting flavor enhancement.

An excellent variant is to coat the cauliflower and cabbage with a Garam Masala (Chapter 2) or curry or other masala spice mixture along with the olive oil, salt, and pepper. At the end of the cooking, add either lemon or lime.

PAN-ROASTED BRUSSELS SPROUTS OR OTHER VEGETABLES

Many people claim that they simply do not like brussels sprouts, but I am convinced that it is because they have not had them properly cooked; this is a vegetable that is becoming more available and popular.

INGREDIENTS

brussels sprouts
½–¾ cup water
olive oil
10–12 cloves garlic, peeled
salt
pepper

Estimation of the amount to cook is not a science; I know how many people I will need to serve and just sort of lay out the vegetable on my board into that many portions. Then I start preparing. I usually prepare extra because I do not want family or guests to leave my table hungry.

Brussels sprouts should be trimmed and cut in half. On the stove top, preheat a pan that has a cover. Place ½ to ¾ cup of water conveniently beside the stove. Add a glaze of olive oil to the pan. Place the brussels sprouts cut side down into the pan. Sear the bottom face of the brussels sprouts. After a couple of minutes in the very hot pan, stir the brussels sprouts, and toss in 10 to 12 cloves of peeled garlic. Immediately after you place the garlic cloves in the pan, salt and pepper the brussels sprouts. Then immediately pour in the water, which will cause the entire pan to sizzle and steam. Put the lid on the pan and lower the heat. Cook for about 5 minutes. Uncover the pan and increase the heat to evaporate all remaining water. Serve.

Variations

An interesting and incredibly easy sort of Asian variation is to add ginger, finely minced, with the garlic. Immediately before all of the water has evaporated, add 1 to 2 teaspoons of hoisin sauce. Stir well. Serve.

An alternative to brussels sprouts for either flavor variation is to substitute bite-sized lengths of green beans (or snow peas or sugar snap peas) with the "strings" carefully removed. Alternatively, you could try sliced radishes. Add chopped garlic as you put these vegetables in the pan. The peas cook very quickly (1 to 2 minutes total), as do the radish slices, while beans need a few minutes on the heat. You will need perhaps ⅛ to ¼ cup of water as you put these delicate vegetables in the pan. Toss until the green vegetables turn bright green and are all still crispy. An excellent trick to crisp and freshen beans—or snow or sugar snap peas—before cooking is to cover and soak them in iced water in the refrigerator for an hour or up to a couple of days.

GRILLED VEGETABLES

Grilled vegetables at room temperature and served with a salad dressing such as aioli, rouille, mustard mayonnaise with lemon or lime (see Mayonnaise recipe in Chapter 8), or Pink Salad Dressing (Chapter 8) as a vegetable dish in lieu of hot vegetables are a wonderful variant for many reasons. One reason for this is very simple: grilled vegetables can be prepared the day before and just merely placed in rows of contrasting colors on a serving platter with fresh tomatoes and cucumbers at the time of the meal. Plus, there is nothing simpler than grilling vegetables outside, and you have no pots to clean. Of course, the flavor is the most important reason.

First, you have to decide what vegetables to grill. The following vegetables are easy to grill: carrots, zucchini, onion, eggplant, portobello mushrooms, asparagus, fennel, green beans, or such other vegetables as you desire. After you clean, peel, and cut the vegetables into the desired shapes (see below for specifics on each vegetable), sprinkle the vegetables with garlic powder, salt, pepper, and olive oil. Stir to coat. Grill and then cool each vegetable separately so that their flavors remain distinct and do not merge.

Carrots should be peeled. Slice off the thin root end of the carrot (perhaps 3–4 inches) and leave it whole. The thicker stem end of the carrot should be sliced in half or quartered, depending on how thick the carrot is. Be very careful not to get your hands in the way of the knife blade or to allow the knife to slip. I find that a chef's knife is best for this process. Do not try this if your knife is not sharp! Keep your hands above the knife blade *at all times* so that you will not be hurt. Once you have sliced the carrot in half, be sure to place the carrot flat side down for stability before you attempt a second slice, if needed, making sure that your free hand is on top of the blade.

For zucchini, after washing, simply slice off the stem and flower tips. Slice the zucchini into at least ¼-inch-thick slices lengthwise (not coins, which will fall through the grill grate).

I always peel eggplant since I do not like the texture of the peel. If you have globe eggplant, slice the eggplant into either ½-inch rounds or lengthwise into long, ½-inch-thick slices.

Onions should be sliced very thick (at least ½ an inch). It is useful to secure the layers of the onion with 2 or 3 toothpicks per slice, inserting from the edge of the slice to the center. Alternatively, you should grill onions on a grill plate so that they do not fall through the grill as they cook, separate into rings, and become soft. Allow the grill plate to get hot on the grill before putting the onions on the grill plate.

For portobello mushrooms, remove the stem, and wash carefully. Reserve the stems for other uses. I do not remove the gills, as I do not find them objectionable, although many TV chefs seem to do so. Just brush the entire mushroom with olive oil, and sprinkle with salt and pepper before grilling.

As the vegetables are cooked, remove them from the grill, and place them into separate bowls to chill. After the vegetables are chilled, you can remove them to a single bowl, or place them on the serving dish and cover with plastic wrap. Particularly during the summer months when you can find great tomatoes and cucumbers from the garden with no wax (added by most grocery stores), add those sliced raw vegetables to the vegetable plate. (Some stores, such as Central Market in Texas, carry unwaxed cucumbers all year round.) And remember—*never* refrigerate tomatoes. Serve with salad dressings in separate bowls to be added by your guests as they desire.

INDIAN-STYLE LENTILS

Lentils are legumes. Lentils are not only healthy, but they are also delicious when properly prepared. However, do not mistake lentils for diet food. Like many legumes, lentils can be quite bland, but these lentils are spicy and flavorful when cooked. While the dish is perhaps not "authentic," the ingredients certainly provide a result as good as any lentil dish in an Indian restaurant. Importantly, you have control over the spice and heat level. And because of the seemingly endless different masalas and spice blends, this recipe can change every time you make it. Search out variations and try them.

There are an incredible variety of lentils with different cooked textures. Indian groceries in particular have a staggering number of types of lentils. You should consult the directions for cooking the variety with which you are working, although some bags are simply not clear. Green or brown lentils need to be simmered for 20 to 30 minutes, while beluga lentils should be cooked approximately 10 minutes fewer. Red or yellow lentils cook only 5 to 8 minutes and can turn to mush quickly. I generally use green lentils or brown lentils, and I buy lentils at an Indian food store. While perhaps not everyone's style, I frequently talk to Indian shoppers I encounter to get their ideas about how to cook these products, since they cook them far more often than I do. People appreciate a genuine interest in their culture, and I invariably get a positive reception.

This recipe is a flavorful amalgam of vegetables and lentils. Other than finely chopping the vegetables so that all ingredients are approximately the size of the lentils, it is a most simple and easy preparation.

INGREDIENTS

1 cup sweet onion or shallot, chopped

1 carrot, finely minced or shredded

2 large cloves garlic, finely minced

2-3 tablespoons fresh ginger, finely minced

1 tablespoon Garam Masala (Chapter 2)

1 tablespoon tikka masala or other Indian spice mix (masala or curry) to your pleasure

1 bay leaf

1¼ cups lentils, picked over and rinsed (about ½ a pound)

4 cups filtered water

1 teaspoon salt

pepper to taste

½ cup or so cilantro, chopped

lemon juice

Lightly sauté the onion, carrot, garlic, and ginger until the onion is sweated, the carrot is softened, and the garlic and ginger flavors reach your nose. Add the spices, cook briefly to bloom flavors, and then add a bay leaf. Add the water, lentils, 1 teaspoon of salt, and ground pepper to taste. Lower the heat to maintain a simmer as soon as a simmer is reached. Cover. Check frequently after 15 minutes if you are using green or brown lentils. Taste for doneness by determining whether the lentils are soft but not mushy. Do not overcook. Once the lentils are just soft to taste, and most of the liquid is absorbed, turn off the heat, and stir in the cilantro.

Rice and beans is a classic combination in multiple cultures, and if you serve these lentils over plain basmati rice, you will surely understand why. I buy basmati rice in an Indian food store. *America's Test Kitchen* tested this rice and preferred the imported Indian brands because of the aging process used by the highly rated brands, a process not used by American brands. I like the Tilda brand. It comes in 10- or 20-pound plastic resealable bags. While it may seem a lot, it stores easily, does not spoil, and is really delicious for most rice needs (but not, of course, risotto).

POTATO KUGEL

Potato kugel is a quintessential part of many Jewish holiday meals and especially Passover, at least in our house. It is essentially a potato pudding but is very much unlike the French potato gratin made with butter, cream, and cheese or the Spanish *tortilla*. It has no milk product but uses chicken schmaltz parsimoniously as a flavoring ingredient. Too much fat will make the kugel greasy. The internet is replete with potato kugel recipes that purport to be "traditional" but use a flavorless vegetable oil and way too much of that; I can only imagine the flavorless, greasy result. Because potato kugel uses chicken fat, it is classically only served with meat meals—typically a braised brisket or roast chicken.

This is a perfect dish for the Passover seder since, properly made, it contains no flour or other chametz. I know many add flour or matzo meal, but the egg acts as a binder, so this is entirely unnecessary. Many recipes add way more than two tablespoons fat, but what you are looking for is the flavor, and two tablespoons provide that. If you use vegetable oil, the kugel will be flavorless and bland.

INGREDIENTS

This recipe makes 10 or more servings.

3 pounds Idaho or baking potatoes, peeled

1 large onion

6 eggs

2 tablespoons Chicken Schmaltz (Chapter 2), melted (plus a teaspoon or so for the pan and to add to brush the top of the partially cooked kugel)

salt

pepper

This amount of ingredients is perfect for a 9x13-inch glass Pyrex baking dish. You do not want the kugel to be too thick, or it will not crisp properly. Grease the baking dish with very little schmaltz, no more than a teaspoon. Line the pan with parchment, leaving extra paper as handles to remove the cooked kugel. Preheat the oven to 350°F.

Grate the potatoes with a box grater or an attachment to a Cuisinart or KitchenAid mixer. The grated potatoes should be in small shreds, not in slices. Once the potatoes are grated, take the potatoes in your hands, and squeeze the liquid out of them, reserving the liquid. Put the dry potatoes into another bowl. (Alternatively, wrap all of the potatoes in a clean kitchen towel, and twist the towel to squeeze the liquid out of the potatoes.) Let the liquid settle; then drain the liquid, leaving the potato starch. Mix the potato starch back into the potatoes to act as a binder. The reason to use Idaho or baking potatoes is that they are starchier than other varieties; this helps the cooked dish maintain its integrity as it is served.

Grate the onion into the now squeezed potatoes. Break and beat the eggs. Mix them into the potatoes and onions with no more than 2 tablespoons of melted schmaltz. Add salt and pepper to taste and mix well. (For this amount of potatoes, you will probably need at least 2 teaspoons of kosher salt). You might want to sauté a bit to taste for salt. Remember, potatoes absorb a lot of salt, but too much is too much and cannot be removed. Add to your taste.

Place the potatoes into the baking dish. Bake the potatoes for about 30 minutes at 350°F until almost done. With a pastry brush, lightly brush a little melted schmaltz over the surface of the kugel to aid browning.

At this stage you have 2 choices: (1) you can let the potatoes cool, cover them tightly, and freeze until ready to use; or (2) you can complete the cooking process. The potatoes are done when the top is very crispy and well browned. The longer you cook the potatoes, the crispier they will get, and this makes the potatoes much more delicious. Take the kugel out of the oven, and slice into squares to serve.

For those who turn up their noses at the thought of rendered chicken fat, remember that for calories, fat is fat. This small amount of fat adds a desirable flavor. Since a tablespoon equals 3 teaspoons, and the recipe makes at least 10 servings, each serving will have less than ½ teaspoon of fat—far less than a pat of butter.

This potato kugel shares a lot of characteristics with latkes, except that latkes are fried in vegetable oil. Latkes, even well drained, far exceed potato kugel in the use of fat. Also, latkes are best served with sour cream. With chicken schmaltz on the potatoes, you cannot serve them with sour cream, a forbidden combination of milk and meat.

SWEET POTATO "SOUFFLÉ" OR PUDDING

Sweet potatoes are delicious at any time but are particularly traditional at Thanksgiving and especially when serving turkey. They are very nutritious, and that is an added fillip. Most of the year, we simply roast sweet potatoes and serve them with cinnamon and, perhaps, butter. At Thanksgiving, I generally make a sweet potato pudding or "soufflé," which has no egg and is really not a soufflé in the classic French sense but is most certainly delectable, qualifying for the *Deep Flavors* label.

INGREDIENTS

This recipe will serve 10 guests.

```
5½–6 pounds sweet potatoes
1 can (12–15 ounces) crushed pineapple, packed in water, not syrup
1–2 apples or pears
1–2 oranges, zested and juiced
1 lemon, zested and juiced
½ cup brown sugar, or to taste
1 teaspoon ground cinnamon, or to taste
pinch of salt
```

Streusel

```
2 cups pecans
½ cup brown sugar
1 teaspoon cinnamon
```

Wash the sweet potatoes carefully, poke the sweet potatoes with a fork liberally, put them on a tray, and roast them at 350°F until well roasted, browned, and very soft. Turn every 20 to 30 minutes. There are other ways to cook and soften the potatoes, but none creates the same rich caramel flavor.

Let the sweet potatoes cool. Scrape the sweet potatoes out of the skin. (If you do not want to eat the skins, do not throw them out; your dog will love them.) Mash well with a potato masher. Mix the sweet potatoes with the crushed pineapple. Peel, core, and finely chop the apple (and/or pear), and mix it in. Add in brown sugar, a pinch or so of salt, and cinnamon.

Add the grated zest and juice of 1 or 2 oranges and 1 lemon. Mix well, and taste for the desired level of cinnamon spice and sweetness.

Place into a 3-liter Pyroceram or other oven-safe baking dish. The pudding can be frozen at this stage and thawed when you need it. Bake uncovered for about 1 to 1½ hours at 350°F, until it is very hot and slightly browned.

If there are little children in the house, they will want marshmallows on top of the sweet potato soufflé, and it is certainly permissible to do this. Sometimes the inner child remains: my daughter, who is an adult, still prefers marshmallows on top of hers. Some people just do not outgrow this tradition.

An adult alternative if the meal does not include meat is to top with a streusel mixture. If you do not mix milk and meat, you cannot use a traditional streusel, which is made with butter, but a liberal mixture of brown sugar, pecans, and cinnamon works well. Place the streusel mixture on top of the potatoes when you are ready to start heating the dish. The sugar will caramelize, and the crust will be delectable—sweet and crunchy. At 3½ years old, my grandson could not get enough of the sweet potatoes at Thanksgiving, even without the marshmallows.

PAN-ROASTED POTATOES

Who doesn't like roasted potatoes? This version is not only simple but is delicious and quick to cook with very little prep time, other than the peeling of garlic. I like to make extra amounts of these potatoes so that there are leftovers that can be chilled in the refrigerator. The next day, the chilled potatoes can be sliced and sautéed in butter (if you use olive oil in the initial cooking and not goose or duck fat) or other fat until crispy for wonderful garlicky panfried potatoes—served with eggs.

INGREDIENTS

enough potatoes to fill the fry pan (2-3 pounds, depending on the size of your pan. Really young potatoes freshly picked, or as close to that as you can get, can really step up the result. Use smaller Yukon Gold or new potatoes—white or red—with thin skins, but not starchy baking or Idaho potatoes.)

salt

pepper

olive oil—or, even better, rendered goose or duck fat (butter has too low a smoke point)

1 whole bulb of garlic, peeled

½ cup or so of water

fresh herbs such as thyme, oregano, or rosemary (optional)

Preheat the oven to 350°F. First, wash and dry the potatoes well. It is not necessary to peel the potatoes. Cut the potatoes into approximately golf ball–sized pieces. Lightly coat a nonstick fry pan with just enough olive oil or rendered fat to barely coat the bottom. Heat the pan so that the oil is shimmering and place the potatoes in the pan. Salt and pepper the potatoes. Sauté until the cut sides are golden. Then add the bulb of peeled garlic cloves. Add a few sprigs of fresh herbs if desired.

Add ¼ to ½ cup of water so that there is about ¼ inch of water in the pan. Place the pan in the preheated oven and cook for approximately ½ hour or until the water is evaporated and the potatoes are well browned.

Alternatively, clamp on a lid after adding the water, and lower the flame. Cook for 15 to 20 minutes covered. Remove the cover and increase the heat to evaporate any remaining liquid. Shake the pan to recrisp the potatoes.

CRANBERRY SAUCE

Cranberry sauce is an essential accompaniment to any Thanksgiving dinner, at least in our house. As I was growing up, the only cranberry sauce that my mother served was the canned cranberry sauce, with which we are all familiar. It can be so much better! This recipe is a gelatinized sauce that is like a Jell-O mold. Cranberries are available fresh in the grocery stores in the fall, before Thanksgiving, but individually quick-frozen (IQF) cranberries work well here too. Many varieties of fresh cranberry sauce can be made. Many are not strained, and you may not like that texture.

You can do the principal amount of work on this dish weeks ahead of Thanksgiving. The result can be easily frozen to stand ready for final assembly and use in the final day or two before Thanksgiving. Sealed in an airtight container, it will last frozen at zero degrees Fahrenheit indefinitely (more than a year).

INGREDIENTS

You can multiply this recipe easily. I generally make 3-recipe supply of this cranberry sauce.

```
12-ounce package fresh cranberries
1 large apple
1 lemon
1 orange
1 (12-16-ounce) package IQF raspberries
2-4 cups orange juice
2 cups white cane sugar, or to taste
1-2 packages powdered, unflavored gelatin
¼-½ cup water or orange juice to bloom the gelatin
1 (12-16-ounce) package IQF sweet cherries
```

The cranberries must be carefully sorted, and any cranberries that have bad places or appear to have been frozen or are otherwise not firm should be discarded. There will invariably be a few cranberries to be discarded. Cranberries that appear to be underripe are perfectly fine and should be used. Wash the cranberries carefully and place them in a pot.

Chop an apple, removing the seed core, and add to the pot. Quarter a lemon and an orange, and squeeze the juice into the pot, discarding the seeds. Then place the remaining lemon and orange rinds into the pot so that the flavor from the rinds can be extracted into the mixture. Add a bag of frozen raspberries (or 2 bags for 3 batches). Add sufficient orange juice to cover liberally.

Bring the pot to a low simmer (not a boil), with the lid slightly cracked. Be careful to pay attention to the pot lest it boil over with a resulting mess. When the cranberries start to pop, add a pinch of salt, and start adding sugar—stirring, tasting, and adding sugar until the levels of sourness and sweetness are balanced to your taste. Simmer until the apple is fully cooked and very soft and the cranberries are fully popped. The cooking should take about ½ an hour or so.

When the mixture is fully cooked, squeeze juice out of the lemon and orange rinds into the pot. Discard the rinds. Then put the remaining mixture through a food mill or sieve. I personally do not like the texture of cranberry skins—or, in this context, apple skins—so this is not merely an exercise in elegance. Carefully scrape any of the thick portion of the fruits that are exuded through the bottom of the food mill (or sieve) into the strained cranberry sauce. The apple skin, raspberry seeds, and cranberry skins may be discarded. What you are left with is a slightly thickened syrup/juice mixture that should taste delicious. Adjust if you need to add sugar. This can be frozen for further use in measured portions, or it may be processed into a completed gelatin at this time.

To finish and jell the cranberry sauce, measure enough sauce to go into the container in which you will be serving, taking into account additions such as the cherries. Sometimes I put the mixture into a Jell-O mold for decanting, and sometimes I just serve the Jell-O-like mixture in a beautiful serving dish.

At this stage you need to add unflavored gelatin, measuring the amount of gelatin as required and using directions provided with gelatin. I use gelatin powder that is unflavored, and you should be able to find kosher gelatin. I have never used gelatin sheets. It is critical to soak the gelatin powder in a small amount of room-temperature and nonheated liquid (such as orange juice) for at least 5 minutes so that the gelatin will soften and swell. Only then does the gelatin become amenable to mix into a hot liquid with subsequent proper jelling. Heat is essential after the gelatin is fully soaked for the mixture to properly jell. Bring the cranberry mixture to a boil in a pot.

Turn off the heat before stirring the gelatin into the very hot cranberry mixture, making sure that the gelatin is fully stirred in and fully dissolved. You can test this by using a spoon and allowing the mixture to drip off of the spoon. If the material left on the spoon is completely clear, without any signs of beading, then it should be ready for final preparation.

Finally, empty a package of still-frozen sweet (no sweetener added) IQF cherries into the serving container before pouring in the hot cranberry sauce that has been mixed with gelatin. You can certainly vary the fruit variety to add to your taste. I made a mistake one year of using IQF mixed sweet and tart cherries, and the result was way too tart. Refrigerate the mixture to cool completely. I allow 24 hours to make sure the process is complete, although 3 or so hours should be sufficient.

REFRIED BEANS (FRIJOLES REFRITOS)

Frijoles refritos are a common item on almost every plate in a Mexican restaurant, at least in Texas, and are common in many, if not most, Mexican households as a staple item. However, at the risk of being accused of blasphemy, I will state that they are, for the most part, so bland as to be inedible without substantial enhancement, at least to my taste. In restaurants, I frequently mix in the spicy salsa to add flavor, if I eat them at all. However, at home, it is possible to make a much more enticing product that is worthy of the effort and quite delicious. It has the additional advantage of being a very inexpensive and healthy dish, although do not confuse beans with a low-calorie diet food. Despite translation of the name *refried beans*, frijoles refritos can be made deliciously without any frying, with very little oil, and without any degradation of flavor (although that is not common practice among Mexican cooks, at least in Texas, who use Crisco, which is kosher, or lard, which is not kosher). The process is quite simple and produces a tasty and flavorful result that is not only kosher but is worthy of being eaten as a side dish or used as an enhancer—not just a filler—in soft tacos of every sort, as well as in Quesadillas (Chapter 12), Seven-Layer Dip (Chapter 5), and more.

This recipe can be easily multiplied. I make extra with the plan to freeze the unused portion since this is a useful and delicious ingredient.

You can cook your own dried beans from scratch, but for this purpose I think it is hardly worth the effort. Buy canned beans that have no additional flavorings at all. If you purchase already mashed refried beans, make sure that they are not flavored other than with salt and do not contain lard or other fat. Read the label carefully because many of these products use pork lard and other undesirable ingredients. A kosher product should not be hard to find. There are many brands with vegetarian refried beans available in their product lines.

INGREDIENTS

2 (1-pound) cans plain whole beans (I prefer black beans for this use, although pinto or red beans are certainly good)—or ½ pound dried beans

1 small onion, diced

3-4 large cloves garlic

1 teaspoon commercial chili powder (I prefer McCormick's flavor, but it is a matter of taste. Penzeys has a chili powder blend with a delicious flavor profile similar to McCormick's, albeit somewhat more spicy, and 2 even more potent chili powder blends.)

1 teaspoon ancho chile powder, or to taste

1 teaspoon ground cumin, or to taste

1 teaspoon thyme, or to taste

1 teaspoon oregano, or to taste

¼-½ teaspoon chipotle chile powder or some canned chipotle in adobo (extra can be frozen in a glass container and thawed for later use)

fresh chile such as jalapeño (optional)

1-2 dried guajillo chiles (optional), reconstituted in hot water, drained, seeded, and chopped, reserving the liquid to substitute for the water needed in the cooking process

about ½ cup fresh cilantro, chopped

salt

freshly ground black pepper

If using canned whole beans, put the beans into a strainer, and rinse thoroughly.

Lightly sauté the onion and garlic in a minimal amount of olive oil (less than a tablespoon). Add a commercial chili powder blend, ancho chile powder, chipotle chile powder (or canned chipotle chile in adobo), salt, pepper, cumin, oregano, and thyme, all to taste. Cook very slightly to "bloom" the flavor of the spices.

A fresh, finely minced jalapeño is also a good addition. Remember to remove the seeds and ribs inside the pepper unless you want the heat, noting there is no lack of opportunity to add heat with other ingredients. Serrano chiles are somewhat spicier than jalapeños but have a significantly different flavor that I do not like. Chipotles (either as chile powder or canned in adobo) are delicious but quite spicy and should be added carefully. Ancho chile powder is less spicy and has a nice fruity flavor. Chipotles are, in essence, smoked, dried jalapeños and add a wonderful, very different smoky flavor to the dish but are spicier than fresh jalapeños. For 2 cans of beans, I never use more than 1 or 2 chipotle chiles if I use the canned version rather than powder. Taste as you add because chipotles are quite spicy.

Different chiles have very different flavors, not just different heat levels. Some TV chefs will use bell peppers (which are, of course, a type of chile) in substitution of, for example, poblano peppers, but the bell pepper flavor profile is just wrong for most Mexican food.

Next add the drained and washed canned beans (or, if you are cooking dried beans, your freshly cooked beans) to the pan with the spices. Add some filtered water—perhaps $\frac{1}{2}$ cup or as needed. Mash with a potato masher to the desired texture. A blender or food processor would produce a wrong texture. Cook the mixture at medium heat to the desired thickness. If it is too thick, add water; if it is too thin, keep cooking, stirring constantly, evaporating water until it reaches the desired thickness, and adjusting as needed. Be careful to not burn the beans, as they will do so if you leave them unattended on the heat.

When desired texture is reached, add some finely chopped cilantro stems, and cook just to heat. I know that some people like my daughter do not like cilantro, but it really adds a nice flavor that does not taste as cilantro in the final product. The finely chopped stems are soft and edible and have the same flavor as the leaves, some of which should be reserved for a more refined use such as a garnish or as a raw condiment in soft tacos.

I assure you these beans are anything but bland and are quite delicious.

*German's Sweet Chocolate Cake with
Coconut-Pecan-Caramel Filling, p. 316*

Chapter 15: *Desserts*

PIES

BOBBIE'S PIECRUST

There is no reason to be afraid of piecrust. This is the absolute, number one, best piecrust recipe in the world, and it is foolproof. Bobbie, my wife, a world-class piecrust maker, claims that it is actually my mother's recipe, but as I told her, my mother did not execute it nearly as well as she does. Bobbie says that is because Mom did not roll the dough thin enough. I have never had piecrust that can match the flakiness and deliciousness of Bobbie's Piecrust. I understand that this is a high standard, but piecrusts are not difficult if you follow the process, and the results will make your reputation as a baker. A store-bought crust cannot compare.

INGREDIENTS

The ingredients in this recipe make crust for a 2-crust 10-inch pie.

2½ cups unbleached flour, sifted

1 teaspoon regular table salt (not kosher salt)

¾ cup plus 2 tablespoons Crisco vegetable shortening, solid at room temperature (If you wish to use some unsalted butter in the recipe for flavor, you may do so, but the piecrust texture will be somewhat compromised and will not be as flaky as when using 100 percent Crisco shortening. Do not use more than 50 percent butter. Butter should be refrigerator cold and cut into chunks.)

about 1 cup of ice-cold tap water (We use only filtered water, adding ice for this purpose. Take care to avoid any ice in the dough.)

Measure the flour and salt into the sifter or strainer, and sift into a bowl. Cut the shortening into the flour until it is well distributed and until there are no pieces of shortening left that are larger than small english peas. Use a pastry cutter or 2 knives—the pastry cutter is easier. *Do not use a food processor.* I do not care how many TV chefs use a food processor for piecrusts; it may seem easier, but it is not when you consider the extra cleaning, and the result is not the same.

Sprinkle the water over the mixture and fluff it quickly with a fork until it sticks together when pressed gently and the water is well distributed throughout. Use only enough water to make the flour mixture stick together. This is a matter of judgment. *Do not* overmix or knead. Place a piece of plastic wrap over the mixture and press it together. The mixture should not be wet but should stick together when pressed into a flat square or round shape. Wrap in plastic wrap, and place in a refrigerator for at least 2 hours to chill and rest. This cooling period in the refrigerator allows the flour to absorb the water fully and allows the shortening to set, ensuring flakiness and tenderness in the pie dough. Do not omit this step.

After the dough is rested and cold, cut the dough in about half, with 1 portion slightly larger than the other because the bottom crust needs to be slightly larger than the top crust. The dough for the top crust should be rewrapped and placed back into the refrigerator.

Preheat the oven to 400°F. Place the dough for the bottom crust on a well-floured piece of wax paper on your cutting board or counter. The rolling pin should be well dusted with flour. Bobbie uses a French rolling pin, which is 18 inches long and slightly tapered. Turn the dough frequently as you roll it out, and use flour as needed so that it does not stick. The dough should be less than ⅛ inch thick when it is fully rolled out.

Place the rolled-out dough into a Pyrex pie dish, press in lightly, and scallop the edges using your finger and thumb. Prick the bottom very well with a fork and cook in the preheated oven for 10 minutes. (You can use pie weights.) Clear-glass Pyrex is the best material for a pie plate, not metal and not some other opaque Pyroceram—and the price is right. I know that many recipes do not call for prebaking the bottom crust, but it prevents a bottom shell that is undercooked and that absorbs too much liquid; this process makes all the difference in the world to the finished product.

If you are filling it with something that does not require further baking, bake the crust at 400°F for 20 minutes with a cover over the edges to keep them from overbrowning. Then remove the cover, prick the crust again if it is puffing, and return the crust to the oven until it is lightly browned.

If you are filling with a custard and not baking the pie after filling, a nice touch is to make a caramel, and coat the already baked bottom crust with the caramel by tilting the shell around. Do not touch the caramel—it will burn you. A caramel is simple cane sugar cooked to a light to medium brown over heat, but not to smoking point. Start the process by adding a small amount of water to the sugar. The water will evaporate before the sugar caramelizes. Pour the caramel immediately into the baked crust, or it will continue to cook and overcook in the saucepan. This makes a nice crunchy bottom and prevents a soggy crust (unless you wait too long to eat it after it is filled). A melted bittersweet chocolate coating is also a delicious alternative. Pour the chocolate into the pie shell with the same tilting process. For a 10-inch pie shell, melt 6 ounces of bittersweet chocolate. After pouring into the shell, chill it before proceeding with other fillings.

Finish the pie as necessary, filling the pie and—if you are using a top crust—placing the top crust on, pressing into the edges of the prebaked bottom crust. Cut holes into the top of the pie so that steam will escape during the cooking process. For any fruit pie, brush the top crust before baking with some of the syrup that is exuded from whatever the filling is made of, or use an egg white–simple syrup mixture, flavored if you have flavoring available. Sprinkle the top with some large crystal decorative sugar, and you will have not only a wonderful-tasting pie, with a flaky, tender crust, but a beautiful pie as well. This is a no-fail recipe if you follow the directions.

Interestingly, neither Pyrex nor Anchor Hocking now make a 10-inch pie plate; the largest generally available is $9\frac{1}{2}$ inches. However, there are websites where older 10-inch pie plates can be acquired. The formula for conversion to a different-sized plate is simple; it is a proportion based on the areas of the plates. The area of a plate is pi (about 3.14) times the radius squared. For a 10-inch plate, that is a result of just more than 75 square inches. A $9\frac{1}{2}$-inch pie plate has an area of almost 71 square inches. An 8-inch pie plate has an area of just under 50 square inches. Thus, a 10-inch plate uses 75/50 or about $1\frac{1}{2}$ times the filling of an 8-inch plate, and a $9\frac{1}{2}$-inch plate comes close to a 10-inch plate.

Additionally, you should be aware that sometime after 1995, Corning changed the glass formula for Pyrex from borosilicate-based glass to soda lime–based glass to improve the hardness of the glass; unfortunately the new formula is somewhat more heat sensitive and can shatter with a rapid heat change such as refrigerator to oven. I understand this is a similar glass formula to that used by Anchor Hocking, the other major US manufacturer of glass kitchenware.

APPLE PIE

There is a saying, "As American as apple pie." I do not know whether this came around because of Johnny Appleseed, but I think that for good reason, apple pie is certainly a favorite American dessert. At the risk of being accused of jingoism, while the French know how to bake, they certainly do not know how to flavor an apple pie or tart. Unfortunately, most commercial versions and many homemade pies have poorly made crusts, use the wrong kind of apples, are not properly flavored, or, even worse, use canned filling.

INGREDIENTS

```
10-inch pie shell (see Bobbie's Piecrust earlier in Chapter 15)
65 ounces (approximately 6 apples) tart cooking apples such as
Honeycrisp or Granny Smith (cooking apples retain some crispness
and do not disintegrate into mush or sauce while baking the pie)
1 teaspoon cinnamon
½-¾ cup white cane sugar, to taste
½-¾ cup brown sugar to taste, to taste
pinch of salt
4 tablespoons cornstarch
2 lemons, zested and juiced
1 tablespoon or so vanilla
1 cup apricot jam and/or 1 cup dried raisins, tart cherries, or
apricots, reconstituted in liqueur, water, or juice (optional)
butter to dot the filling before adding the top crust—about 2
tablespoons—unless this accompanies a meat meal (optional)
crumb topping (optional variation to top crust; see ingredients at
the end of recipe)
```

Preheat the oven to 350°F. First, make a 10-inch pie shell, or if you do not have a 10-inch pie plate, make a 9½-inch shell. (I do not understand why someone would spend the time making a 9-inch or 8-inch pie.) Prebake it for 10 minutes.

Preparation of Filling

For a 10-inch pie, peel and core 6 large cooking apples. I like a generous amount of filling. By large apples, I mean apples that are at least 11 ounces each. Apples come in all sizes, and for each variety there are large and small apples, depending on local growing conditions. Honeycrisp apples are, at least in my view, by far the best apples to make a pie, but there are times when this variety is unavailable. You should use 1 or more varieties of tart, crisp cooking apples that will not lose their texture and turn into applesauce. (We are fortunate in Texas to have Central Market; this store, year round, has 25 to 30 apple varieties available for sale, and growers are continuously bringing new varieties to market.)

I peel the apples with a vegetable peeler. Then I cut the apples in half and take out the blossom end and the stem end with a short paring knife (with a 3- or $3\frac{1}{2}$-inch blade). With the paring knife, remove the core by placing your thumb less than 1 inch up from the point and turning around the core (or use your preferred method). Then slice the apples into $\frac{1}{8}$-inch slices so that they are evenly sized. Put the apple slices into a large mixing bowl that will be sufficient to contain all of the apples. Add the cinnamon, sugar to taste, salt, cornstarch, grated zest and juice, and vanilla. Stir well so that the lemon covers each of the apple slices and the cinnamon is well distributed. (I find that smaller, thin-skinned lemons are frequently juicier.)

An optional and delicious addition is a cup of apricot jam. If you decide to add optional dried fruit such as raisins, tart cherries, or apricots (1 to $1\frac{1}{2}$ cups), you need to macerate or rehydrate them in a liquid such as rum, amaretto, apple juice to your taste, or even water so that the pie will not be dry. Cut larger fruit such as dried apricots into quarters.

Assembly and Baking

Make the filling at least $\frac{1}{2}$ an hour before the pie is filled to go into the oven so that the apples can exude juices—reserve about $\frac{1}{4}$ cup of the juice to brush on the top crust. One technique that minimizes the cooked pie's overjuiciness is to fill the pie shell with the apple slices, holding back the exuded juices; then heat and reduce the already exuded juices (with some butter if the pie is not to be pareve) in a sauté pan until they are thickened. Then add the thickened juices to the pie before adding the top crust and baking.

The cooked pie is frequently even better after it has been cooled or even chilled for a short time, particularly since otherwise it is difficult to serve; chilling causes the juices to become viscous enough so that they will not run everywhere.

You can either make this pie as a double-crust pie, or you can use a crumb topping. If you are using a top crust, fill the bottom crust with filling. Then dot the filling with butter (unless you want the pie to be pareve), and cover with the top crust. Cut holes in the top crust to release steam, brush the crust liberally with the liquid from the filling, and sprinkle with a coarse decorative sugar. Bake until brown and bubbling in the preheated oven, about 45 to 50 minutes or more (depending on the amount of filling used), checking for doneness after 45 minutes. Place a tray covered with foil on the rack under the pie to catch dripping juice. The pie should be bubbly and the crust golden when done.

If you do not use a top crust, don't add butter to the filling. Bake the pie for 30 minutes before sprinkling liberally with a crumb topping (recipe below). Bake an additional 15 minutes or until the pie is bubbly and the topping browned.

Crumb topping

6 tablespoons butter at room temperature
1 cup pecans, chopped (not toasted)
1 cup brown sugar, firmly packed
½ cup unbleached flour

Mix brown sugar, flour, and nuts, and cut the butter in as for biscuits or a piecrust.

GERMAN'S SWEET CHOCOLATE COCONUT PECAN PIE

This recipe is derived from the original recipe on the inside of the Baker's German's Sweet Chocolate wrapper. This wrapper recipe is identical to the one that I got from my sister out of my mother's recipe collection (my sister still had Mom's wrapper with the recipe) when I was with her after her granddaughter's bat mitzvah in June 2010. We have improved it as indicated.

It is interesting that Baker's claimed (in response to my request for the recipe) to no longer have this recipe. The recipe can be found in various postings on the web, although you have to sort through multiple variants using materially different ingredients.

While I am sure that any chocolate would be good, the flavor profile of any recipe using a chocolate other than German's Sweet Chocolate would obviously be somewhat different.

INSTRUCTIONS

This recipe makes a 10-inch pie.

1 (4-ounce) package Baker's German's Sweet Chocolate

¼ cup unsalted butter

2–3 ounces bittersweet chocolate (optional—definitely not in the original recipe)

1½ cups regular white cane sugar (some brands specify that they contain pure cane sugar, but other brands do not and presumably contain sugar from other sources)

3 tablespoons cornstarch

½ teaspoon salt

1⅔ cups (14½ ounces) evaporated milk (not sweetened condensed milk)

2 eggs (we use jumbo eggs, although I am sure the original recipe intended the use of large eggs)

1 teaspoon vanilla extract (Use only real extract and not artificial flavor "extract." Also, my wife, Bobbie, who actually makes this pie, has confessed that she does not actually measure the vanilla, and she probably uses closer to 1 tablespoon than 1 teaspoon.)

1 10-inch pie shell (See Bobbie's Piecrust recipe earlier in Chapter 15. The original recipe calls for an unbaked shell; however, we believe that pie shells should be blind-baked for 10 minutes at 400°F.)

1⅓–1⅔ cups flaked, sweetened coconut, toasted (Although the original recipe did not call for toasting the nuts, you should always toast coconut or other nuts before using, as this improves the flavor dramatically. See Chapter 2 for coconut-toasting instructions.)

½–1 cup pecans, chopped and toasted

Preheated the oven to 375°F.

Melt the chocolate with butter over low heat, stirring until blended. (The butter and chocolate can be melted in the microwave at high for 1 minute in 30-second stages; if not melted when stirred, microwave for another 15 seconds. You should break the chocolate into pieces, but it is unnecessary to chop it.) Be careful not to burn the chocolate. Remove from heat.

In a separate bowl, mix the sugar, cornstarch, and salt. Gradually blend in the evaporated milk. Beat eggs and vanilla into the mixture. (You cannot leave sugar and eggs together unbeaten for any extended time because the eggs will be denatured—i.e., cooked—by the contact with sugar if the mixture is left unbeaten.) Gradually blend in the melted chocolate. Then pour the mixture into the pie shell. Mix the coconut and pecans. Sprinkle that nut mixture over the filling in the piecrust. Fill the pie shell as it sits on the oven shelf to avoid spillage, and carefully slide the shelf back into the oven.

Bake the pie for 45 minutes or until the top is puffed. The filling will be soft and the middle slightly jiggly, but it will set while cooling. Do not overbake. Cool at least 4 hours before serving.

CHERRY PIE WITH LEMON-COCONUT CUSTARD TOPPING

I love a variety of pies, but I think this is the absolute best pie you will ever eat. The cherry pie filling was my mother's recipe and was made with a traditional two-crust pie. It was always a favorite. Many years ago, we found a recipe with the lemon-coconut custard topping instead of the top crust in the *Virginia Beach Beacon*, a weekly newssheet. Bobbie clipped the recipe, and it languished for a number of years until she tried it, modified to include Mom's filling and piecrust recipe.

INGREDIENTS

This recipe fills a 10-inch pie.

1 batch piecrust, partially prebaked (see Bobbie's Piecrust recipe earlier in Chapter 15)

Filling

2 (14-ounce) cans red, tart, pitted cherries, packed in water (not syrup and absolutely not cherry pie filling)
4 tablespoons cornstarch
1 tablespoon cinnamon
1⅓ cups sugar
4 tablespoons butter
½ teaspoon salt

Topping (optional if not using top crust)

2 eggs, beaten
½ cup sugar
¼ cup butter, melted
1 cup coconut, toasted
2 teaspoons lemon juice, or more if desired
zest of 1 lemon
2 teaspoons vanilla

One brand of cherries we have used is Oregon, or you may find this product in the Comstock brand. You may have to search to find this product canned or bottled. If you can find only IQF tart cherries, fiddle with bottled sweet (or sour) cherry juice (½ to 1 cup) plus sugar to make the filling. Any extra filling is good served warm over ice cream.

Drain to separate the canned cherries from the juice, reserving the liquid. Mix cornstarch with some of reserved liquid to make a slurry. Set aside. Boil the remaining liquid with the cinnamon, salt, and sugar. Then whisk the cornstarch slurry into the boiling liquid. Add butter and stir in until smooth. Stir the cooking liquid constantly until thick and clear. If it is too thick, add water (or sour cherry juice that is available bottled) slowly as necessary until it is not a paste but is still very thick and not soupy.

Add the cherries and pour into a 10-inch partially prebaked pie shell. Cover with a top crust only if you are making a traditional 2-crust cherry pie. After rolling out the top crust, you can cut the dough into strips to make a lattice top—a very traditional presentation. Brush the top with a mixture of egg whites and cherry juice. For the 2-crust pie, bake in a 400°F oven for only 30 minutes or until the top crust is brown and the filling bubbly.

To complete the pie with coconut-lemon custard topping, do not use a top crust or lattice, and bake the pie 30 minutes at 375°F before adding the topping. Combine all of the topping ingredients. Then carefully pour the lemon-coconut mixture over the baked cherry pie and cook for an additional 20 to 25 minutes.

LEMON MERINGUE PIE AND CITRUS VARIANTS

Citrus pies come in many variants. This recipe is based on a citrus curd filling that, except for the butter, does not use any milk or cream product such as sweetened condensed milk. It is derived from my mother's recipe, which she gave to Bobbie. This is not an issue of kosher rules; it is merely a matter of taste. Most of the lemon or lime pies I have eaten in restaurants include a milk product, and I think these fillings have a less-than-clean flavor. Bobbie's citrus curd, on the other hand, is sublime. Of course, it is quite tart (not bitter or sour), which I happen to like. It is all a matter of taste. It goes without saying that the only acceptable juice is freshly squeezed.

The meringue topping makes a spectacular presentation and is an effective use of the whites of the eggs, the yolks of which are used in the filling.

INGREDIENTS

1 fully baked 10-inch pie shell (see Bobbie's Piecrust recipe earlier in Chapter 15)

Curd

¾ cup cornstarch
4 cups water
2 cups sugar
¼ teaspoon salt
6 egg yolks, beaten
4 teaspoons lemon zest
6 tablespoons unsalted butter
⅔ cup lemon juice

Meringue topping

6 egg whites
1½ teaspoons lemon juice
6 tablespoons white cane sugar

Making the Curd

Place the cornstarch in a bowl, and slowly stir in just enough water to wet it. Set aside. In a saucepan, combine the sugar and the remaining water. Heat to boiling. Lower the heat. Whisk in the moistened cornstarch slowly, being careful to make sure it does not clump. Simmer slowly for another 6 to 8 minutes. Remove from the heat. The mixture should be very thick.

Stir a small amount of the hot mixture into the egg yolks to temper the yolks so they do not curdle or scramble. Return the tempered yolks to the rest of the hot mixture, whisking in carefully to avoid lumps. Stir constantly while bringing to a boil over high heat. Reduce immediately to low, and cook, stirring, for another 4 minutes.

Remove from heat and stir in the lemon zest and butter. (Cut the butter up into pieces to reduce melting time.) Gradually stir in the lemon juice. Cover surface of curd with plastic wrap to prevent a skin layer from forming on top. Chill in the refrigerator for at least 1 hour. Put the now chilled curd in the fully baked pie shell, cover with plastic wrap, and chill for another hour.

Caramel Variant

If desired, you can make a caramel with ½ to ¾ cup of sugar (really just cooked in a pan until it melts and becomes a tan liquid), and pour it hot into the prebaked pie shell before adding the curd, tilting the shell to spread the caramel before it quickly hardens as it cools. This caramel shell makes a very nice and unusual sweet and crunchy taste/texture addition and contrast to the tart curd.

Lime and Lemon-Lime Variants

While the base recipe is for a lemon pie, use this to make other citrus pies. I love lime pie, but my favorite citrus pie is with a mixed lemon-lime curd, a variant that I have never seen outside of our house. The recipe for a lime pie is identical to the lemon pie, substituting lime juice and zest for the lemon. Similarly, a lemon-lime pie is also identical with the sole exception that you use lemon and lime juice and zest in equal proportions; that is, ⅓ cup of each freshly squeezed juice and 2 teaspoons of each zest.

Making the Meringue Topping

Beat the egg whites with the lemon juice (which substitutes as an acid in place of the normal cream of tartar) until the egg whites form soft peaks. Gradually add the sugar and beat until the egg whites form stiff peaks and the sugar is dissolved. Spread over pie, making sure it reaches and seals to the edge of the crust. With the spatula, form little peaks in the topping for decoration. Bake in a 350°F oven for 12 to 15 minutes, just until the meringue browns lightly. The browning will not be even, and the peaks will brown first. Cool before serving.

PECAN PIE

I grew up in Georgia, and we had pecan pie frequently. It is a staple dessert throughout the South and still a favorite in our house. Perhaps one of its advantages (other than that it is great to eat) is its ease of preparation. It is great hot, room temperature, or cold. Vanilla ice cream is a more-likely-than-not addition to be served with the pie. While I have seen chef-driven restaurants use other ice cream flavors, for this pie nothing beats a really good vanilla ice cream. I suggest looking for an ice cream with natural and not artificial flavorings.

There are actually two alternative sweetener varieties noted here: light corn syrup and molasses. Molasses has a more dominant flavor, and you will have to choose. Bobbie uses light corn syrup.

INGREDIENTS

1 10-inch pie shell, partially baked at 400°F for 10 minutes and cooled (see Bobbie's Piecrust recipe earlier in Chapter 15)

⅓ cup butter

1¼ cups light brown sugar, firmly packed

4 eggs

⅔ cup Karo light (not dark) corn syrup or molasses (see note regarding brands)

1¼ teaspoons vanilla extract

⅔ teaspoon salt

2 cups raw pecans, broken (not toasted; the pecans will toast as the pie bakes)

Cream together the butter and brown sugar. Add the eggs 1 at a time, and then stir in the corn syrup (or the molasses) and vanilla. Bobbie does not measure vanilla, so I am sure she uses more than the indicated amount. Add salt. Finally, stir in the pecans. Fill the shell and bake for 40 minutes or until a knife or toothpick inserted in the filling comes out clean.

Note: There are several varieties of molasses on your grocer's shelf. Use only unsulfured molasses here or in any other recipe. We only use Grandma's Molasses. Brer Rabbit brand, unsulfured, is also acceptable. Blackstrap molasses is made with immature sugar cane, and the flavor is "enhanced" with chemicals, including sulfur. You do not want this because the flavor is harsh and will dominate your dish.

BLONDIES

This is my variant and very simple recipe for blondies, which is modified to my philosophy of *Deep Flavors*.

INGREDIENTS

This recipe is intended for a 10x15-inch glass Pyrex pan.

```
1 cup unsalted butter at room temperature
½ cup white granulated sugar
1½ cups dark brown sugar, packed (dark brown sugar adds a richer
flavor than light brown sugar)
2 eggs (I use jumbo)
1 tablespoon vanilla
2 cups flour
¾ teaspoon baking powder
1½ teaspoons baking soda
½ teaspoon salt
1 teaspoon cinnamon
12 ounces sweetened coconut flakes, toasted
12 ounces butterscotch chips (preferably Guittard brand)
12 ounces pecans, toasted
12 ounces bittersweet or semisweet chocolate chips

Preheat the oven to 325°F.
```

Prepare the pan by adding a piece of parchment paper long enough so that it fits crosswise into the pan with handles at least 3 to 4 inches above the edge of the pan to serve as a cradle for the blondies. It is unnecessary to add any butter, as there is an adequate amount of butter in the mixture.

To bring 2 sticks of butter to room temperature, it is easy to slice the butter from the refrigerator (or freezer) into pieces in a KitchenAid bowl, and add both the white and brown sugar. Then let the butter-sugar mixture sit at room temperature for an hour or so. Do not be tempted to use the microwave to accelerate this softening of the butter, or the end product may wind up greasy, and the butter-sugar mixture may not properly whip. When the butter is room temperature, beat the butter-sugar mixture with a beater (not a whisk) attachment until the butter and sugar are well mixed and fluffy and the color changes slightly. Extra beating (over about 3 minutes) will hurt the mixture by causing the air bubbles in the butter-sugar mixture to break down. Add eggs 1 at a time. Add vanilla. (I add this liberally and do not measure; I suspect I use more than 1 tablespoon.)

In a separate bowl, whisk together the flour, baking powder, baking soda, and salt, and then add the cinnamon. Slowly add the flour mixture to the butter mixture, turning the mixer down to its very lowest speed and stopping as needed. If you do not turn the mixer down to its very lowest speed, I assure you that you will have a big mess in your kitchen. Then slowly stir in the toasted coconut flakes, toasted chopped pecans, butterscotch chips, and bittersweet or semisweet chocolate chips, using the mixer by turning it to the lowest speed and cycling to off and then back on until the ingredients are mixed. (If you do not have a scale, I suggest using the following measure: a package of butterscotch chips, 1½ cups or so of bittersweet or semisweet chocolate chips, and 1½ cups or so of each of the nuts. I chop the pecans in a bowl, using a very heavy-duty pastry cutter; you can use your own favorite method.)

After the nut mixture is mixed into the batter, add the batter to the pan prepared with the parchment cradle. Tear off lumps of the blondie batter using your clean fingers and plop them throughout the pan. After all of the mixture is scooped out of the mixing bowl and into the baking pan, smooth the top with those same fingers so that the mixture is roughly evenly spaced, and the pan is completely covered. The mixture will spread as it cooks, so perfection is not required at this stage. You will have to lick your fingers before washing them to get the mixture off—a hard duty.

Bake the mixture for 35 to 40 minutes, checking at 35 minutes to see if it is cooked (lightly browned and somewhat firm to the touch, with a toothpick inserted and coming out clean). Do not overcook. Cool in the pan. If you can resist eating some at this time, do so. Carefully lift the cooked blondies out of the pan, or you can cover the pan with aluminum foil, and refrigerate until cold. If you refrigerate first, you may have to use a spatula to sort of pry the mixture off the bottom of the pan, being careful, of course, not to crack the pan or break the blondie cake apart. The mixture will come out. It is far easier to let the blondies cool in the pan for about an hour, and then lift them out carefully so as not to break the cake apart before refrigerating. Place on a cutting board, cover, and chill before cutting. Then slice the blondies into the desired sizes. A sharp, serrated bread knife is the best for this purpose. I freeze the blondies (as I do all of my cookies), because that is how I like to eat them, but of course, that is a personal choice. They will not last long enough to go bad.

DEEP FLAVORS CHOCOLATE BROWNIES

There are brownies that are unctuous, moist, rich, intense, chocolaty, and almost fudgy, and then there are those that are dry, cakey, and not very chocolaty. These brownies will never be the dry sort unless you overcook them, which would be criminal. I prefer the interior portions of the brownie, which are even more fudgy and intense then the outer portion, although all parts of these brownies are better than good. For a variation, the use of Grand Marnier and candied orange zest (see instructions for making your own under the Chocolate-Orange-Almond-Coconut Biscotti recipe on page 287) combined with intense chocolate is a flavor combination that must be eaten to be believed!

INGREDIENTS

This recipe should be cooked in a 9x13-inch Pyrex dish.

8 ounces (½ pound) unsweetened chocolate

8 ounces unsalted butter, plus butter for the pan

5 eggs (large or jumbo)

3¾ cups white cane sugar

1 tablespoon or more vanilla extract

1 teaspoon almond extract

2½ tablespoons liqueur—Grand Marnier, bourbon, dark rum (such as Myers's Rum), amaretto, or other desired flavor of liqueur (optional variation: if you are using Grand Marnier in the brownies, add 1 teaspoon of orange oil and 1 cup finely chopped candied orange zest)

1⅔ cups unbleached flour, sifted

8 ounces (½ pound or 2 or more very generous cups) pecans, large pieces toasted

¼ teaspoon salt

Preheat the oven to 425°F.

The pan should be double lined with aluminum foil. Heavy-duty aluminum foil with a width of larger than 12 inches is desirable here because otherwise the foil will not fit to the rim of the Pyrex dish, which is 2 inches deep. Butter the foil with melted butter.

Melt the unsweetened chocolate with the butter in a large double boiler or in a heavy saucepan over a low flame, being careful not to burn the chocolate. Stir occasionally until the chocolate and butter are melted. Mix to combine. Set aside.

Beat the eggs, sugar, vanilla, almond extract, and liqueur (and orange oil, if using) in an electric mixer, using the whisk attachment until well mixed and the sugar is dissolved (at least 10 minutes). The eggs will change color. Slowly whisk in the chocolate-butter mix. Then mix the salt into the flour, and slowly add the flour mix to the eggs, again beating slowly only until mixed. Remove the bowl from the mixer and stir in the nuts. Pour the mixture into the prepared pan, smoothing the top.

I suggest placing the pan on top of a cookie sheet to cook to avoid burning the brownie bottom, noting the cooking time may be increased. You may have to experiment with your oven for all recipes to figure out how your oven cooks.

Bake for no more than 30 minutes, checking at 25 minutes to ensure that the brownies do not overcook. For the first 15 minutes, loosely cover the brownies with aluminum foil so that the brownies will not overbrown. Even when the brownies are cooked, a toothpick will come out wet and covered with chocolate. These brownies are so rich that the mixture will solidify as it cools. Do not bake the brownie cake more than 30 minutes and bake less if it appears to be done. The hot, cooked brownies might appear slightly jiggly in the middle.

After you remove the brownies from the oven, they should cool at room temperature. Since the brownies must be chilled to avoid excessive runniness, cover the brownies tightly with aluminum foil at this point, and refrigerate. After the brownies are thoroughly chilled, remove them from the refrigerator. Then to remove the brownies, invert the baking dish with a board tight against the pan as you invert; remove the foil, and slice the brownies into the desired sizes. It is preferable to slice the brownies with a serrated bread knife. If the brownies at this stage survive immediate eating, freeze them for future enjoyment. Frozen brownies should be maintained in an airtight container.

CHOCOLATE CHERRY BARS

These bars are dense and wonderfully chocolaty and intensely cherry flavored, a classic flavor combination, but unless they are cold or frozen, they do not really hold together like a blondie or other traditional bar-shaped cookie. They can, of course, be served on a plate with a scoop of vanilla ice cream.

INGREDIENTS

```
2-plus cups dried sour cherries
10 ounces unsalted butter, split use
1 cup cane sugar, split use
⅔ cup sour cherry juice
1 tablespoon vanilla
½ teaspoon cinnamon (optional)
2 cups plus 2½ tablespoons unbleached flour, split use
¾ cup light brown sugar, packed
½ cup dutch-process cocoa
1 cup shredded coconut, toasted
1 teaspoon kosher salt
about ½ cup ice water
2 eggs
½ cup Kirsch or other cherry-flavored liqueur
½ cup bittersweet chocolate chips
```

Butter a 9x9-inch baking pan. To double, use a 10x15-inch Pyrex pan; be aware that the cooking time for the larger pan is about 75 minutes rather than 50 minutes.

On the stove top, cook the cherries, 2 tablespoons of butter, ¼ cup of cane sugar, and the cherry juice. Simmer, stirring as needed, until the juice is mostly absorbed. Remove from heat. Add vanilla. Add another ¼ cup cane sugar (or more to taste) and stir to dissolve. Add ½ teaspoon cinnamon, if desired. Cool.

In a food processor, pulse together the flour, brown sugar, cocoa powder, coconut, and salt, or whisk by hand. Blend in the remaining 8 tablespoons of butter until the mixture resembles coarse crumbs, and press until the mixture just comes together. Line the baking pan with parchment. Measure out 3 cups of the flour mixture, reserving the rest for a topping, and slowly add up to ½ cup of water, stirring gently with a fork until the dough just holds together when squeezed in your hand. Press 3 cups of the dough (which is, in essence, a shortbread) into the bottom of the pan, pricking the layer with a fork. Chill for at least 30 minutes in the refrigerator. Bake the shortbread in a preheated 325°F oven until firm to the touch and just beginning to pull away from the sides, about 20 minutes. Cool.

Beat the eggs, ½ cup cane sugar, and Kirsch with whisk attachment until the mixture is pale (4 to 5 minutes). Stir in 2½ tablespoons of flour with the cooled cherry mixture; then fold it into the egg-sugar mix. Stir in chocolate chips. Spread over the baked crust. Crumble the remaining shortbread mixture over the top. Bake until set, about 50 minutes. Cool and remove from pan. It is better to refrigerate before cutting into squares.

CHOCOLATE HERMITS

Chocolate hermits are a variant of a molasses cookie, and there are many hermit cookie variations in various recipe books and on the internet. Most versions do not have enough spice flavor (as opposed to "hotness") to my taste, nor do they have enough chocolate flavor. My modifications epitomize the concept of this book, *Deep Flavors*. Most recipes use ground black pepper; this recipe does not—the goal is flavor, not heat. I have seen recipes that suggest making this into bar cookies, but I do not like the result with this recipe.

INGREDIENTS

8 ounces unsalted butter at room temperature

1 cup white cane sugar, plus more sugar crystals to top the unbaked cookies

1 cup light brown sugar

1 teaspoon kosher salt

1 egg, beaten

1 cup buttermilk

¾ cup dark unsulfured molasses

1 tablespoon vanilla extract

½ cup liqueur for soaking or macerating, depending on the fruit (Rum for raisins, cherry liqueur for cherries, and amaretto for apricots. After the fruit has macerated and plumped, there should still be a residual amount of liqueur, which is incorporated in the recipe as additional liquid.)

3 ounces unsweetened chocolate, melted

4 cups unbleached all-purpose flour
1 teaspoon baking soda
2 teaspoons baking powder
½ cup cocoa powder
2½ teaspoons cinnamon
½ teaspoon allspice
½ teaspoon nutmeg, freshly grated
½ teaspoon ground clove
½ teaspoon mace
2½ teaspoons ground ginger
12 ounces bittersweet or semisweet chocolate chips
1½ cups pecans, chopped and toasted
2 cups raisins, chopped apricots, or dried sour cherries

In a KitchenAid mixing bowl, cream the room-temperature butter and both sugars well. Add salt, egg, buttermilk, molasses, and vanilla to the creamed butter and sugar. Drain the liqueur from the macerated fruit and add the remaining liquid to the wet ingredients. Mix the melted chocolate into the wet ingredients.

In a separate bowl, mix the dry ingredients, including the spices and cocoa. Stir the nuts and chocolate chips into the dry ingredients. Slowly mix the dry ingredients into the wet ingredients, being careful not to coat the kitchen by mixing too vigorously as the dry is poured into the wet ingredients. The dough should be thick and relatively stiff. If not, add in some additional flour until the texture is correct and not too sticky. Scrape the bowl with a spatula to mix thoroughly.

After the mixture is well blended but not overbeaten, gently stir in the macerated fruit. Make sure the mixture is consistently mixed all the way to the bottom of the bowl. Chill the dough for 2 hours to overnight to stiffen the dough *and* keep it in the refrigerator between baking batches; if the dough is warm, the cookies will spread too much.

Preheat the oven to 350°F. Line a cookie sheet with parchment or Silpat. I use an insulated cookie sheet (with an air center) or 2 half sheet pans (one inside the other) so the cookie bottoms do not burn. Roll the cookies into golf ball–sized balls and press to flatten slightly. Leave room for the cookies to spread, as they will. Sprinkle the top of the cookies with a liberal amount of crystallized sugar. Bake the cookies for about 12 to 15 minutes. The cookies should appear slightly underdone but will firm as they cool. Take the cookies out of the oven and move to a rack after 5 to 10 minutes to continue cooling. Continue baking batches until all of the dough is used and all of the cookies are baked. As with all cookies, I freeze in an airtight container.

CHOCOLATE-ORANGE-ALMOND-COCONUT BISCOTTI

These biscotti certainly are not your Italian grandmother's cookies, but they are delectable and, once you collect the ingredients, simple to make, albeit with a number of steps. They are a favorite of anyone who has tasted them and may be the best cookie you will ever taste. The candied zest, toasted coconut, and toasted almonds can be prepared days, weeks, or months in advance and frozen or refrigerated.

INGREDIENTS

4 cups (18 ounces) all-purpose flour

1 teaspoon baking powder

1 teaspoon kosher salt

¾–1 cup dutch-process cocoa powder

8 ounces unsalted butter, softened

1 cup light brown sugar, packed

1 cup granulated sugar

4 eggs (jumbo), plus egg white from 1 additional egg for egg wash

¼ cup orange simple syrup, plus a little for the egg wash (The orange simple syrup is a byproduct of making the candied orange zest. Refrigerated in a Ball jar, it keeps indefinitely.)

2 teaspoons pure almond extract

1 teaspoon pure coconut extract (omit if what is available is synthetic, which adds an odd flavor)

1 teaspoon lemon oil

1 teaspoon orange oil (available from King Arthur Flour)

1 teaspoon pure orange extract

1 tablespoon pure vanilla extract

1 cup candied orange zest (not packed), chopped finely with some of the sugar it is packed in (see recipe instructions—the zest is different from a candied peel since the white pith is not used)

2 cups almonds, toasted and roughly chopped

1½–2 cups shredded sweetened coconut, toasted

12 ounces bittersweet chocolate, chopped or chips

King Arthur Flour is an excellent online source for high-quality chocolate, including chips and cocoa. Different cocoas have different fat contents, and cocoa with higher fat content has better flavor. I always order chocolate while the weather is cold, so it does not melt in shipping.

In a bowl, whisk together flour, baking powder, salt, and cocoa powder.

In a separate bowl, cream butter with both sugars until fluffy. Then add and beat in eggs 1 at a time. Finally, add and beat in all of the extracts, flavored oils, and orange simple syrup. Always scrape down the sides between additions to ensure everything is mixed. Then mix in the chopped candied orange zest and the flour mixture. If the mixture is too sticky, add a little extra flour. Mix in nuts and chocolate at the end. The final mixture should be stiff and very slightly sticky. Cover and let rest in the refrigerator for at least ½ hour up to 2 hours. If you let it rest overnight, the dough will be very stiff and hard to work.

Preheat the oven to 350°F. With parchment paper or Silpat, cover a half sheet pan with sides. (Because of the egg-white glaze, Silpat or a similar surface is preferable to make the baked logs easier to slide off onto a board for cutting.)

Roll the rested dough into logs on a sugared (not floured) surface. The logs should be about 1½ to 2 inches wide and 1 inch tall by 13 to 15 inches long. Place the logs carefully on the pan. Leave at least 3 inches between the logs. They will expand in baking. The dough will make 3 to 3½ logs and will need 2 batches to cook. After you form the logs and place them on the baking sheet, brush the tops and sides liberally with a mixture of egg white and orange simple syrup. This gives the biscotti a slight sheen when baked and helps stabilize the biscotti for cutting after the first baking. Sprinkle more sugar on top after brushing on the glaze. You can purchase crystalline sugar that is attractive on the finished cookies for this use.

Cook at 350°F for 35 minutes (or 45 minutes if you refrigerate overnight), rotating the pan halfway through. (I think you get a better result if you only use 1 pan in the oven at a time.) Remove from the oven, and cool until logs can be handled—about 15 to 30 minutes. As they cool, the logs become easier to cut without crumbling, so cooling is very important.

Carefully move the cooled logs onto a cutting board, using a spatula to assist. Carefully cut at an angle with a serrated knife. Pieces should be thick enough (½ inch at least) so that individual pieces will stand up for the second baking. Place the sliced cookies standing up and slightly separated on the baking pan. Lower the oven temperature to 275°F (or 250°F convection) and bake again for 25 to 30 minutes. Remove from the oven, and cool. The cookies will crisp as they cool. Store in freezer for longer life (if they last that long).

Making the Candied Orange Zest

Make the candied orange zest by zesting 3 or more oranges (carefully using no bitter white pith) with a vegetable peeler. Cook the zest at a simmer in a couple cups of simple syrup (a mixture of equal parts of filtered water and cane sugar) until the liquid thickens slightly and the zest is tender, about 15 to 20 minutes. Notwithstanding every recipe I have read that suggests blanching the zest in plain water, discarding the liquid (sometimes repeatedly) before cooking in the simple syrup, I do not do this and regard it as a senseless waste of time, effort, and flavor. Lift out the cooked, softened zest with tongs, letting them drip. Remove the softened, still wet but not dripping zest to a generous bed of dry cane sugar, tossing until separated and well coated. Let the zest dry in this sugar for a couple of hours.

Refrigerate (1) the zest and remaining coating sugar in a Mason jar and (2) the reduced orange simple syrup in a second Mason jar to be used for flavoring. (Mixed in equal parts with egg white, this flavored simple syrup makes an excellent glaze.) Reuse the stored orange simple syrup, adding equal parts as needed of water and sugar to make future batches of candied orange zest; as it is reused, the orange flavor becomes more intense. As with honey, if the stored syrup starts to crystallize, simply heat to refresh, adding water if needed.

COCONUT MACAROONS

At Passover, it is not permissible to eat any leavened product. Since that includes products made with flour other than matzo, other sweets came to the fore. Macaroons do not contain flour and are a traditional delicacy served at Passover. However, this is a treat that transcends cultural or holiday boundaries. In addition, the macaroons are an outstanding way to use excess egg whites generated by the many recipes that call for egg yolks separated from egg whites (that are not then used). Although vanilla macaroons unmodified by additional flavors are great, they are even better when modified by adding chocolate flavor or a citrus flavor. Although commercial macaroons are available, they are simply not in the same league with homemade macaroons as far as taste is concerned.

This recipe is a very different "cookie" from French-style almond macarons, and since it has no flour, it is perhaps not even a cookie. As I look at my mother's recipe, the base recipe called for three egg whites, two tablespoons sugar, and half pound fresh, grated coconut, a product I seriously doubt Mom had access to.

INGREDIENTS

Depending on added flavorings, proportions indicated may vary; see below for variations.

1¼–1½ cups egg whites
½ teaspoon cream of tartar
½ teaspoon salt
1½ cups white cane sugar
at least 1 teaspoon vanilla extract
28 ounces grated, sweetened coconut, toasted

Preheat oven to 350°F.

28 ounces of the toasted coconut will almost fill a 4½-quart KitchenAid mixing bowl. See Chapter 2 for instructions for toasting nuts. This recipe will yield about 48 macaroons using the small muffin tin method described in the instructions.

Beat the egg whites until they are stiff, adding the salt and cream of tartar as the whites are being whipped (assuming you are not using a copper bowl, in which case cream of tartar is not needed). Slowly add the sugar and vanilla extract as the whipping proceeds. One of my basic philosophies is that vanilla can never hurt a dish, and more is better. A KitchenAid mixer with the whisk attachment is excellent to beat the egg whites. Then thoroughly but gently stir in the coconut by hand.

There are 2 alternative baking methods for use with any flavor variant.

Baking Method 1

With a spoon, drop the coconut mixture into mounds on a greased cookie sheet (or a sheet covered with Silpat or parchment). This method permits the macaroons to spread, and the egg whites will separate slightly from the coconut. When the macaroons are toasted until light brown (about 12 to 14 minutes in a 350°F oven), take them out of the oven, and cool them on a rack. After they have cooled slightly, remove them from the pan or Silpat or parchment with a spatula, and sort of mold them back into mounds.

Baking Method 2

There is a much better and easier method of baking macaroons. If you use a muffin tin with holes for very small muffins that will accommodate 24 macaroons or muffins (with holes slightly less than 2 inches in diameter), you eliminate the spreading problem. Spray the muffin-tin holes with a neutral-flavored vegetable oil spray (not olive or peanut) that is kosher for Passover, if that is when these are made. Then simply fill the muffin holes, being careful that the amount of raw macaroon is not so great that it slops over to the next muffin hole.

An even better plan is to eschew the spray; use mini parchment cups to hold the mixture for baking, storage, and service. These cups fit the muffin-tin holes and are a cinch to fill. They easily lift out after cooking. Google "parchment-paper mini-muffin cups" to locate sources. Bake at 350°F for 14 to 15 minutes (a couple of minutes longer for chocolate) until toasted light brown. After removal from the oven, let the macaroons cool very slightly (about 5 minutes), and then remove them carefully from the little muffin holes, prying them out gently with a breakfast knife or butter knife (prying not needed if you use the parchment cups). Repeat as necessary to use up the recipe. Cool on a rack.

Chocolate Macaroon Modification

You should make flavored coconut macaroons in addition to the vanilla variety. The basic recipe is substantially the same, modified as follows: For chocolate coconut macaroons, mix 1¾ cups of sugar with ¾ cup of dutch-process cocoa (sifting the cocoa to eliminate lumps), the salt, and cream of tartar. (Dutch-process cocoa is available from King Arthur Flour at a price significantly less than the brand carried by most retail grocers and is most delicious and intensely chocolaty. I use Dutch-process cocoa because I think it is seriously superior in taste to the brands of regular cocoa generally available.)

As the egg whites are almost fully whipped to soft peaks, gradually add the cocoa mixture to the whipped egg whites. The egg whites may deflate and not whip up into the light fluffy texture that one is familiar with; however, this is not a problem for completing the macaroons. The baked macaroons will be somewhat denser than nonchocolate varieties and will have a very intense chocolate flavor.

If you want to add a citrus flavor (lemon and orange meld wonderfully with chocolate), add grated zest of 1 to 2 oranges or lemons along with the cocoa mixture.

After the egg whites and cocoa mixture are whipped together, add the toasted coconut by hand, stirring thoroughly. Then proceed to shape and bake as indicated (either on a cookie sheet or in the muffin tin). The cooking time for these chocolate macaroons is on the longer end of the indicated cooking period and can extend to perhaps 17 or 18 minutes. If you undercook the macaroons, they will not come out of the tin easily.

Lemon or Orange Macaroon Modification

For lemon-coconut or other citrus macaroons, the process is identical with the following modifications: Beat the egg whites with 1½ cups of sugar to soft peaks, adding the grated zest and juice of 3 lemons, being careful not to add the piths at the end of this process. Alternatively, you could use a mixture of lemon and orange (also delicious) or just orange, using the zest of whatever citrus you desire. This is really good using navel oranges. I have not made lime or grapefruit macaroons, but if that thought floats your boat, go for it. Lemon and lime combined is delicious. The egg-white mixture will beat nicely, and the coconut is then mixed in by hand. The result is lighter in texture than the chocolate macaroons. The whites will deflate—not a problem. Baking time is not more than 15 minutes.

After the macaroons are cooled on a cooling rack, I freeze the macaroons. I usually make 2 batches—1 chocolate and 1 citrus—which produces more than 100 macaroons. As with most cookies, I prefer to eat frozen macaroons, or you can defrost them.

GINGERSNAPS

If you like ginger, you will love these cookies. These cookies have the most intense, wonderful ginger flavor; they leave a lingering and satisfying gingery aftertaste. Most commercial cookies are deficient on the ginger flavor—as with most homemade cookies, these have more flavor and are far better than anything you can purchase.

INGREDIENTS

It is easy to double this recipe. A double recipe will produce about 35 cookies.

9½ ounces all-purpose flour

1½ teaspoons baking soda

1 tablespoon ground ginger

½ teaspoon ground cloves

½ teaspoon kosher salt

7 ounces dark brown sugar

5 ounces unsalted butter at room temperature

3 ounces molasses

1 large egg at room temperature (I use jumbo eggs)

2 teaspoons fresh ginger, finely grated (a microplane grater is excellent for this purpose)

2 ounces candied ginger, finely chopped

sanding sugar for sprinkling (optional)

Preheat the oven to 350°F, or alternatively, use convection heat at 325°F.

In a medium mixing bowl, whisk together the flour, baking soda, ground ginger, ground cloves, and salt. It is easy to weigh the bowl, zero the scale, and then scoop in the correct weight of flour.

Separately, place the brown sugar and butter into the bowl of a stand mixer fitted with the paddle attachment. It is easy to add the butter, and then weigh the brown sugar as you did the flour; that is, zero the scale with the bowl with the butter in it, and then add brown sugar to desired weight. (This avoids using extra measuring cups and is very easy to accomplish.)

Cream the butter and sugar on low speed until light and fluffy, 1 to 2 minutes. Add the molasses, using the same weighing process, then the egg and fresh grated ginger, and beat on medium for 1 minute. Add the candied ginger (really finely chopped—it will take a couple of minutes with a chef's knife, with a hand on the handle and the other on top of the blade). Using a rubber spatula, stir to combine. Add the dry ingredients to the wet, and stir (with mixer, then finishing by hand) until well combined.

Use an insulated cookie sheet with air between layers to avoid burning the bottoms—or use 2 cookie sheets, one inside the other. With a 2-teaspoon-sized scoop, drop the dough onto a parchment-lined half sheet pan, approximately 2 inches apart. If you make the cookie balls by hand, they should be about ¾ the size of a golf ball. These really spread to become thin and crisp, so do not crowd. Sprinkle on sanding sugar, and press in slightly so that the dough is a disk about ½ an inch high and about 1 inch in diameter. Bake on the middle rack of the oven for 15 to 17 minutes for crisp cookies. Rotate the pan halfway through cooking. Use only 1 pan at a time in the oven. Let cool for at least a minute after removing from the oven before moving the cookies because the cookies are still really soft while warm; they will crisp up nicely when they fully cool. I reuse parchment paper for later batches.

After removing from the oven, and after allowing the cookies to stay on the sheet pan for 60 seconds or so, transfer them to a wire rack with a metal spatula to cool completely. Store the cookies in an airtight container for up to 10 days. I freeze all my cookies after they cool. If desired, you may scoop and freeze the cookie dough on a sheet pan and, once frozen, place in a resealable bag to store. Bake directly from the freezer as above, taking out about ½ to 1 hour in advance for the dough balls to thaw.

SHAKER LEMON BARS

This recipe uses the entire lemon—rind, zest, juice, and all (except the seeds, which are never good to eat). The result is an unusually tart lemon bar, a taste that I find quite delicious, with a very intense lemony flavor. The texture is not smooth like a normal lemon bar made with a lemon curd, as it contains little fragments of lemon rind. It can be made somewhat smoother by using a blender rather than a food processor to grind the lemon mixture as discussed next. It is the use of the whole rind and not just the zest that gives these cookies their unusual intensity. It also requires a several-day process because the lemons must macerate in sugar.

INGREDIENTS

This recipe fits in a 9x13-inch glass pan.

Filling

5 medium lemons, or 3 lemons and 3 Persian limes (Persian limes are the regular green limes that are the size of small lemons, as opposed to the very small key limes that are mostly available in ethnic Mexican stores. Select smaller, thin-skinned lemons.)

2 cups granulated sugar

½ teaspoon salt

6 jumbo eggs

Crust

13 ounces or so of lemon snaps or wafers

3 cups grated coconut, toasted .

½ cup sugar

10 tablespoons unsalted butter, melted and cooled

the whites of 2-3 eggs (4-6 tablespoons), brought to room temperature and lightly beaten, not whipped

Preparing the Filling

Around 4 or 5 days before starting on the cookie crust, wash the lemons carefully with detergent to remove any wax or other undesirable items that might be on the surface of the lemon, rinsing well. Dry with a paper towel. Detach any stem remaining and dispose of it. Very thinly slice the lemons and limes (paper thin), removing and disposing of the seeds from the lemons. Put all of the lemon and lime slices into a CorningWare, glass, or Pyroceram container with a cover, and toss with 2 cups of granulated sugar and a pinch of salt. After 1 day, the mixture will have exuded significant liquid. Stir daily for at least 4 or 5 days. The reason for the waiting period is that the sugar extracts the bitterness (as opposed to sourness) out of the lemon or lime rind so that the objectionable flavor is eliminated from the final cookie.

Then take the lemon-sugar mixture out of the refrigerator. In either a food processor or a blender, blend the mixture with 6 whole jumbo eggs and the salt.

When you are ready to bake the cookies, prepare the crust.

Preparing the Crust

For the crust, crush the lemon (or chocolate) wafers and the coconut with ½ cup of sugar in a food processor. Drizzle in 10 tablespoons of cooled, melted butter until thoroughly combined. Prepare the dish for baking by making a cradle out of parchment set crossways in the 9x13-inch Pyrex dish, and press in the cookie crust. Cook the crust for about 15 minutes at 350°F, opening the oven and brushing on the beaten egg whites at about 8 minutes. The beaten egg whites will then finish cooking and will seal the crust lightly so that the filling does not leak through the crust to make the crust soggy. Take the lightly browned crust out of the oven, and let it cool in the pan for at least 30 minutes. Lower the oven temperature to 325°F.

Put the pan with the cooked and cooled cookie crust on a shelf in the 325°F oven. Pour the blended lemon slurry from the blender gently and evenly over the cookie crust. Spread gently with an offset spatula if necessary.

Bake in the 325°F oven for 15 to 20 minutes, checking at 15 minutes. If the mixture is still liquid (wobbly) in the center, continue cooking for 2 to 3 minutes, checking at that kind of interval until the mixture is just set. Do not overcook. Take the cookie out of the oven, and let it cool in the pan for at least 30 minutes. Carefully lift by the parchment cradle onto a cutting board. When fully cooled, cut into squares of the desired size. As with all cookies, I freeze the final result, leaving the "cake" on the cutting board until it is frozen, then cutting before putting into a sealed container. If you do not freeze these cookies, they should certainly be refrigerated because of the amount of egg in the cookie.

BAKLAVA

Baklava are, in my view, one of the Greek civilization's great contributions to human food culture. The original recipe for this came from my wife's cousin, Phyllis Cohen, who is a terrific cook. With some slight modifications, the result is truly unctuous.

INGREDIENTS

This recipe is intended for a 10x15-inch baking pan and calls for foil cupcake holders.

2 pounds pecans, walnuts, or pistachios, toasted and chopped, but not too fine

1 cup sugar

1 tablespoon cinnamon

2 pounds fresh phyllo packages (Frozen if necessary. Alton Brown asserts that frozen is the only way to go, but Phyllis is clear that fresh is easier to work with. Fresh phyllo will probably be available only from a Middle Eastern market.)

¾-1½ pounds salted butter, melted (for this recipe only, use salted butter)

cloves

Syrup

3 cups sugar

2 cups water

1 lemon, juiced

2 sticks cinnamon

½ cup honey

Put all syrup ingredients in saucepan. Gently boil for 20 minutes, and then cool.

Mix together nuts, sugar, and cinnamon.

Brush baking pan with butter. Lay 16 sheets of phyllo in the pan, 2 at a time, buttering each. When placed as indicated, these sheets are the bottom layer of the baklava. The sheets should hang over the sides of the pans, about 2 inches on each of the 4 sides. Go in a circular fashion around the pan so you have extensions over all 4 sides. Make sure the phyllo has enough melted butter on the sides to keep it from drying out.

Sprinkle a layer of nut filling over the phyllo. Top with 2 buttered phyllo sheets that are folded to fit within the pan size. Repeat 8 times. Fold the flaps of phyllo over the stuffing. End with 14 phyllo sheets on top, laid within the boundaries of the pan 2 at a time and buttered.

Cut fairly deeply into the baklava with a large, very sharp knife. It is hard to describe how to cut them, but basically you make 4 equidistant vertical rows down the length of the pan.

Next make 5 or 6 horizontal rows, about 2 inches apart. Third, to form triangles, slice at a 45-degree angle, starting at the bottom left through 1 piece. Then move up 2 inches and cut through 2 pieces. Then move up 2 inches and cut through 3 pieces. Continue until each of the squares have been cut into 2 triangles.

Put a whole clove on each triangle. Cook at 350°F for about 1 hour until golden or when the contents of whole pan move when shaken. After you have taken the baklava out of the oven, set the timer for 7 minutes. Re-cut the baklava triangles during this period. After 7 minutes, slowly pour the cooled syrup over the baklava. It is important that you pour cooled syrup over hot baklava or hot syrup over cooled baklava. Never hot into hot or cold into cold. Cover and refrigerate overnight.

When thoroughly cooled, place into foil or paper cupcake holders. The baklava may be frozen at this time.

If you use frozen phyllo, it should be defrosted overnight in the refrigerator and then left (sealed) at room temperature for 2 hours or so before assembly. Keep covered with moist tea towels after opening.

DEEP FLAVORS CHOCOLATE CHIP OATMEAL COOKIES

These cookies, sometimes called "everything" cookies, are a variant of a chocolate chip oatmeal cookie stuffed with lots of good stuff. They are quite delicious and somewhat unique. I particularly like the effect of the reconstituted dried fruit. Every cookie monster in your house will love them.

INGREDIENTS

This recipe makes approximately 30 cookies.

1½ cups raisins or dried sour cherries
brandy or cherry liqueur for macerating
1½ cups unbleached all-purpose flour
pinch of salt
1 teaspoon baking soda
½ pound unsalted butter, room temperature
¾ cup dark brown sugar, packed
¾ cup granulated sugar

> **2 large or jumbo eggs**
>
> **1 tablespoon pure vanilla extract—be liberal**
>
> **1½ cups old-fashioned rolled, not steel-cut, oats—the texture is important**
>
> **1½ cups bittersweet chocolate chunks or chips**
>
> **1½ cups pecans, toasted and lightly chopped**
>
> **1½ cups coconut, toasted**
>
> **decorating sugar to finish**

A couple days in advance, macerate the fruit in the brandy or cherry liqueur at room temperature, stirring from time to time. Use enough liqueur or juice so that the fruit fully plumps, and the bowl still has some residual liquid. Add liquid as needed, depending on how dry the fruit is to start. This can take a couple of days, or you can speed the process by heating the liquid in the microwave.

Preheat the oven to 350°F (or 325°F if using convection).

I use insulated cookie sheets, which allow the cookies to fully cook without burning the bottoms. Line the cookie sheets with parchment paper or Silpat. Set aside.

In a large bowl, sift together flour, salt, and baking soda. Separately, in the bowl of an electric stand mixer fitted with the paddle attachment, cream together the butter and both sugars at medium speed until the mixture is light and fluffy. Scrape the sides of the bowl once or twice during the mixing. When mixture is light and fluffy, add the eggs 1 at a time, and mix to combine. Add the vanilla, and mix to combine, again scraping down the sides of the bowl. Slowly add the flour mixture to the butter mixture, and mix until well combined. Add the oats, pecans, raisins or cherries, chocolate, and coconut, and mix well to combine.

Chill the mixture well before cooking. When the mixture is well chilled, it will be quite stiff. Spoon out the dough and roll into approximately golf ball–sized balls. Top with some large crystal decorating sugar. Bake for 14 to 16 minutes or until lightly browned. Remove the cookies to a cooling rack, continuing the process until all of the dough is used. The cookies while hot will be quite fragile. It is much easier to slide the parchment onto the cooling rack and wait to remove the cookies until 15 to 20 minutes have elapsed and they are somewhat cooled and set. These cookies freeze well.

CANDY

DARK CHOCOLATE GANACHE BAR (WITH CHERRY, ORANGE, OR RASPBERRY)

As everyone is aware, the US Department of Agriculture made a grievous error when they failed to create a food group for chocolate. Chocolate, notwithstanding the efforts of the commercial candy industry, can be a most complex and satisfying treat! While most chocolate is good, it is better to search out the best-tasting bars to work with. Wonderful sources abound. Different brands can have wildly varying taste profiles, and you should use what you like. There are highly rated and expensive brands I simply do not like as much as others—it is a matter of taste.

This is a most delicious dense bar.

INGREDIENTS

Ingredients are for an 8-inch square pan. Double the amounts for a 9x13-inch pan. Use Pyrex for this purpose.

1½ cups unbleached flour

⅞ cup confectioners' sugar

⅜ cup unsweetened dutch-process cocoa

½ teaspoon kosher salt

12 tablespoons unsalted cold butter

1 tablespoon vanilla extract

12 ounces bittersweet or semisweet chocolate, finely chopped

⅔ cup heavy cream

3 tablespoons Kirsch (or other cherry-flavored liqueur if you are making a cherry-flavored bar), rum, brandy, or other spirit (such as Grand Marnier if making an orange flavor or a raspberry liqueur such as Chambord if making a raspberry-flavored bar, etc.)

> *if making orange-flavored bar:* ¼ cup (or so) candied orange zest, very finely chopped (see instructions for making your own under the Chocolate-Orange-Almond-Coconut Biscotti recipe in Chapter 15)

> *if making cherry-flavored bar:* ¼–½ cup dried sour cherries, macerated in cherry liqueur (or sour cherry juice) and chopped after maceration

> *if making raspberry-flavored bar:* ¼–½ cup raspberry jam

In a food processer, pulse together the flour, sugar, cocoa powder, and salt. Add the butter and vanilla, and pulse until the mixture just comes together. Line the baking pan with parchment paper. Press the dough (which is, in essence, shortbread dough) into the bottom of the pan, pricking the layer with a fork. Chill for at least 30 minutes in the refrigerator.

Preheat the oven to 325°F and bake the shortbread until firm to the touch and just beginning to pull away from the sides—about 25 minutes. Cool. Heat the heavy cream on the stove top. Add the chocolate into the cream, letting it sit in the cream for a couple of minutes before stirring to make a ganache. Mix the choice of fruit (macerated cherries, chopped orange, or raspberry jam, as appropriate) into the ganache. Whisk in the appropriate liqueur. Spread over the shortbread. Cool, slice, and serve.

ICE CREAM AND SAUCES

CHOCOLATE ICE CREAM (AND VARIANTS)

A prime manifestation of chocolate is chocolate ice cream or frozen custard.

Once you have the custard base mastered, you can move forward to any number of variants with ease. In the case of ice cream, it is hardly worth the effort if you are not going to make ice cream that is richer and better than anything you can buy in a store. Needless to say, you will not use any unpronounceable chemicals.

In the case of chocolate ice cream, if you do not use the best-quality chocolate and cocoa, you cannot come to a final resolution of an outstanding chocolate ice cream. Similarly, you need to use the highest-quality vanilla (because vanilla is a prime ingredient in chocolate ice cream). Also, you must use high-quality milk and heavy cream, noting that some brands of heavy cream skimp on the butterfat—read the labels.

This is a matter of taste, but a product where the chocolate is going to be the star is not the place where you want to start skimping on the quality. Better quality does not necessarily mean significantly higher price. For example, the cocoa and vanilla extract that I buy from King Arthur Flour is, in my experience, cheaper and better quality than what I can get in a grocery store. The flavor of chocolate, like that of grapes used to make wine, is very much influenced by terroir, and your ice cream's taste will change by your selection of chocolate.

This version uses eggs because an egg-custard–based ice cream simply has a better texture and flavor after it is frozen. Make the custard and assemble the final mixture a number of hours before processing the custard into ice cream—you want the custard to be as cold as the refrigerator will get it before freezing in your ice cream maker to facilitate the freezing process. The average home ice cream freezer only whips air into the custard and gets it cold enough that it is semifrozen. The ice cream at this stage resembles soft serve, and your Thermapen should read twenty-one degrees Fahrenheit. Once this is done, you then need to remove the mixture and put it in a container for proper freezing and storage in your freezer.

Once you have the ice cream base made and have frozen it in the ice cream maker, you can then mix in flavorings and other ingredients to make variants. For example, I frequently make a chocolate Oreo ice cream. I use a package of chocolate-filled Oreos (that is, Oreos filled with chocolate cream as opposed to the original white cream)—the cream filling is no longer lard and, therefore, no longer prohibited. The lemon Oreo cookies also are a wonderful addition. Break the cookies up into small pieces; then freeze the cookie bits before mixing into the freshly churned ice cream.

Flavorings can get more sophisticated, such as by adding orange extract or liqueur and finely chopped candied orange zest. You can make chocolate-coconut ice cream by adding a couple cups of toasted coconut to the churned ice cream, chocolate-cherry ice cream by adding dried cherries macerated in cherry liqueur, or chocolate-rum-raisin ice cream by adding a couple cups of raisins macerated in a dark rum such as Myers's. If you want chocolate-cinnamon ice cream, add a teaspoon of ground cinnamon to the custard before churning. The options are endless, and you are limited only by your imagination. Liqueurs and liquid flavorings can be added to the base at the start of the churning process. Be judicious in your selection of flavorings: some extracts (coconut comes to mind) are artificial and harsh flavored and can ruin the final result. Others can be so intense (such as almond extract or citrus oil) that, although delicious in moderation, too much can have the same deleterious effect.

Freeze the container into which you are going to transfer the ice cream in the freezer so that it is already cold and will not melt the ice cream as you transfer it for storage and final freezing. Everything should be freshly out of the freezer.

The process is not difficult, nor is it particularly time consuming, although it will take up to three days to complete the process. When you make the custard, it takes a day to refrigerate it. It also takes two days to churn the ice cream in batches, unless you have a lot of freezer capacity for ice cream (I use a Cuisinart ice cream maker, which requires that the freezing container be frozen for twenty-four hours first before it can be used to freeze the ice cream; thus, a wait time between batches. This recipe makes three batches using this particular ice cream maker.) If you use an ice cream maker that operates with the classic process where you add salt and ice around the freezing container, or if you use a machine with a built-in refrigeration unit, you can freeze multiple batches in one day. In any event, the result will be a luxurious, wonderful, chocolaty product.

INGREDIENTS

```
1 quart whole milk
up to 4 vanilla pods, split and scraped (or 2 tablespoons vanilla
extract)
12 eggs (6 whole eggs and 6 egg yolks)
2 cups cane sugar, split use,
½ teaspoon salt
½ cup dutch-process cocoa
1 quart heavy cream, split use
1 pound of your favorite bittersweet chocolate, chopped finely
```

Heat 1 quart of whole milk, into which you have added the scraped vanilla pods, including both seeds and pods. (If you do not have vanilla pods, use 2 tablespoons of vanilla at the *end* of the custard recipe, after all cooking is finished, immediately before refrigerating. If you heat vanilla extract, it will drive off flavor.)

Once the milk is heated to a bare simmer, turn the heat off, and let the milk, vanilla seed, and pod mixture rest for ½ an hour to allow the vanilla to infuse and flavor the milk.

Whisk the 6 egg yolks and 6 whole eggs with 1½ cups of cane sugar and ½ teaspoon of salt until thoroughly combined and the sugar is dissolved. Strain the milk mixture slowly into the eggs, whisking constantly to temper the eggs. Take care that you do not do this process too fast, or you can scramble the eggs. Then immediately pour the combined mixture back into the saucepan. Heat slowly, stirring constantly, making sure to reach the corners of the pan, until the mixture thickens into custard. This will occur at about 175°F. Remove immediately from the heat. It is important that you do not leave the stove or stop stirring. Do not heat the mixture so rapidly that the eggs curdle and scramble. Since the pot is hot, in order to stop the cooking immediately after the mixture thickens into custard, strain the mixture into a bowl that is large enough to accommodate another quart of liquid (the cream and chocolate).

In a separate bowl, mix ½ cup of dutch-process cocoa and ½ cup of cane sugar. Vigorously but carefully, stir just sufficient cool water into this powder in order to make the cocoa and sugar come to a smooth, heavy syrup or paste. You need to mix this carefully until all of the cocoa and all of the sugar is worked into a syrup or paste with no lumps. The cocoa resists hydration, and you need to be diligent to avoid lumps.

You can rinse and reuse the pan that you just used to make the custard. Add and heat 2 cups of heavy cream to a bare simmer. When the heavy cream is heated, immediately pour it over the chopped bittersweet chocolate in a bowl. Let it sit for a minute, and then stir until the ganache is smooth and consistently dark brown. Add the ganache and the cocoa mixture into the custard. Stir in the 2 remaining cups of cold heavy cream. At this point, if you did not use vanilla pods to infuse and flavor the milk, stir in 2 tablespoons of vanilla extract.

Cover the mixture with plastic wrap so that the plastic wrap rests directly on the surface of the custard. This process prevents a film from forming on the surface of the custard. Refrigerate overnight or until it is well chilled. After the custard is well chilled, follow the directions for your ice cream churn to morph the custard into an ice cream.

When the churning process is complete, you may mix in other ingredients into the still somewhat soft ice cream to make the variant flavors of ice cream—and there are endless varieties. (Of course, this is great ice cream as it is.) If you are adding liquid flavors such as extracts or a liqueur, they may be added before the churning process, but any solid flavorings such as chopped candied orange peel, nuts, dried fruits, etc. should be mixed in after the custard is frozen in the churn. The ice cream then needs to be frozen further in a freezer. You may well never want to buy another commercial ice cream.

SWISS HOT FUDGE SAUCE

There are many brands of chocolate sauce or fudge sauce to be found in the grocery store. So far as I am aware, all of these contain artificial ingredients and, in my opinion, are not appropriate for human consumption. A reading of the label of a leading brand of chocolate syrup discloses high-fructose corn syrup, sugar, water, and corn syrup (that is, water and sugar) as principal ingredients—and then and only then as a fifth ingredient, cocoa, followed by potassium sorbate, salt, mono- and diglycerides from vegetable oil, polysorbate 60, xanthan gum, and vanillin (an artificial vanilla flavor), with a small print notation that, notwithstanding a big statement on the front of the label that it is a fat-free food, one of the ingredients adds an allegedly "negligible" amount of fat.

This recipe does contain fat and is not low calorie, but it may be the best chocolate sauce you will ever taste. It replicates a fudge sauce that I remember from an ice cream shop in Silver Spring, Maryland, that is unfortunately now nonexistent. It does not contain any of those chemicals of which the food industry is fond. Thus, it will spoil, so I freeze it in Ball jars until I am ready to use it. The inspiration for this recipe comes from Maida Heatter.

INGREDIENTS

1 Batch

½ cup heavy cream
3 tablespoons unsalted butter
⅓ cup granulated sugar (taking care to make sure it is cane sugar)
⅓ cup dark brown sugar, firmly packed
pinch of salt
½ cup unsweetened dutch-process cocoa, sifted to remove all lumps (sifting is critical)

This recipe can be multiplied easily, and I usually make enough to freeze—4 or more

4 Batches

2 cups heavy cream
12 tablespoons butter
1⅓ cups granulated sugar
1⅓ cups dark brown sugar
large pinch salt
2 cups unsweetened dutch-process cocoa

Heat the cream and butter over moderate heat, stirring until the butter is melted and the cream comes to a low boil. Add the sugars and stir for a few minutes until they are dissolved. Reducing the heat, add salt and cocoa, stirring briskly with a wire whisk until smooth. (You may wish to mix the cocoa with a small amount of water to make a thick paste prior to mixing into the hot liquid to facilitate amalgamation and removal of any lumps of undissolved cocoa.)

As soon as the mixture is smooth, remove it from the heat. The mixture will be very thick and will thicken if it is reheated. To thin, you may add a small amount of water, stirring in carefully.

When you store the sauce, use widemouthed Ball jars that are straight sided, not the type with a cap that is smaller than the sides of the jars. If you use a small-mouthed jar, the sauce is so thick that it will be impossible to get it out of the jar effectively. Reheat by placing the jar in a pan with boiling water or reheat gently in the microwave.

Serve over ice cream or with berries or in any other desired fashion.

CAKES

ORANGE FUDGE PUDDING CAKE

This "cake" will sound most improbable, but it is easy to make and delicious by itself or served with ice cream, either vanilla or chocolate. Orange and chocolate are a classic combination.

INGREDIENTS

This recipe is for an 8-inch square pan. If you double the recipe, use a 9x13-inch pan. I use Pyrex and not metal for this recipe.

⅔ cup dutch-process cocoa, sifted, split use
⅓ cup light brown sugar, packed well
1 cup white cane sugar, split use
6 tablespoons unsalted butter
2 ounces dark semisweet or bittersweet (not milk) chocolate, chopped
¾ cup unbleached flour
2 teaspoons baking powder

```
¼ teaspoon salt
1 teaspoon vanilla extract
⅓ cup milk (not skim)
1 egg yolk
1½ cups orange juice
1 teaspoon orange extract
no more than 1 teaspoon orange oil

Preheat the oven to 325°F.
```

Butter or spray the pan. In a small bowl, whisk together ⅓ cup of sifted cocoa, all of the brown sugar, and ⅓ cup of white cane sugar.

Melt the butter and chocolate in a double boiler (or microwave), being careful to just melt the chocolate so that it does not burn, and whisk till smooth. Whisk in the remaining ⅓ cup of cocoa. Cool slightly.

In a separate small bowl, whisk the flour, baking powder, and salt, and set aside.

In a medium bowl, whisk the remaining ⅔ cup of white cane sugar, vanilla, and milk until dissolved and combined. Whisk in the egg yolk. Add the melted chocolate mixture and whisk to combine. Add the flour mixture and stir until evenly moistened. Pour the batter into the baking tray and spread evenly. Sprinkle the dry cocoa mixture evenly over the batter so that it covers the entire surface of the tray.

Now comes what will seem to be a very strange process. Mix together the orange juice, orange extract, and orange oil; then gently pour it over the cocoa mixture. Put the pan in the oven. Bake until the cake is puffed and bubbling and just beginning to pull away from the sides of the baking dish (about 45 minutes). Do not overbake. Cool the cake in the dish for 25 to 30 minutes before serving. The cake will have a wonderful orangey, fudgy, saucy bottom with a cake topping—a most strange result, but delicious.

BANANA NUT BREAD (WITH CHOCOLATE)

This is one of the most delicious recipes for banana nut bread (although my family insists that because of all of the ancillary ingredients, it is not really banana nut bread) that you will ever taste. It has an incredible banana flavor. It depends on two very basic and easy but critical requirements. First, you need a lot of very ripe bananas with heavily speckled skins, and second, you microwave the bananas, drain them, and simmer the drained liquid to seriously reduce the liquid volume, intensifying the banana flavor.

INGREDIENTS

This recipe makes 2 intensely flavored 8.5x4.5-inch or 9x5-inch loaves.

1¾ cups unbleached all-purpose flour (8¾ ounces)

1 teaspoon baking soda

½ teaspoon salt

1 teaspoon cinnamon

2½ pounds very ripe bananas, peeled (approximately 6-8 bananas)

1 teaspoon or more vanilla extract

½ cup unsalted butter, melted and then cooled

2 jumbo eggs

¾ cup light brown sugar, packed (5¼ ounces)

2 cups raisins (or tart dried cherries)

2 cups pecans, chopped lightly and toasted

2 cups coconut, toasted (optional)

2 cups semisweet or bittersweet chocolate chips (optional)

⅓ cup dutch-process cocoa (optional)

⅓ cup white cane sugar (optional if adding cocoa)

Preheat the oven to 350°F. Place the oven rack in the middle position. Spray your loaf pans with nonstick cooking spray. Set aside.

Whisk flour, baking soda, salt, and cinnamon (and cocoa and white cane sugar, if using), in a large bowl. Set aside.

Peel the bananas and weigh them. Cut into 1-inch pieces, and place them into a microwave bowl, and cover it with plastic wrap or a glass cover. (A CorningWare dish with a glass lid is excellent for this purpose.) If you are using plastic wrap, cut steam vents into the plastic with a knife. Microwave on high for 5 minutes until the bananas are soft and release liquid. Stir and let sit for 5 minutes until the bananas fully exude their liquid. Drain the bananas in a stainless steel mesh strainer over a bowl. Allow the bananas to drain fully, stirring occasionally. The bananas should be cooled, and you should have about ¾ cup or so of watery liquid in the bowl. Reduce this liquid in a pot on a stove burner, being careful to not let the liquid boil over, as it will if you do not watch it constantly, stirring and moderating the heat from time to time. The liquid should be reduced to a syrup (about ¼ to ½ a cup, depending how much liquid you start with). This reduction will take about 10 minutes, and it will have an intense banana flavor. Cool.

Mash the cooked bananas, and mix them with the vanilla, melted butter, eggs, brown sugar, and the cooled banana syrup.

Add the liquid ingredients into the dry flour mixture and stir until just combined. A machine is not needed. Fold in the fruit, pecans, coconut, and chocolate chips. Divide the batter, now mixed, into the 2 pans. (While I would normally be inclined to soak the dried fruit for texture—and flavor—it is not only not necessary but soaking here would add too much liquid and make the loaves difficult to bake.)

Bake for 55 to 75 minutes, until a toothpick inserted into the middle of the loaf comes out clean. The larger pan cooks slower than the smaller pan, so start testing at 55 minutes, and continue baking until the toothpick comes out clean. Undercooked banana nut bread will be mushy and not satisfactory in texture. When the bread is baked, cool it in the pan on a wire rack for about 15 minutes. Gently remove from the pan and continue to cool on the rack.

Serve warm or at room temperature (or frozen). Slice any excess and freeze it. As with cookies, I think it is excellent chilled or frozen. This is a matter of taste. I can assure you that this banana nut bread will meet your expectation of *Deep Flavors*.

CHERRY PAN CAKE

This recipe is not clafouti, nor is it a classic cake; it is more in the southern tradition of a sheet cake with a lot of fillings. It is reminiscent of the Fresh Apple Cake (Chapter 15) that my wife makes but is, at the same time, very different. When I make it, I cut it into squares and freeze it because I like the texture when it is frozen. In an unfrozen state, it is very, very moist and sticky and should be eaten with ice cream on the side, and indeed, it is wonderful served warm with ice cream.

INGREDIENTS

This recipe fits in a square 9x9-inch baking dish. If you double the recipe, use a 10x15-inch baking dish.

Cake

1 cup sugar

2 tablespoons butter at room temperature

1 egg

2 teaspoons pure vanilla extract

1 cup unbleached all-purpose flour

1 teaspoon baking powder

¼ teaspoon salt

½ cup whole milk

1 (24-ounce) can or bottle of tart cherries in light syrup (I sometimes use Zergut, which is available online and from specialty shops. Oregon and Comstock each make a canned version of tart cherries packed in water and only 14½ ounces, which are also delicious. Do *not* use canned cherry pie filling.)

1 cup or so pecans, roughly chopped and toasted

1 cup coconut, toasted (optional)

Sauce

juice from tart cherries (Zergut yields 1¼ cups of liquid per bottle, and the cans—Oregon or Comstock—each yield less than 1 cup. You can add a sufficient amount of sour cherry juice to bring the total amount of liquid up to 1¼ cups)

¾ cup sugar if you are using cherries packed in light syrup (or 1 cup sugar if you are using cherries packed in water)

½ teaspoon cinnamon

pinch of salt

1 teaspoon vanilla

Before the process of baking the cake, combine the cherries, juice, cinnamon, and sugar for the sauce. Heat until boiling. Whisk to combine the cinnamon, which is somewhat resistant to incorporating into the liquid. Add a pinch of salt. Let the mixture cool for at least 30 to 45 minutes or refrigerate overnight. Cook until when you test a cherry by tasting it, it has a desired flavor: tart but not overly sour. Drain the cooked cherries well when you start to make the cake, reserving the liquid into a bowl.

Baking the Cake

Preheat the oven to 325°F.

Generously butter your baking dish. (I use Pyrex.) Then pour some flour into the dish and move the dish around to have the flour coat the butter. Pour out any extra flour for use in the cake.

Cream the sugar and butter for 2 minutes, using the beater attachment for a KitchenAid mixer. Add the egg and vanilla and mix well. In a separate bowl, sift the flour, baking powder, and salt together. Then add the flour mixture to the creamed butter, alternating with the addition of milk. Scrape off the beater with a rubber spatula. Then add in the drained tart cherries and chopped nuts, including the coconut if you are using it. Fold the solid ingredients into the cake mixture.

Pour the batter into the buttered pan and smooth the surface. Bake the cake for about 45 minutes, checking at 40 minutes. Bake until golden brown on the surface and a toothpick comes out clean. The cake may need to cook for longer than 45 minutes, particularly if the recipe is doubled, but check frequently so that it does not overcook. While the cake is baking, begin to make the sauce.

When the cake has cooked, remove it from the oven, and with a sharp knife, release the cake as necessary from the sides of the pan. Let the cake sit for 5 to 10 minutes to cool slightly, and then remove the cake to a plate to finish cooling. Poke the cake liberally with a cake tester or toothpick; then immediately spread the warm, reduced sauce (instructions below) onto the cake, and let it soak in. If you do not do this while the cake is warm, the cherry sauce will not soak through the cake. Cool. The cake can be served at this time with ice cream, or it can be cut into squares and placed on a double layer of wax paper and frozen.

Making the Sauce

For this sauce, use the reserved cherry-cooking liquid. As the cake is baking, reduce the cherry "simple syrup" until it is very syrupy and coats a spoon thickly. You will need to watch the syrup so that it does not boil over, because if it does, you will have a royal mess on your hands. Turn off the heat, and only then do you add vanilla to the syrup. Add carefully, as the vanilla will cause the syrup to boil up. You should have about ¾ (or slightly less) of a cup of syrup per recipe from the 1¼ cups that you started with. This warm sauce is used to soak into the cake after it is baked.

FRESH APPLE CAKE

I have had many apple cakes over my lifetime. This one is absolutely the best, moistest, most apple-flavored, and most redolent of cinnamon anywhere. It is also perhaps one of the tastiest and most appreciated coffee cakes of any type that I have ever eaten. Bobbie got this recipe from a friend many years ago. This rendition may be the only remaining version.

INGREDIENTS

```
4 large (11 ounces or more each) cooking apples (Honeycrisp
variety preferably, or other good cooking apples)
1 cup pecans, toasted and chopped
7 teaspoons cinnamon, split use
⅔ cup butter
½ teaspoon salt
2 cups sugar, plus sugar for topping
2 eggs
2 tablespoons vanilla
1 heaping teaspoon baking powder
1 teaspoon baking soda
2 cups flour

Preheat the oven to 350°F.
```

Peel, core, and chop apples into ¼-inch cubes. Chop the nuts—mix them with about 2 teaspoons of the cinnamon, stir them with the apples, and set aside. By adding the cinnamon, you will not see as much browning on the apples.

Cream the butter, salt, and sugar with the KitchenAid beater attachment, and continue until the butter changes color—1 to 2 minutes. Do not overbeat, because the goal is only to whip air into the butter mixture. Add eggs and vanilla, and beat until fluffy, scraping the bowl to ensure even mixing.

In a separate bowl, whisk the baking powder, baking soda, and 2 teaspoons of cinnamon into the flour. Add the flour mixture to the butter mixture in 3 or 4 additions, mixing well. The batter will be thick. Remove from mixer. Pour into a very large mixing bowl (to cut down on strays). Then add the apples and nuts, and mix using a large spatula until well mixed. The batter will be a very thick mixture, but you want the batter well distributed among the apples and nuts.

Pour into a 13x9x2-inch Pyrex pan that you have lined with aluminum foil and well oiled or buttered ahead.

The topping is a most important part.

Make a mixture of cinnamon and sugar totaling about ½ cup. Make the topping mixture look really dark brown. The ½ cup will contain 3 teaspoons of cinnamon. Sprinkle it liberally and evenly over the top of the raw apple cake.

Bake in the preheated oven for 50 minutes. (Depending on your oven, it may need to be cooked longer if it turns out too moist; trial and error testing may be required.) The mixture will still be moist when done, so the toothpick test does not work. Let cool on top of stove, and serve either warm or cold. I like it frozen. It will not matter; even somewhat undercooked, it will be yummy. It will get eaten any way it is served. Enjoy!

CHOCOLATE PINWHEEL CAKE

This cake was my mother's recipe, and I remember eating it for at least sixty years. I am not sure that I have ever had a better pure chocolate cake. It is very chocolaty, with a moist and excellent crumb. Some modifications have been made; for example, Mom used Crisco solid shortening, and we now use unsalted butter. Although this cake uses only unsweetened chocolate, it is delightfully sweet. If you use high-quality chocolate, the resulting cake is improved. For many years we used a chocolate brand from the supermarket, but King Arthur Flour carries superior unsweetened chocolate in disks rather than squares. A digital kitchen scale is very helpful here. As a historical note, the large cans of evaporated milk have been reduced by, I believe, four ounces to the current size of twelve ounces so that multiple cans are required to supply the thirteen ounces needed in the recipe. A five ounce can is also available. This cake, along with the German's Sweet Chocolate Cake (Chapter 15), has served well as many a birthday cake and is one of the go-to chocolate cakes in our house.

INGREDIENTS

5 ounces unsweetened chocolate, split use

1¾ cups cake flour (not all-purpose), sifted

2½ cups cane sugar, split use

2 teaspoons baking powder

¼ teaspoon baking soda

1¼ teaspoons salt, split use

1 1/6 cups unsalted butter, split use (typically 2 sticks plus 2 tablespoons plus 2 teaspoons)

13 ounces evaporated milk, split use (preferably Carnation, and not sweetened condensed milk)

2 teaspoons pure vanilla extract, split use

1 tablespoon water

2 eggs

Preheat your oven to 350°F.

Making the Cake

Melt 2 ounces unsweetened chocolate.

Sift together cake flour, 1½ cups sugar, baking powder, baking soda, and 1 teaspoon salt. In the bowl of a KitchenAid mixer with the beater attachment, stir ½ cup room-temperature butter. Add half the flour mixture, then ½ cup undiluted Carnation evaporated milk and 1 teaspoon vanilla, mixing to dampen the flour. Add the rest of the flour mixture and another ½ cup of the evaporated milk. Beat in the KitchenAid mixer for 2 minutes at low speed. Add the eggs, an additional ¼ cup evaporated milk, and 2 ounces of melted chocolate, and beat for 1 minute. Pour the batter into two 9-inch round cake pans, lined on the bottom with waxed or parchment paper and also buttered and floured. Then add the topping before baking.

Making the Topping

Carefully melt 2 ounces of the unsweetened chocolate. Pour the melted chocolate in concentric circles on top of the batter in each pan. Make a swirl design in each pan by moving the tip of your pointed knife gently through the drizzled chocolate. Bake at 350°F for about 30 minutes. Test with a toothpick for doneness, noting that the chocolate swirl will still be liquid. While the cake cools, make the buttercream filling.

Making the Buttercream Filling

Combine the following in a bowl: 1 ounce of unsweetened chocolate, melted and cooled; ⅔ cup (1 stick plus 2 tablespoons plus 2 teaspoons) of butter; 1 cup granulated white cane sugar; ⅓ cup undiluted evaporated milk; ¼ teaspoon salt; 1 teaspoon vanilla; and 1 tablespoon water. Whip the mixture for 10 minutes or until fluffy. *Note*: Use of granulated sugar in this buttercream leads to a filling with a somewhat gritty texture because the sugar does not totally dissolve, which my family likes; if this is a problem to your taste, substitute superfine sugar for a perfectly smooth buttercream.

After the cakes have fully cooled, split the 2 cakes into layers to make 4 layers. Spread about ⅓ of the whipped buttercream mixture (about ⅔ cup) between each layer, leaving the top layer to be one of the pieces with the drizzled chocolate design. It is important to chill the cake to firm the buttercream before serving so that the layers do not slide.

PUMPKIN PECAN CHEESECAKE

INGREDIENTS

1 batch of crumb topping (see recipe under Apple Pie recipe earlier in Chapter 15)

Crust

1½ cups crushed vanilla wafers or graham cracker crumbs

¼ cup sugar

6 tablespoons butter, melted

Filling

3 (8-ounce) packages Philadelphia cream cheese, room temperature

¾ cup sugar

¾ cup brown sugar, packed

5 eggs

16 ounces canned pure pumpkin

¼ cup heavy cream

1 teaspoon cinnamon

½ teaspoon nutmeg

¼ teaspoon cloves

To make the crust, combine the crushed wafers, sugar, and butter, and press firmly into the bottom of lightly greased 9-inch springform pan. Spread the crust halfway up the sides. Bake about 15 minutes at 350°F.

To make the filling, mix the cream cheese, sugar, and brown sugar together in a KitchenAid mixer with the beater attachment. Beat on high speed until light and fluffy. Add eggs 1 at a time. Beat well after every addition, scraping the bowl. Stir in the pumpkin, heavy cream, and spices. Double wrap the springform pan in aluminum foil so that water will not leak in. Then pour the filling into the prebaked crust. Place the pan into a larger pan and move it to the oven shelf. Fill the larger pan with boiling water to half the height of the springform pan, and carefully slide the rack in, and close the oven door. Bake in the water bath at 350°F for 1 hour. Then add the crumb topping and bake for an additional 15 minutes in the water bath.

Remove it from the water bath and allow it to cool to room temperature. Then refrigerate overnight before loosening and decanting to a plate for serving.

GERMAN'S SWEET CHOCOLATE CAKE WITH COCONUT-PECAN-CARAMEL FILLING

I have heard this cake described as "better than sex," and while I am not sure that I would use that degree of hyperbole, this cake is certainly a longtime favorite in our house. Bobbie, my wife, is the principal cake and pie baker in our house and has been making this cake since we were married in 1968, a long time ago, and my mother made the cake as I was growing up. This recipe includes Bobbie's practical suggestions and modifications from the wrapper recipe to make the perfect cake-and-frosting combination. I have had many examples made by other bakers, but Bobbie's version set forth below is the gold standard.

Like many wonderful things, the origin of this recipe is Texan. It was included in a letter to the *Dallas Morning News* in the 1950s. As with the German's Sweet Chocolate Pie earlier in Chapter 15, the recipe was eventually printed inside the wrapper of Baker's German's Sweet Chocolate and became widely available. This chocolate product was fortuitously developed by a Mr. German, and it has nothing to do with the country of Germany or the Pennsylvania Dutch. As a historical note, the cake was reputedly served by President Johnson at his ranch on the Pedernales River to the chancellor of Germany.

While it is true that this chocolate is not of the intense, often even bitter variety now so popular, and it does not produce the most intensely chocolate cake, the resulting cake stands on its own. The cake's texture is wonderful, and the flavor melds perfectly with the unique frosting combination of a "caramelly" base combined with pecan and coconut to produce a sweet and irresistible result. You will devour the cake and the frosting! I have seen recipes on the internet using other chocolate products to bake this cake, and Bobbie once substituted a semisweet chocolate, but the taste just does not work. However, addition of the optional bittersweet chocolate steps the recipe up a notch.

INGREDIENTS

This recipe makes 16 servings.

Cake

1 (4-ounce) package Baker's German's Sweet Chocolate

½ cup filtered water

2 cups unbleached all-purpose flour

1 teaspoon baking soda

¼ teaspoon salt

1 cup unsalted butter, softened to room temperature

2 cups sugar

4 eggs, separated

1 teaspoon or so quality vanilla extract

½ cup buttermilk

an additional 4 ounces of a quality bittersweet chocolate, with an additional 3 tablespoons of water (optional—if you go with this option, add an additional ¼ cup of flour)

Coconut-pecan-caramel filling

1 (12-ounce) can evaporated milk

1½ cups sugar

¾ cup unsalted butter

4 egg yolks, slightly beaten

1½ teaspoons vanilla (Bobbie really doesn't measure)

1 (7-ounce) package Baker's Angel Flake Coconut, toasted (about ⅔ cup)

1½ cups pecans, chopped and toasted

Making the Cake

Preheat the oven to 350°F.

Butter and line the bottoms of three 9-inch cake pans with parchment or wax paper; butter the sides of the pans and the paper. (Actually, Bobbie uses unflavored Pam spray.) When Mom and then Bobbie started making this cake, parchment paper was not available, but it is now the preferred product for oven use.

Break up the chocolate. Melt the chocolate in the filtered water either in a double boiler or by microwaving the chocolate and water in a large, covered, microwavable bowl on high for 45 seconds, then stirring, or until chocolate is almost melted. You have to stir because the chocolate may not look melted, even though it is. Stir until melted. If you are using the microwave, restart for another 30 seconds, and stir again as necessary, being careful to not burn the chocolate.

Whisk the flour, baking soda, and salt in a bowl. Set aside. Then beat the butter and sugar in large bowl with the beater attachment, not the whisk, in an electric mixer such as a KitchenAid. Use the medium speed until light and fluffy—a couple of minutes. Add the egg yolks, 1 at a time, beating well until combined after each addition. Stir in the melted chocolate and vanilla. Add the flour mixture slowly, alternating with buttermilk and beating until well blended after each addition. Beat egg whites in another large bowl with the electric mixer on high speed until stiff peaks form. Gently stir into the batter. Pour evenly into the prepared pans. (This is a perfect time to use a kitchen scale.)

Bake at 350°F for 30 minutes or until a toothpick inserted into the centers comes out clean. Immediately run a knife or spatula between each cake and the sides of each pan. Cool for 15 minutes. Remove the cake layers from the pans by placing a flat board or plate over the cake pan and quickly inverting. The cakes should slip out of the pans. Remove the paper from the now exposed bottoms of the cakes. Cool completely on wire racks. Spread coconut-pecan filling and frosting between the layers and on the top of the cake.

This cake can be frozen when finished or before filling and frosting. In fact, you can make the cakes weeks ahead and freeze them for later use. Simply make the frosting the day you will be serving the cake, take the cakes out of the freezer, frost them, and let the now completed cake come to room temperature.

Making the Coconut-Pecan-Caramel Filling

Mix the milk, sugar, butter, and egg yolks in large saucepan. Cook on medium heat, stirring constantly, for about 12 minutes or until just thickening and turning golden. Remove from heat. While cooking longer does not ruin the frosting, it makes it much harder to spread, and the cooled result can be firmer, resulting in a less luxurious cake-and-frosting combination.

Add the coconut, pecans, and vanilla, and mix well. Cool to room temperature, checking to make sure it is of a desired spreading consistency. This recipe makes about $4\frac{1}{2}$ cups or enough to fill and frost the top of a 3-layer cake or frost tops of two 13x9-inch cakes or 24 cupcakes. The sides do not need to be frosted, but if you desire to do so, double the frosting recipe, although the result would be very sweet.

FRUIT AND CUSTARDS

FRUIT CRISP

Fruit crisps are perhaps one of the easiest desserts to make and are uniformly delighted in by anyone who likes fruit—and who does not? It bears resemblance to clafouti except that there is no egg or milk mixed with the fruit, plus there is a crispy topping. One of my favorites is plum crisp, and I await the time each year that these wonderful stone fruits are in season. I like to use two or three varieties mixed for the plum crisp.

INGREDIENTS

Filling

your choice of fruit (for example, it takes 12-15 plums to make a 13x9-inch crisp)

sugar to taste (brown sugar and/or granulated cane sugar; depends on the ripeness and sweetness of the fruit you are using and whether you favor more or less sweet fruit desserts)

pinch of salt

vanilla

1 lemon, zested and juiced

cinnamon

4 tablespoons or so cornstarch

Crisp

¾ cup flour

¾ cup white sugar or packed brown sugar (or a mixture)

½ teaspoon salt

1 teaspoon ground cinnamon

4 ounces cold unsalted butter

¾ cup or so pecans, chopped and untoasted, or uncooked old-fashioned rolled oatmeal.

The basic crisp is just fruit of your choice in sufficient amount to mostly fill the baking dish you are using. Cut the fruit to bite-sized pieces. Add sugar to taste, 1 or 2 pinches of salt, vanilla, lemon zest and juice, cinnamon, 4 tablespoons or so of cornstarch—all to taste. The amount of cornstarch used in the fruit filling will vary depending on the fruit used, the juiciness of the fruit, and the desired texture of the finished product. Since the crisp will be served in a bowl, generally with ice cream, it may not really matter to you if the filling winds up very juicy and does not hold together (as you would desire a pie to do). Thus, for a 9x13-inch Pyrex dish, I suggest no more than 3 or 4 tablespoons of cornstarch for apples, plums, apricots, raspberries, strawberries, etc. Be generous and use enough fruit to mostly fill the baking dish that you are working with. Always taste the fruit mixture after it is macerated with the sugar and before baking (and, again, just before adding the crisp topping after 20 minutes in the oven) to adjust seasoning, as necessary, particularly to add more sugar or cinnamon if necessary. I have had crisps in restaurants where the chef seemed to have an aversion to sugar; it is my taste that there should be sufficient sugar in the filling so that this dessert is not overly tart—adjust to your taste.

The fruit recipes in this book disclose my strong preference to flavor fruit with cinnamon and lemon—very different from the French predilection. If you are using a delicate fruit such as blueberries, you should err on the side of moderation in adding lemon zest, lemon juice, and cinnamon so as to not overpower the wonderful fruit flavor.

Making the Crisp Topping

The crisp topping is not a precisely measured constituent; just make enough to completely cover the fruit. The crisp topping is seriously improved by adding the pecans or oatmeal.

Combine the flour, sugar, salt, pecans or oatmeal, and cinnamon, and then cut the butter into the mixture as you would for a biscuit dough or piecrust.

Baking the Crisp

Put the crisp filling without the topping in the oven at 350°F. Bake for 20 minutes. After 20 minutes, remove the filling briefly from the oven to add the crisp topping after tasting to make sure you have enough sugar. This ensures that the topping will not be overcooked or the fruit filling undercooked. Crumble the topping generously and evenly over the entire surface of the fruit. Bake for another 30 to 40 minutes, or until the crisp is bubbling and the topping browned. Because of the liquid exuded by the fruit, it will not overcook before the topping is cooked. Always put a baking sheet under the crisp to avoid messy oven spillover.

LIMONCELLO TIRAMISU

Tiramisu is an Italian word that means "pick me up." This incredible variant of the normal cocoa-coffee-marsala tiramisu has an intense lemon flavor that is a true pick-me-up. This sounds very fancy and will wow your guests, but it is incredibly easy to execute. (You can convert this to an orange tiramisu by the simple expedient of substituting orange for lemon and Grand Marnier for the limoncello.) The inspiration for this dessert is from Chef Rocco Sacramone, originally from Abruzzi in Italy and now the chef and owner of an outstanding Italian restaurant in Queens, New York—Trattoria L'incontro.

INGREDIENTS

Lemon-infused simple syrup

```
1 cup water
1 cup sugar
1 lemon, zested and juiced
3 ounces limoncello (an Italian lemon liqueur)
```

Filling

```
4 eggs, separated, split use
¼ cup limoncello
2 lemons, zested and juiced
1 cup sugar, split use
pinch of salt
1 teaspoon cream of tartar
1 pound mascarpone
40-45 ladyfingers
```

Making the Simple Syrup

Heat 1 cup of water to dissolve 1 cup of sugar. After the sugar has dissolved, add the juice of 1 lemon plus the freshly grated zest (not the white part of the rind, which is bitter). Simmer for 2 to 3 minutes to infuse the simple syrup with the lemon flavor. A microplane grater is really the best tool for grating lemon zest. Alternatively, you could just zest a lemon with a vegetable peeler and take the peel out after the simple syrup cools. Cool and refrigerate the lemon simple syrup. Add 3 ounces of limoncello to the cold simple syrup.

Making the Filling

In the top of a double broiler, mix 3 egg yolks with the limoncello, lemon zest, lemon juice, ½ cup of sugar, and a pinch of salt. You could also use a big stainless steel bowl set over a pot with about an inch of boiling water. The boiling water should not touch the double boiler, or you will have scrambled eggs and not custard.

Whisk promptly so that the sugar does not "cook" the yolks. Heat the mixture, whisking constantly to make a zabaglione (an Italian custard). Move the bowl on and off the heat to control the heat and avoid curdling the eggs. The zabaglione is done when the custard thickens and will coat the back of a spoon. Cool immediately over some ice, stirring for a short period to stop the cooking. Cover with plastic wrap by laying the wrap directly on the zabaglione to prevent a skin from forming. The zabaglione should then be refrigerated.

In a mixing bowl, beat 4 egg whites to stiff peaks along with a pinch of salt, ½ cup sugar, and the cream of tartar.

Fold the cooled zabaglione into 1 pound of mascarpone, and then fold in the egg whites.

Dip the ladyfingers into the simple syrup mixture. Do not oversoak—you do not want the ladyfingers to fall apart. Other products such as pound cake are not suitable because they will not hold together. Place a single layer of dipped ladyfingers into a 9x13-inch serving dish that is 2 or 3 inches deep. Layer half of the mascarpone mixture on top of the first ladyfinger layer. Add another layer of dipped ladyfingers and then the second layer of the mascarpone mixture. Cover and refrigerate the mixture to set. You may dust with cocoa powder for decoration. Serve. This is excellent served with a dessert wine or port.

PLUM CLAFOUTI

Classically, clafouti is a variant of flan from the Limousin area of France and is made with sweet cherries. Julia Child's books have recipes using a number of different fruits including cherries, pears, plums, apples, and berries, as do *The Joy of Cooking* and other sources. The number of delicious combinations is limited only by your imagination. A few include an apple-and-dried-tart-cherry mixture, a pear-and-dried-apricot mixture, and an assembly using an assortment of seasonal varieties of plums. I think that for any fruit dessert such as this, after seasoning with sugar, the fruit should not be overly tart but should taste luxuriant to the tongue.

This is one of those dishes that is incredibly simple to execute and will be a hit with any of your guests.

INGREDIENTS

fruit (For a 9x13-inch pan, use 12–15 plums. The fruit should be in a generous single layer.)
3 eggs
½ cup flour
1–2 lemons, zested
1 teaspoon cinnamon
⅓ cup granulated cane sugar, plus extra for sweetening fruit
1¼ cups whole milk
⅛ teaspoon salt
1 tablespoon vanilla extract

Preparing the Fruit

If you are using plums or other stone fruits, you may want to use 2 or 3 varieties, testing for ripeness and also firmness in season. Cut the flesh off of the pits so that each fruit is cut into 7 or 8 spoon-sized pieces. Place the pieces of fruit into the baking dish, squeezing the juice from the lemons that you zested. Add sugar until the mixture is adequately sweet and flavored. Prebake the fruit in a 350°F oven for about 25 minutes. A significant amount of juice will be released that should be used in the custard in lieu of some of the milk. Taste the fruit for sweetness before adding the custard and add sugar if needed. Finish the custard mixture and add it to the fruit to complete cooking.

Similarly, for an apple-and-dried-tart-cherry mixture, peel, core, and dice the apples into bite-sized pieces. Mix with an adequate quantity of dried cherries (perhaps 2 parts apple to 1 part dried cherry). Use a good cooking apple such as Granny Smith, Honeycrisp, or any of the multitudinous new and delicious varieties of crisp and tart but sweet apples that hold together well when cooked. As tasty as the venerable Red Delicious variety is, for example, it will not work here. Mix the apples with sugar and lemon juice to a desired level of sweetness.

If you are using dried apricots, they need to be diced into smaller pieces.

Pears need to be peeled and cored. Bartlett pears will work for this purpose, but they should be firm to the touch and not overripe. Bosc will be crisp and should be prebaked to slightly soften before adding the custard.

If you do not prebake, let the fruit macerate for 15 to 20 minutes so that the juices exude from the fruit before adding the custard. Dried fruit in the filling will tend to absorb exuded liquid from the fresh fruit.

Preparing the Custard

Break the eggs into the flour, and whisk until the mixture is smooth. Add the lemon zest and cinnamon (not traditional) to the egg mixture. Then slowly add the sugar and milk (substituting some of the exuded fruit juice for milk, if possible), whisking constantly to avoid any lumps. Add the salt and vanilla extract. If necessary, for the size of the baking dish that you are using, double or triple the custard recipe.

Add the custard to the fruit, mix in any exuded juices, and bake in a preheated 350°F oven. When you bake the clafouti, it will solidify, puff slightly, and lightly brown. Cooking time will depend on the size of the pan and how full it is with fruit. You should start checking after 30 minutes until the custard mixture is cooked but not overcooked. Test with a toothpick in the center to confirm the custard is not liquid. The custard may still be somewhat jiggly and will firm as it cools.

Use your imagination for other fruit and berry combinations with the custard mixture, but do not use fruit that totally collapses when cooked, such as strawberries.

COLD CHOCOLATE SOUFFLÉ

The original idea for this recipe was in *The Gourmet Cookbook*, which we bought about fifty years ago. We have modified it so that it is lighter, fluffier, and better tasting. Since it has no leavening, flour, or other grain product, it is an excellent dessert for Passover—but, if you do not eat milk after meat, only if your meal is not fleishig. (I have never had a matzo-meal dessert that I thought was worthy of eating or serving to anyone else.) It is a favorite of all who eat it. It is very chocolatey and has an incredibly fluffy texture. Luxuriant is an excellent description.

INGREDIENTS

This recipe doubles easily.

4 whole eggs

3 egg yolks

½ cup cane sugar

¼ teaspoon salt

1½ tablespoons unflavored gelatin

¼ cup water

2 teaspoons orange juice

7 ounces bittersweet or semisweet chocolate

⅓ cup Myers's dark rum, Jack Daniels, Grand Marnier, or limoncello.

½ teaspoon orange oil or lemon oil (if you are using Grand Marnier or Limoncello, use orange oil or lemon oil, respectively)

2 cups heavy cream

First, combine 4 whole eggs, 3 egg yolks, the cane sugar, and the salt in the bowl of a KitchenAid or other mixer. Whip the mixture with the whip attachment for about 15 minutes or until it is very thick and pale in color. Alternatively, you could put the bowl over hot water and beat vigorously with a rotary beater or handheld beater.

Soften the gelatin in a mixture of the water and orange juice. Dissolve in a bowl set over hot water to activate it, and after it has warmed, turn off the heat, and let it sit over the hot water for a few minutes. This amount of gelatin merely keeps the chilled final dessert from being runny, but it does not create a texture like Jell-O.

Chop the chocolate, and mix in the rum and oil. Unlike vanilla extract, citrus oils should be carefully measured because in excess, they detract from rather than enhance flavor. Melt the chocolate mixture using your preferred method (either in a double boiler or in a microwave for 1 minute on high). Remember, do not overcook and burn the chocolate, because it will not taste good after that.

With the back of a spoon, agitate the softened gelatin thoroughly but gently until there are no lumps, and then mix it into the chocolate mixture. Stir thoroughly but gently; you do not want unmixed gelatin, which would spoil the texture. Fold the chocolate mixture carefully into the beaten egg mixture.

In a separate bowl, whip the heavy cream until it forms soft or medium-stiff peaks. Add the chocolate mixture, and fold in until smooth and light and there are no pockets of just cream or just chocolate. Place into a decorative bowl, and chill for at least 2 to 4 hours so that the soufflé will hold its shape.

BERRY BUCKLE

Buckles are a classic American dish and can be made either with fresh or frozen berries. For this purpose, blackberries, raspberries, blueberries, or strawberries all work wonderfully. There is nothing better than a warm, baked fruit dessert, particularly served with vanilla ice cream.

INGREDIENTS

This dish can be made either in a 9x9-inch pan or a 10-inch heavy-duty skillet, or it can be doubled for a 10x15-inch Pyrex pan.

Filling

```
4 cups berries
1 cup sugar, or to taste
1 teaspoon cinnamon
1 lemon, zested and juiced
pinch of salt
```

Batter

```
1 cup unbleached flour
1 cup sugar, or more to taste, depending on the tartness of the
berries
1 cup whole (not skim) milk
2 teaspoons or more vanilla extract
2 teaspoons baking powder
½ cup unsalted butter, melted
```

```
Preheat the oven to 350°F.
```

For the filling, slightly mash the berries, and sprinkle with the sugar. Mix all of the filling ingredients lightly. Place the filling into the cooking pan, including all of the juices.

For the batter, mix the dry ingredients with the milk, vanilla extract, and the melted butter. Stir well. Pour the batter over the berries. Bake until the top is golden and the batter tests done by putting in a toothpick that comes out clean. This will take about 1 hour.

POACHED FRUIT

There are many recipes for baking apples and pears, but for me, there is something lacking in many of these recipes for several reasons. It is difficult to properly core the fruit if it is left whole, particularly for pears, which have a tough stem that extends through the fruit and really needs to be removed. Also, the skin is frequently left on, and while this does provide for structural integrity, the skin impedes transfer of flavor from the sauce to the fruit, and I personally do not particularly like the texture. Actually, unless you start with a soft and very ripe fruit, structure is really not a problem—you just do not have the beautiful whole fruit for presentation purposes. Finally, the added flavoring mixture leaks out of the center of the whole fruit and is not in contact with the fruit long enough to be absorbed to flavor the fruit. This recipe solves those problems and leaves you with a bountiful, delicious sauce to use over the fruit and, if you want, ice cream. There are many wonderful ice cream flavors, but for this purpose, I think vanilla is best. Poached fruit is another perfect Passover dessert.

INGREDIENTS

5-6 apples or pears, depending on the size of the pan you are using. (This lasts well in the refrigerator, so I make enough for a number of desserts. Apples should be a good cooking apple; that is, Granny Smith, Honeycrisp, or other tart, crisp apple that will retain its shape for poaching. Pears may be either Bartlett, Anjou, or Bosc and should be firm and not overripe or soft to the touch.)

1 teaspoon cinnamon, or to taste

½ teaspoon salt

1-2 cups of sugar, or more to taste

1 cup orange simple syrup (optional—see the process for making the simple syrup under the Chocolate-Orange-Almond-Coconut Biscotti recipe earlier in Chapter 15.)

1 orange and/or a lemon, zested and juice

1-1½ bottles of drinkable red or white wine of your choice, but not sweet or dessert wine

1 tablespoon vanilla extract

Peel the fruit. (My dogs love the peel from pears and apples.) Then cut the fruit in half, core it, and stem it. Fit the fruit, preferably in a single layer, into the pan that you will be using, cutting the fruit into quarters if necessary to fit into your pan. I suggest a pan with as wide of a bottom as will fit on your stove top. You want the fruit to be in full contact with the wine.

Add the cinnamon, salt, sugar, orange simple syrup if you are using it, and the zest of the orange and/or lemon. Pour in sufficient wine to barely cover the fruit. The final flavor will vary with the wine you choose. (If you are using vanilla bean instead of extract, add the seeds and pod right after you add the wine, but don't add extract at this time.) Heat the fruit and wine to a simmer on the stove top. Cover, and maintain the temperature of the liquid at a bare simmer. Flip the fruit at about 10 minutes to get full contact with the sauce. Taste the sauce to ensure that it is adequately sweet; if not, add sugar. Cook for 20 to 30 minutes, testing the fruit by inserting a knife. Once the knife slips in and out of the fruit easily, turn off the heat, and remove the fruit from the cooking liquid to a storage pot or bowl. (CorningWare is excellent for this purpose.)

Return the cooking liquid to high heat and reduce the liquid until it starts to become thicker. You can reduce to a point where the liquid starts to become syrupy, or you can stop short of that point. It will thicken some as it cools. Taste the liquid. Squeeze in lemon and/ or orange juice at the end of the reducing process, to taste. Turn off the heat and stir in the vanilla extract. Pour the still hot, reduced cooking liquid over the fruit. Cover and cool. You can serve the warm poached fruit at this point over ice cream. Refrigerate any fruit that is not utilized while warm. The fruit can be rewarmed by nuking it briefly, or it is also wonderful served cold over ice cream.

Cheese (and other) Blintzes , p. 171

About the Author

During fifty-one years in a general tax and transaction practice as a CPA and lawyer, Ken Horwitz developed a creative and focused approach to finding and fixing problems—a skill that translates well to the development and modification of recipes based on traditional family favorites but tailored to one's personal tastes and dietary needs. His professional drive and the care given to his work has earned him multiple awards, including being awarded an Honorary Fellow for lifetime distinguished service as well as being awarded the 2017 Chairperson of the Year by the Texas Society of CPAs. Currently residing in Dallas, Texas, Ken enjoys sharing his passion for cooking with his wife and his children's families.

Chocolate-Orange-Almond-Coconut
Biscotti, p. 287

Index

B

C

E

F

S

T

V